JUAN PABLO FORNER AS A CRITIC

This dissertation was conducted under the direction of Alessandro Crisafulli, Ph.D., and was approved by David Rubio, Ph.D., and Helmut Hatzfeld, Ph.D., as readers.

The Catholic University of America

Juan Pablo Forner as a Critic

A DISSERTATION

SUBMITTED TO THE FACULTY OF THE GRADUATE SCHOOL OF ARTS AND
SCIENCES OF THE CATHOLIC UNIVERSITY OF AMERICA IN PARTIAL
FULFILLMENT OF THE REQUIREMENTS FOR THE DEGREE OF
DOCTOR OF PHILOSOPHY

BY

SISTER MARY FIDELIA LAUGHRIN, M.A.

OF THE

SISTERS, SERVANTS OF THE IMMACULATE HEART OF MARY

OF

MONROE, MICHIGAN

THE CATHOLIC UNIVERSITY OF AMERICA PRESS
WASHINGTON, D. C.
1943

To
MY FATHER
in memory of
MY MOTHER

PREFACE

Juan Pablo Forner, eighteenth century Spanish scholar, philosopher, jurist, satirist, polemist, and critic, although only a minor writer, is of interest because of the important part he played in the Spanish opposition to the spread of the Encyclopedic ideas in Spain.

Although Spanish scholars generally regard Forner as an outstanding figure in the field of criticism in Spain in the eighteenth century, no detailed study of the man and his work appears to have been made. Quite in keeping with what one might expect, Menéndez y Pelayo seems to be the most reliable source of information regarding Forner, whom he considers, in spite of his faults, as the embodiment of the most intelligent and violent reaction against the French Encyclopedic movement and the most tireless polemist of eighteenth century Spain.[1]

Based on an intensive study of his two most outstanding works, the *Oración apologética* and the *Exequias de la lengua castellana*, the dissertation presents Forner as a critic. The study reveals the standards by which Forner judged the literature of Spain and France in his day. It shows to what extent and in what respects he exalted the literary and scientific glory of Spain's past, defended the *purismo* and *españolismo* of her language and literature, and protested against her acceptance of *galicismo* with its manifold implications—aesthetic, philosophic, and scientific.

To Dr. David Rubio, who suggested the subject, to Dr. Alessandro Crisafulli, who directed the work, and to Professor Helmut Hatzfeld, I extend my sincere appreciation for their careful reading of the manuscript and their helpful suggestions. I wish also to express my indebtedness to my religious Superiors for making this study possible.

---

[1] M. Menéndez y Pelayo, *Historia de las ideas estéticas*, V (Madrid: Hernando, 1933), p. 323.

CONTENTS

CHAPTER		PAGE
	PREFACE	vii
I.	FORNER, THE MAN	1
II.	THE EXEQUIAS AND THE ORACIÓN APOLOGÉTICA	13
III.	PHILOSOPHY, RELIGION AND SCIENCE	32
IV.	ART PRINCIPLES	70
V.	LITERARY FORMS AND TYPES	93
VI.	CONCLUSION	126
	APPENDIX I	131
	APPENDIX II	134
	BIBLIOGRAPHY	191
	INDEX	196

CHAPTER I

FORNER, THE MAN

Juan Bautista Pablo Forner y Segarra was born in Mérida, a province of Extremadura, in February, 1756.[1] He was endowed with remarkable intellectual gifts, and from his earliest years he was offered every cultural advantage. His father, Augustín Francisco Forner y Segarra, a native of Viñaroz in Valencia, was a learned man, interested particularly in historic antiquities, inscriptions, medals, and ancient monuments.[2] His mother, Manuela Piquer y Zaragoza, a native of Madrid, was the niece of the celebrated physician, philosopher, and humanist, Andrés Piquer, to whom the major direction of Forner's education was intrusted.

At the University of Salamanca where Forner went at the age of fourteen, and where he studied for nine years, with the view of becoming a lawyer, he pursued courses in philosophy and jurisprudence, applying himself at the same time to the study of Spanish literature, Hebrew, Latin, and Greek, particularly, to the reading of the Greek classical authors. Forner's study was not confined to the mere acquisition of facts, but was always accompanied by a critical sagacity and a keen discernment, powers which he attained from the study of his favorite authors, Vives and Bacon.[3] During his stay at the university he made the acquaintance of Iglesias, Estala, and Meléndez, who encouraged him in his literary endeavors.[4]

---

[1] Sainz y Rodríguez gives the date of his birth as February, 1756 ("Introducción" in Juan Pablo Forner, *Exequias de la lengua castellana*, Madrid: La Lectura, 1925, p. 10). Sotelo gives as the date February 17, 1756 ("Elogio del señor Don Juan Pablo Forner" in Cueto, *Poetas líricos del siglo XVIII*, Biblioteca de autores españoles, LXIII, 2, Madrid: Rivadeneyra, 1871, p. 273). Villanueva in his "Noticia biográfica" states that the baptismal record shows February 23 to be the date (Cueto, *op. cit.*, p. 253).

[2] Sotelo, *op. cit.*, p. 273.

[3] *Ibid.*, p. 274.

[4] Sainz y Rodríguez, *op. cit.*, p. 11. Sotelo notes that José Cadalso, who lived in Salamanca at the time, gave him valuable help with his poetry (*op. cit.*, p. 274).

1

Forner, the Man

The author's .literary and scientific interests fostered at the university persisted throughout his life; and though the duties of his profession were manifold, he always found time to write and to take an active part in various literary and scientific societies, particularly while he was in Seville.[5] His relations with these groups made both friends and enemies for him, since, naturally, there were those who were in agreement and those who were at variance with his strongly national views and his uncompromising expression of them.

Forner's interest in literature was always such that it is hard to conceive it as a secondary occupation and not his profession. Fundamentally, it was not secondary, for his one aim, whether through law or letters, was to promote the common good.[6] As a lawyer, he seems to have been successful from the very beginning of his career.[7] At the age of twenty-two, he went to Madrid,[8]

---

[5] He lived in Seville between the years 1790 and 1796. He was director of the "Amigos del País" and a member of the "Sociedad de Buenas Letras," of a Canon Law society, and an Ecclesiastical History group (Villanueva, *op. cit.*, p. 265). While living in Seville he also encouraged many social reforms (Sotelo, *op. cit.*, pp. 288-289).

[6] Sotelo, *op. cit.*, p. 288. Even in Forner's polemics, his aim was to do good *(ibid.*, p. 275).

[7] In his "Elogio" (p. 287), Sotelo, a contemporary of Forner, writes of him: ". . . Forner . . . aun cuando ignorase algunas voces o fórmulas de estilo, no ignoraba los decretos de las leyes, ni la historia de su patria, ni los elementos del derecho de gentes, ni las opiniones o sistemas políticos adoptados entre los pueblos cultos de la Europa, ni las fuentes de donde se deriva el derecho público convencional de las naciones, ni las verdaderas reglas de la interpretación, ni el arte de discurrir con solidez y con exactitud; y por lo mismo supo hacer triunfar gloriosamente la justicia de su causa, hasta entonces ignorada o torpemente confundida, mientras que quizá era reputado por un mero humanista entre aquellos que han intendido reducir la ciencia legal a una fastidiosa y estéril nomenclatura." (The standard modern accentuation and spelling will be used throughout this study.)

[8] The statements made regarding this part of Forner's life appear somewhat conflicting. Sainz y Rodríguez states clearly that Forner went to the court at the age of twenty-two *(op. cit.*, p. 11), which would mean that he went in 1778. Then when setting up Forner's picture of himself, he writes: "Por el año 1783, 'había acudido a la corte con el fin de concluir la carrera de sus estudios . . .'" *(op. cit.*, p. 10). It is apparent that these statements are contradictory. Villanueva in his "Noticia biográfica" re-

Forner, the Man 3

where he continued his studies and became an assistant in the office of Miguel Sanelda.[9] He was admitted to the "colegio de abogados," August 28, 1783; and on April 19, 1784 he was named "abogado honorario e historiador" of the house of Altamira with an annual pension of 10,000 reales.[10] In 1790, he was appointed "fiscal del crimen" in Seville.[11] Having been assigned the office of "fiscal" of the Consejo Supremo in 1796, he returned to Madrid, where he was named "socio de mérito" in the Academia de Derecho Español, of which body he was elected president in 1797.

He never entered upon the duties of this office, however, as he died on March 17 of that year, at the age of forty-one. Besides his widow, he left three sons, two of whom died in their youth and the third, at the age of thirty-one.[12]

While Forner's personality and character will manifest themselves in his literary works, yet, before passing to our review of these works, it might be well to give some little consideration to his pen picture of himself and to a few comments made by critics regarding him. In *Los gramáticos: historia chinesca,* he writes of himself, when as a young man, he went to Madrid.

Había acudido a la corte con el fin de concluir la carrera de sus estudios un joven adusto, flaco, alto, cejijunto, de

---

marks that in the year 1782, while still a student at the University of Salamanca, Forner received the award of the Spanish Academy for his *Sátira contra los abusos introducidos en la poesía castellana.* In the next sentence the biographer writes that Forner went to Madrid at the age of twenty-two after finishing his course in jurisprudence, which would again mean that he went in the year 1778 *(op. cit.,* p. 264). Cueto, in a note, remarks that Forner wrote this work in 1782 while he was a professor of jurisprudence at Salamanca *(op. cit.,* p. 304, n. 1). Sotelo in his "Elogio" notes that Forner attended both the University of Salamanca and the University of Toledo, that he received his degree in Civil Law from the latter university and that he went immediately from Toledo to Madrid *(op. cit.,* p. 274). In a note, Sotelo states that Forner lived in Madrid with an uncle, Juan Crisóstomo Piquer from 1779-1783 *(ibid.,* n. 4).

[9] Sainz y Rodríguez, *op. cit.,* p. 11. Villanueva gives the name Sarralde *(op. cit.,* p. 264).

[10] *Ibid.,* see also Sotelo, *op. cit.,* p. 287, n. 3.

[11] In 1791 he married Doña María del Carmen Carassa, who belonged to a distinguished family in Seville (Sainz y Rodríguez, *op. cit.,* p. 12); see also this study, p. 2, n. 5.

[12] Villanueva, *op. cit.,* p. 266.

4 *Forner, the Man*

una condición tan insufrible y de un carácter en sumo
grado mordaz. . . . Su genio, naturalmente seco y ajeno
de toda adulación servil, le llevaba a atropellar por todo
inconveniente por el gustazo de ajar la vanidad y bajar
el toldo a cualquiera que se complaciese en ajar a todos.[13]

Although, because of his polemics, Forner is usually referred to
as a man of aggressive and violent character,[14] it appears from
the information which the Counsellor Nava gave to Floridablanca
that he lived for a long time in retirement and obscurity.

Yo solamente le he visto una vez en mi vida; pero
según me han asegurado hombres de juicio y de bien, que
le conocen de Salamanca y de Madrid, y, según mani-
fiestan sus papeles, es mozo de grandes principios y
esperanzas, de quien con el tiempo se puede sacar mucha
utilidad para el adelantamiento de la literatura. Dicen
que es de muy buenas costumbres, melancólico y tan re-
tirado y entregado a los libros, que ya es vicio; por lo cual
son pocos en Madrid los que le conocen personalmente.[15]

Once he came out from his retirement, he apparently gave full
vent to his aggressive spirit, for his life became a series of dis-
putes which prevented him from writing the type of works that
his talent and learning warranted.[16] He paid no attention to the en-

---

[13] Bibl. Nac. Manusc. Dd. 196 of the *Obras de Forner* as quoted by Sainz
y Rodríguez, *op. cit.*, p. 10. In all probability, he went to Madrid in 1778;
see this study, p. 2.

[14] Sainz y Rodríguez, *op. cit.*, p. 9. This author speaks of Forner as a
man of "pasiones reconcentradas" *(ibid.,* p. 10), as a man tormented by
his surroundings, by an atrabilious and melancholy disposition, and by an
excessive ambition for glory *(ibid.,* p. 13). Sotelo, however, would take
exception to the fact that Forner was proud and conceited. He points out
that Forner was never taken with flattery, and that he was one who did
not think he knew everything simply because he knew a few things *(op. cit.,*
p. 275).

[15] Bibl. Nac. Manusc. Dd. vol. II of the *Obras de Forner* as quoted by
Sainz y Rodríguez, *op. cit.*, p. 13. Nava wrote this to Floridablanca when
Forner was trying to get the permission to publish *Los gramáticos (ibid.,*
p. 13). Sotelo also attests to Forner's retirement because of his interest
in his studies *(op. cit.,* p. 274).

[16] Sainz y Rodríguez, *op. cit.*, p. 11. Forner engaged in these polemics
between 1783 and 1790; see this study, p. 11.

Forner, the Man 5

treaties of his friends, who sought to dissuade him from participation in these controversies, but he showed himself set in purpose, stubborn, unmoved by fatigue or punishment.[17]

As Sainz y Rodríguez notes, however, the reader will form a "lamentable idea" of the character of Forner if he judges him exclusively by his polemics.[18] He believes that if one will look beyond the implacability which Forner displayed toward his enemies, he will find in him a spirit of uprightness and justice, which on occasions made him sacrifice his own self-love, and an affection and gratitude that were never dissembled toward the few people with whom he contracted a friendship.[19] Sainz y Rodríguez cites, as examples of Forner's tenderness and gratitude, a couple of letters that the author wrote—one to Iglesias, in which he begged Iglesias to put an end to the enmity that had kept them apart for a year; and another letter to an old professor, Francisco P. de Lema, in which he relates that he is doing well, that his writing is progressing, that he has married and is very happy.[20]

Menéndez y Pelayo, who was likewise disposed to look beyond

---

[17] Sainz y Rodríguez, *op. cit.*, p. 19. In a letter to Forner, his friend Moratín begged him to give up his quarrels and to occupy himself with tasks that would bring him esteem rather than persecution and unhappiness. (Moratín, as quoted by Sainz y Rodríguez, *ibid.*, p. 12.)

[18] *Ibid.*, p. 33. Apparently basing his opinion of Forner's character on the author's polemics, Cotarelo y Mori considers him capable only of the bitterest satire (*Iriarte y su época*, Madrid: Sucesores de Rivadeneyra, 1897, p. 223). It is his belief too that Forner's character and personal appearance interfered with his success *(ibid.*, p. 258). Deriving his opinion from Cotarelo y Mori's study, and disregarding Menéndez y Pelayo's view that Forner was a fearless defender of the purely Spanish ideals, Robert E. Pellissier writes that "he was a barefaced opportunist, a kind of literary 'spadassin,' a man ready to strike any one at any time if there was any promise in these blows of either personal advancement or the satisfaction of envy. The man who attacked at once Iriarte, García de la Huerta . . . cannot for a moment be thought to have been a person of character and with an honest purpose" *(The Neo-Classic Movement in Spain during the XVIII Century*, Stanford: University Press, 1918, p. 114).

[19] Sainz y Rodríguez, *op. cit.*, p. 33. The Frenchman Florian held Forner in great esteem both as a learned counselor and an obliging, generous friend (Sotelo, *op. cit.*, pp. 283-284).

[20] "Epistolario español," Colección Rivadeneyra, II, 213, as quoted by Sainz y Rodríguez, *op. cit.*, pp. 33-34.

6   *Forner, the Man*

the sputtering of Forner's polemics, also observed some quite remarkable traits in his character, for he wrote of him:

> ... en las polémicas de Forner, hasta en las más desalmadas y virulentas, hay siempre algo que hace simpático al autor en medio de sus arrojos y temeridades de estudiante, y algo también que sobrevive a aquellas estériles riñas de plazuela con Iriarte, Trigueros, Huerta o Sánchez, y es el macizo saber, el agudo ingenio, el estilo franco y despreocupado del autor, el hirviente tropel de sus ideas, y, sobre todo, su amor entrañable, fervoroso y filial a los hombres y a las cosas, de la antigua España, cuyos teólogos y filósofos conocía más minuciosamente que ningún otro escritor de entonces.[21]

Sotelo, in his comments on Forner's criticism of Borrego's *Historia* sets Forner up as a model of kindness and sympathy.

> Pero esta impugnación vigorosa de las falsas opiniones de Borrego iba accompañada de la mayor dulzura, respeto y urbanidad hacia el mismo a quien refutaba; reconocía y confesaba sinceramente el mérito de la obra, recomendaba al Gobierno su publicación luego que estuviese purgada de los errores en que había incurrido, y él mismo se ofrecía voluntariamente a corregirlos; manifestando de este modo el aprecio y estimación que se le debía, y enseñando con su ejemplo a todos los censores a unir la severidad crítica con la indulgencia y la moderación.[22]

Forner's literary career really began in 1782 when, as a student, he won the first prize awarded by the Spanish Academy for his *Sátira contra los abusos introducidos en la poesía castellana*.[23] In this work, he points out the reasons for the decline of Spanish

---

[21] Menéndez y Pelayo, *op. cit.*, p. 331.

[22] Sotelo, *op. cit.*, p. 283.

[23] Sainz y Rodríguez, *op. cit.*, p. 11. In his edition, Cueto uses in the title *vicios* instead of *abusos* (*op. cit.*, p. 304). According to this editor, Forner received the award of the Academy at a meeting on October 15, 1782 (*ibid.*, n. 1). D. Leandro Moratín also wrote a satire on the same subject, which Forner thought better than his own. Moratín, however, favored the decision made by the Academy. It is interesting to note that the friendship between these two men began with this event (Sotelo, *op. cit.*, p. 275). Cotarelo y Mori, stressing the fact that the work is a satire, remarks "no podía ser otra cosa" (*op. cit.*, p. 258).

Forner, the Man

poetry. He shows how writers have abused the art by their poor imitations and their obscure, affected style. He attributes to them the corruption of ideas, of good taste, and of the Spanish language. He discerns the beauties, defects, and vices of the principal poets.[24] In his condemnation of the defects and vices of the seventeenth century theatre, he does not spare Lope or Calderón.[25] In this work he also assails Tiraboschi, Bettinelli and Quadrio for their unjust exaggeration of Spanish ignorance.

From this time the various types of works which came from the pen of Forner give evidence of the versatility of his genius and the extent of his labors. His scholarly, philosophical, and professional interests found expression in the fields of history, law, poetry, drama, and criticism.[26]

In the field of history there are two rather outstanding works. In his *Reflexiones críticas sobre la Historia universal,* which he wrote in 1788, Forner shows his impartial judgment, his critical ability, his erudition in ecclesiastical matters, and his knowledge of the history of Europe.[27] His *Discurso sobre el modo de escribir y mejorar la historia de España* is a work in which he displays not only his profound knowledge of the history of Spain through first sources, but also his exact critical judgment and historical method, in which respects he was far in advance of his times.[28]

His two best works in jurisprudence are the *Observaciones sobre la perplejidad de la tortura* and the *Plan sobre unas instituciones de derecho español.* In the former work, he shows himself the advocate of just reform;[29] in the latter, he sets forth

---

[24] Sotelo, *op. cit.,* p. 275.

[25] Sainz y Rodríguez, *op. cit.,* p. 11. See this study, pp. 100-101.

[26] The complete works of Forner have not been published. The *Obras de Forner* (7 vols.) are found in manuscript form in the Biblioteca Nacional. Some of his poems and other works were published in Madrid in 1871 by Cueto in his *Poetas líricos del siglo XVIII.* The *Exequias de la lengua castellana* was included in this volume. In 1925 it appeared as a separate work in the collection "Clásicos castellanos." For further comment on this edition see this study, p. 13, n. 2.

[27] Sotelo, *op. cit.,* p. 282. See also this study, p. 2, n. 7.

[28] Sainz y Rodríguez, *op. cit.,* pp. 39-40. Menéndez y Pelayo classes this work with the author's *Exequias* as among the best works in Spain in the eighteenth century *(op. cit.,* p. 335).

[29] Menéndez y Pelayo, *op. cit.,* p. 335.

8   *Forner, the Man*

a careful philosophic study of the views of Spaniards who have written on law, comparing their ideas on civilization and progress with the state of civilization in his time and with the scientific progress of the most learned nations.[30]

Among his other didactic works are the *Carta de don Antonio Varas, El Paralelo de las dos églogas premiadas por la Real Academia Española,* and the *Discurso sobre la poesía dramática,* the prologue to his comedy *El filósofo enamorado,* which was written in 1796. In the first of these he presents the principal rules of epic poetry; in the second, the rules of bucolic poetry; in the third, those of dramatic poetry.[31]

His work entitled *Discursos filosóficos sobre el hombre* not only gives evidence of profound philosophical knowledge and classical scholarship,[32] but also shows the spirit of philosophical analysis which was predominant in the eighteenth century, particularly in the last half of it.[33] The work consists of the *Discursos,* a didactic poem similar to Pope's *Essay on Man* and the *Illustraciones,* in prose.[34] In his *Elogio,* Sotelo gives an excellent summary of the work, which shows Forner's philosophical views and his appreciation of the necessity of man's knowing himself and his destiny.

> Su genio filosófico y meditador le inclinaba naturalmente al estudio de aquella filosofía sublime que enseña al hombre a conocerse a sí mismo, y el alto fin a que fué destinado; . . . Sabía que el que no estudia profundamente las relaciones que ligan al hombre consigo mismo, con la primera causa de quien depende, y con todos los seres que le rodean, jamás podrá usar rectamente de ellos, ni satisfacer sus deseos, ni conseguir la felicidad a que aspira; sabía que sin estos conocimientos, ni el poeta puede deleitar, ni el historiador instruir, ni el orador mover, ni el político fomentar la prosperidad pública, ni

---

[30] Villanueva, *op. cit.,* p. 266.

[31] Sotelo, *op. cit.,* p. 287, n. 1.

[32] Villanueva, *op. cit.,* p. 264.

[33] Cueto, *op. cit.,* p. 354, n. 1.

[34] Cueto says the *Ilustraciones* were written in Forner's youth. As a continuation of the *Discursos,* they give a clear idea of Forner's special talent, "el de razonador incisivo y profundo" (*ibid.*).

Forner, the Man

el legislador dictar buenas leyes, ni el ciudadano observarlas, ni el magistrado hacer de ellas una justa aplicación, ni
el hombre, en fin, desempeñar las augustas obligaciones en
que lo constituye la misma alteza y dignidad de su ser; y
penetrado de estas ideas, se dedicó a un estudio intenso,
metódico y continuado de los filósofos más célebres. Leyó
atentamente sus libros, investigó el origen de sus opiniones,
analizó sus sistemas, examinó sus principios, observó sus
efectos sobre la felicidad física y espiritual de los hombres,
meditó, comparó y dedujo de todos ellos una multitud
de consecuencias luminosas e importantes al linaje humano. Meditó las inalterables leyes dictadas al hombre
por la razón para conservarse y perfeccionarse en el
orden de su ser, comparó las acciones humanas con estas
leyes, y notando entre ellas una contradicción casi universal, dedujo la corrupción de nuestro entendimiento.
Meditó los extravagantes delirios que bajo el especioso
nombre de sistemas han forjado los hombres en toda la
serie de los siglos para explicar la esencia del Ente supremo y fijar el culto que debe tributársele; comparólas
entre sí, y no hallando en todas ellas más que un tenebroso
laberinto de opiniones inciertas y ridículas, dedujo la
debilidad y flaqueza de la razón humana para conocer
por sí sola la naturaleza de Dios y el modo con que debe
adorarlo. Contempló la immensa cadena de los seres
criados, observó que todos ellos contribuían a la existencia
del hombre, al paso que no necesitaban del hombre para
existir; y de aquí infirió que el hombre no forma una
parte o eslabón de esta cadena, sino que es un ente sometido a otro orden distinto, y destinado para otro fin.
Reflexionó que éste no podía ser la conservación de su
existencia puramente física, puesto que las cualidades
espirituales de que está dotado, y las operaciones intelectuales de que es capaz, no son necesarias para vivir,
y dedujo como una consecuencia necesaria que este fin
debía durar más allá de la vida.[35]

The *Discursos filosóficos* is a work remarkable more for the
philosophical and moral thoughts expressed in it than for its poetic
value. The same criticism applies to Forner's other long poem,
Canto a la paz, which was written in 1796.[36] Most of Forner's

---

[35] Sotelo, *op. cit.*, pp. 275-276.

[36] Sainz y Rodríguez, *op. cit.*, p. 36. Sotelo says this is Forner's poetic
masterpiece *(op. cit.*, p. 203, n. 2).

10 Forner, the Man

poetry, while containing admirable thought, is marked by rigidity and tedium, because of the sterility of his imagination and his natural inclination toward the rational rather than the descriptive.[37] His satiric verse, however, according to Sainz y Rodríguez, approaches the excellence of his prose and may well be placed with the best satires of the period.[38] Sotelo, looking upon the collection of the author's satires, odes, and epigrams as his classic work, remarks:

> Éste no había recibido de la naturaleza una imaginación lozana, amena ni delicada, pero sí sumamente vigorosa y ardiente, de lo cual resulta que así como en las composiciones suaves y plácidas jamás pudo acercarse a la sencillez y gracia nativa de los griegos, en las que requieren un colorido fuerte y golpes de grande energía, sin líneas sutiles, ha igualado y tal vez excedido a los mejores poetas de nuestra nación. No hay más que comparar sus sátiras, epigramas y otras composiciones de esta clase con las de Argensola, Herrera, etc., y se verá que hay en Forner más fuerza en los pensamientos, más energía en la expresión, más singularidad en las ideas, más número en el verso, más riqueza y filosofía en el lenguaje poético, y una imitación de los antiguos muy distante de la servil que se nota con frecuencia en los poetas españoles e italianos del siglo XVI, y aun tal vez en el imcomparable Boileau.[39]

Forner even attempted drama, but his productions in this field suffered from much the same defects as did his poetry.[40] In 1784, his comedy, *La Cautiva española,* appeared; and as it provoked the disapproval of Ignacio López de Ayala, the censor of the theatre, Forner replied with a long letter giving his views on the writing of drama and making personal attacks against the censor

---

[37] *Ibid.,* p. 36. Forner's poetry appears insignificant in comparison with his prose. To Forner as a prose writer, Menéndez y Pelayo applies the adjectives "fecundo, vigoroso, contundente y desenfadado" (*Historia de los heterodoxos españoles,* III, Madrid: Librería Católica de San José, 1881, p. 330).

[38] Sainz y Rodríguez, *op. cit.,* p. 36.

[39] Sotelo, *op. cit.,* p. 286, n. 2.

[40] Sainz y Rodríguez, *op. cit.,* p. 36.

Forner, the Man

and his drama, *Numancia*.[41] Forner's stiff, formal comedy, *La escuela de la amistad o el filósofo enamorado* written in 1796, met with some little success,[42] but it lacked the charm of lightness and laughter that is ordinarily associated with comedy. Forner held that the purpose of comedy was not to entertain and provoke laughter, but to present a true picture of some phase of real life with the idea of bettering society.[43] Among his other dramas are *Los falsos filósofos* and *El Ateísta,* the latter written with intention of combatting the ideas of the Encyclopedists.[44]

Between 1783 and 1790, Forner devoted most of his time to polemical writing, which nearly all of his critics regard as a blot upon his literary career.[45] His literary campaigns became so numerous and the personal attacks contained in them so bitter and violent that a royal decree was issued in 1785, forbidding him to publish anything without the proper authorization. The most important of these diatribes[46] were directed against Tomás de Iriarte,

---

[41] Menéndez y Pelayo, *Historia de las ideas estéticas,* V, 325.

[42] Sainz y Rodríguez, *op. cit.,* p. 36.

[43] Menéndez y Pelayo, *Historia de las ideas estéticas,* V, 328. See this study, p. 102.

[44] Sainz y Rodríguez, *op. cit.,* p. 37.

[45] Montolíu remarks that Forner pitifully wasted his exceptional talent on them (Manuel de Montolíu y de Togores, "El siglo XVIII," *Literatura castellana,* Barcelona: Editorial Cervantes, 1930, p. 696). Menéndez y Pelayo, however, finds a sort of congeniality in them, a certain something, which, in his opinion, outweighs the sterile quarrels themselves and merits pardon and relative vindication today (*Historia de las ideas estéticas,* V. 331); see also this study pp. 4-6.

[46] Menéndez y Pelayo divides them according to the following plan (*Historia de las ideas estéticas,* V, 332-333, note):

Contra Iriarte: *El Asno erudito; Los Gramáticos, historia chinesca; Cotejo de las dos églogas premiadas por la Real Academia Española.*

Contra Huerta: *Fé de erratas del prólogo del teatro español; Reflexiones de Tomé Cecial; El Morión,* poema burlesco; y varios romances, sonetos, epigramas, etc.

Contra Trigueros: *Carta de D. Antonio Varas al autor de la Riada; Suplemento al artículo Trigueros en la biblioteca del Dr. Guarinos.*

Contra varios poetastros menores, Nipho, Laviano, Valladares, etc.: *Carta de Marcial a D. Fermín Laviano; Carta del Tonto de la Duquesa de Alba a un amigo suyo de América; Sátira contra la literatura chapucera del tiempo presente,* etc.

12 *Forner, the Man*

Cándido María Trigueros, Tomás Antonio Sánchez, Vicente García de la Huerta, Ignacio López de Ayala, and José Vargas y Ponce. These controversies were carried on under the various pseudonyms of Pablo Segarra, Bartolo, Varas, Paulo Ipnocausto, Bachiller Regañadientes, Silvio Liberio, and Tomé Cecial.[47]

While practically all of his works are marked by a critical character, in none of them, however, has Forner displayed his powers as a literary critic more effectively than in the *Exequias de la lengua castellana* and the *Oración apologética por la España y su mérito literario,* which form the basis of this study.

Contra D. Tomás Antonio Sánchez: *Carta de Bartolo,* en respuesta a la *Carta de Paracuellos.*

Polémica en defensa de la Oración Apologética: *(Contestación al discurso 113 de El Censor)* ; *Pasatiempo de D. Juan Pablo Forner* (contra *El Apologista Universal*) ; *Lista puntual de los errores de que está atiborrada la primera carta de las que el Español de París ha escrito contra la Oración apologética.*

Contra Vargas Ponce: *La corneja sin plumas.*

Contra varios teólogos andaluces, en defensa del establecimiento de un teatro en Sevilla: *Respuesta a la carta de Juan Perote; Carta dirigida a un vecino de Cádiz sobre otra de un literato de Sevilla; Respuesta a los desengaños útiles y avisos, importantes del literato de Écija; Prólogo al público sevillano,* etc.

Contra varios periodistas; *Diálogo entre El Censor, El Apologista Universal; Demostraciones palmarias de que El Censor, El Corresponsal,* etc.

[47] *Ibid.,* p. 333, note. In connection with the title of the *Exequias,* as also in the preface to the work, Forner uses the pseudonym, Pablo Ignocausto.

CHAPTER II

THE EXEQUIAS AND THE ORACIÓN APOLOGÉTICA

As was previously stated, the purpose of this study is to present Forner as a critic through an intensive study of his two outstanding works, the *Exequias de la lengua castellana* and the *Oración apologética por la España y su mérito literario.* In this chapter, however, we shall confine ourselves to a general discussion of the nature and purpose of these works and to a survey of the estimates which scholars have made in regard to Forner's ability in the field of literary criticism.

The *Exequias de la lengua castellana* is an allegorical fiction, which the author called a "Sátira menipea" because of its intermingling of prose and verse. Just when the work was written is not known. No date has been established, as internal evidence offers little in the way of conclusive deductions. That the author may have planned and begun the *Exequias* shortly after his *Sátira contra los vicios introducidos en la poesía castellana* seems highly plausible. The success of the *Sátira* in 1782 along with the timeliness of its subject matter may have encouraged the author to treat the topic in a more comprehensive manner and to present it in a unique and more pretentious form. Basically, the subject matter is the same in both works. Another factor which supports the assumption that Forner began the work early in his life is his statement in the prologue that he wrote it when he was young— "pienso que aun muy joven"—giving it the title, *Funeral de la lengua castellana.*[1] Since the *Exequias* did not come to light until after Forner's death,[2] it seems quite reasonable to believe that he

---

[1] "Noticia del licenciado Pablo Ignocausto y razón de la obra, todo en una pieza," *Exequias de la lengua castellana* (Madrid: La Lectura, 1925), p. 63.

[2] The work was first published by Cueto in 1871 in his *Poetas líricos del siglo XVIII.* In April, 1924, Sainz y Rodríguez fulfilled, as he said, Menéndez y Pelayo's request that the work be published separately ("Introducción," *Exequias de la lengua castellana,* Madrid: La Lectura, 1925). Unless otherwise specified, the references made to the *Exequias* in this study are to the edition of Sainz y Rodríguez.

14   *The Exequias and the Oración Apologética*

may have worked on it over a period of time. If, according to Cueto's observation, Forner wrote the *Noticia*, or prologue to the work, shortly before his death in 1897,[3] it is also reasonable to believe that the work may have been in process up to that time. His support of the ancient national theatre as expressed in the *Exequias* reveals an attitude toward the drama which he did not have when he wrote the *Sátira contra los vicios* in 1782[4] or when he wrote his letter to Ayala in 1784.[5] Apparently, the steady popularity of the Golden Age drama throughout the century[6] had changed his former views.[7] His satirical description of the drama in the *Exequias* is certainly a faithful delineation of the type of plays produced in the 'eighties and 'nineties; and it shows that the writing of the work, or at least, revisions of it, may have continued well into the 'nineties.

The purpose of the work, as stated by the author himself in his prologue, was to manifest the sources of good taste in the use of the Spanish language and to declare war on its corruptors "antiguos y modernos."[8]   The following comment made in the "Noticia" by Forner's imaginary legatee expresses well the plan of the work:

> En ella investiga las causas y orígenes del que el llama mal gusto en la *literatura española;* hace alarde y reseña de los escritores más famosos que han cultivado o han pervertido nuestra lengua; descubre las raíces del mal,

---

[3] "Exequias," Cueto, *Poetas líricos del siglo XVIII*, II, 378, n. See also Sotelo, *op. cit.*, p. 274, n. 2.

[4] Cf. "Sátira contra los vicios introducidos en la poesía castellana," Cueto, *Poetas líricos del siglo XVIII*, II, 304.

[5] Cf. "Carta de Don Juan Pablo Forner a Don Ignacio López de Ayala sobre haberle desaprobado su drama intitulado *La cautiva española*," Cueto, *ibid.*, p. 374. Menéndez y Pelayo observes that Forner also manifested little sympathy toward the ancient Spanish theatre in 1786 when he wrote the *Reflexiones de Tomé Cecial*, although the critic adds, "Cierto que en lo esencial de la cuestión, Forner no transige nunca . . ." *(Historia de las ideas estéticas*, V, 325-326).

[6] Ivy L. McClelland, *The Origins of the Romantic Movement in Spain* (Liverpool: Institute of Hispanic Studies, 1937), p. 165.

[7] See this study, pp. 6-7.

[8] "Noticia," *Exequias*, p. 63.

The Exequias and the Oración Apologética 15

> mete la tienta en la llaga, corta y trincha despiadadamente,
> y nada escapa de su pluma, sin elogio si lo cree bueno,
> y sin rechifla si lo cree malo.[9]

The story related in the allegory is sufficiently interesting. The author presents Arcadio and Aminta[10] going up to Parnassus accompanied by Cervantes, who was sent by Apollo to act as a guide to them.[11] They had not traveled far when they came upon a large, troubled, muddy lake at the foot of a mountain. Wallowing in the lake and on its banks were a countless number of frogs, which were formerly human beings, "escritores estrafalarios" from all countries.[12] Having been transformed by Apollo,[13] they were croaking away as frogs in this terminus for all useless, pedantic, fantastic, and perverse writers.[14]

In this "tropel confuso"[15] were all those writers who had perverted the ideas of beauty and destroyed the majesty of the Spanish language. There were the translators of French "libritos," who had corrupted the Spanish language in order to satisfy their hunger and their sordid interests;[16] lawyers and jurists, who had obscured the pure Castillian with their "latino-bárbaro" commentaries,[17] and a great number of bad poets, especially those of France who were as noted as the lawyers for their "estambre de la habladuría."[18] Humanists too were seen there, who should have destroyed pedantry, but who, instead, practised it.[19] Besides the loquacious philosophers who did nothing more than increase the number of books on library shelves,[20] there were also representa-

---

[9] *Ibid.*, pp. 63-64.

[10] Arcadio is the poetic name of José Iglesias de la Casa (*Exequias*, p. 72, n. 5) ; and Aminta, that of Forner *(ibid.*, p. 81, n. 10).

[11] *Ibid.*, p. 82.

[12] *Ibid.*, p. 88.

[13] *Ibid.*, p. 87.

[14] *Ibid.*, p. 93. In order to preserve the Fornerian savor many passages in this study are direct translations of the *Exequias* and the *Oración apologética.*

[15] *Ibid.*

[16] *Ibid.*, p. 89.

[17] *Ibid.*

[18] *Ibid.*, p. 91.

[19] *Ibid.*, p. 92.

[20] *Ibid.*

16 The Exequias and the Oración Apologética

tives of the modern philosophasters who engendered the eighteenth century impiety.[21]

As the interested travelers were reaching the summit of the sacred mountain[22] they saw Apollo, a "mancebo gallardo, en cuyo rostro aparecían la majestad y el agrado con una naturalidad casi divina."[23] He was followed by an excited, restless group. This crowd, he learned, was a band of "puros noticieros y habladores de marca, hipócritas de la sabiduría" who were trying to steal their way into the mansion.[24] Boasts of their abilities and their learning, and manifestations of their marked conceit and jealousy were heard in response to Apollo's inquiries.[25] Because Apollo was displeased with them for wasting their talents and making only charlatans of themselves,[26] he almost immediately converted them into frogs and ordered them into the lake.[27]

On the mountain the travelers met all the Spanish "sabios" who, in times past, had cultivated letters and developed the Spanish language. With these renowned personages they carried on a series of interesting and learned conversations which provided the author with a pretext to make a keen critical review of the literature of his country and to condemn its corruptors.[28]

In the temple the travelers beheld the sad spectacle of the beautiful matron, the Spanish Language, lying on a white bed, apparently cold in death.[29] When the time came for the funeral ceremonies, all passed through a spacious court, in the center of which was seen a disorderly pile of books that had been written by the executioners of the Castilian language. These books were to be burned in the pyre that was destined for the body of the language.[30]

---

[21] *Ibid.*, p. 88.
[22] *Ibid.*, p. 95.
[23] *Ibid.*, p. 96.
[24] *Ibid.*
[25] *Ibid.*, p. 97-102.
[26] *Ibid.*, p. 102.
[27] *Ibid.*, p. 103.
[28] *Ibid.*, pp. 106-140.
[29] *Ibid.*, p. 115.
[30] *Ibid.*, pp. 140-141.

The Exequias and the Oración Apologética 17

The detailed description of the funeral cortège[31] again provided a pretext for the continued discussion of the Spanish writers, resulting in praise for those of the past and condemnation for those of the time.

The procession was led by a number of women called "plañideras."[32] Behind these women, and represented by various insignia which were carried by men of letters, was a display of honors which the deceased had received.[33] Among them were symbols of theology,[34] of legislation and power,[35] statecraft, magistracy, and the science of war.[36]

Following this display was a group of Americans who paid their respects to the language for freeing them from the chains of servitude.[37] Behind these freedmen, the progenitors of the language—the Greek, Latin, and Arabic—appeared in wax figures. Forner's description of this part of the procession is very interesting as is seen from the following quotation:

> Representados en bultos de cera, iban en pos de los libertos algunos ascendientes o progenitores de la difunta. Apolo no quiso que fueran todos, porque no en todos hubo méritos para que se honrara con ellos su posteridad. Sobresalían las lenguas griega, latina y árabe, y nadie echó de menos a la goda, al revés de lo que sucedió en el entierro de Junia, hermana de Bruto y mujer de Casio, que toda la ciudad fijó la atención en estos dos célebres republicanos, por lo mismo que no los vió entre las imágenes de la familia. El tipo o fondo de nuestra lengua es latino-gótico; de las demás no heredó sino voces y armonía; pero Apolo dijo que la mezcla del carácter gótico destruyó la energía, variedad y fecundidad latina; endureció sus períodos, y pegó a las lenguas modernas la esterilidad que era consiguiente a la selvatiquez de las gentes del Norte, no de otro modo que desfiguró la belleza de las artes y la civilidad de las costumbres. Notamos allí

---

[31] *Ibid.*, p. 208.
[32] *Ibid.*, p. 209.
[33] *Ibid.*, p. 214.
[34] *Ibid.*, pp. 214-216.
[35] *Ibid.*, pp. 216-218.
[36] *Ibid.*, pp. 218-219.
[37] *Ibid.*, p. 229.

18   *The Exequias and the Oración Apologética*

que habiendo en el Parnaso no poca nobleza española, no hubo ni siquiera un hidalgo montañés que saliese a la defensa de la nación goda. Debió de consistir en que, como los nobles que hay allí son sabios, ninguno debía pensar tan neciamente que creyese haber debido a su genealogía las calidades de su espíritu, ni haber arribado a la inmortalidad por continuar en sí la raza de una gente facinerosa.[38]

Following the progenitors were Luis de León and Bartolomé de Argensola who led the long line of "sabios" that had cultivated, beautified, and perfected the language. The order in which these learned barons moved in the procession was according to the progression of letters in Spain and the degrees of their perfection.[39] The poets came first in the following order—lyric, dramatic, bucolic, epic, historic, didactic, and epigrammatic.[40] Among the prose writers, the sacred orators took the lead,[41] and were followed by the various types of historians and chroniclers,[42] who, in turn, were followed by the novelists, led by Cervantes.[43]

The author's musings and comments on the novelists were interrupted by the festive shouts and acclamations that came from the temple. Suddenly all beheld a marvelous spectacle, for the Spanish Language, the beautiful matron, began to show signs of life. She was presented to the astonished throng, weak and limp, leaning on the shoulders of some illustrious Spaniards.[44] Then Apollo, imposing silence on the group, explained to all, and especially, to Forner and Arcadio, that what had seemed to be death was but a paroxysm which he had brought about as a lesson to Spaniards. The strange event had been directed with the intention of showing the Spaniards how much they would lose if they allowed themselves to be defrauded of their glorious language, and how the evils of the day would bring about the

---

[38] *Ibid.*, pp. 238-239.
[39] *Ibid.*, p. 239.
[40] *Ibid.*, pp. 239-247.
[41] *Ibid.*, pp. 249-250.
[42] *Ibid.*, pp. 254-255.
[43] *Ibid.*, p. 257.
[44] *Ibid.*, p. 258.

The Exequias and the Oración Apologética   19

death of the language if they did not set about at once to correct them.[45]

After Apollo's brief speech, the allegory closes with Apollo's order to throw into the lake the ashes of the books which had been burned in the pyre.[46] He then commands Forner to ascend a peak which nature had made for a pulpit and to read the while from a book that he placed in his hands[47]—a book which proved to be Forner's own *Sátira contra la literatura chapucera de estos tiempos.*[48]

All the critics who pass judgment on the *Exequias* appear to have only words of praise and esteem for it. Menéndez y Pelayo styles it "la obra maestra de Forner, y una de las más notables del siglo XVIII."[49] He compares it to the *República literaria* of Saavedra Fajardo and the *Derrota de los pedantes* of Moratin. While Menéndez y Pelayo admits that the *Exequias* is inferior to these two works in amenity and grace, yet he thinks it superior to them in the transcendency of views and ideas. Forner's originality and penetrating analysis win this scholar's esteem and admiration. He also praises the honest, resolute criticism which Forner makes of the whole field of Spanish literature, his study of its progress and decadence, the accurate judgments which he forms of the literature, the incomparable exactitude and beauty in which he, at times, expresses his judgments, his severe condemnation of the tastes of his time, his literary doctrines, and his ardent love and defense of Spain's past grandeur.[50] It is Menéndez y Pelayo's belief, too, that nothing was written in the eighteenth century with a greater plenitude of ideas, with more abundant diction, greater energy of style, with more vivacity of imagination, and with more Spanish savor than some passages of this Menipea. According to this critic, its only defect lies in the extraordinary extension of the work and the earnest desire of the author to accumulate in it all the treasure of his vast

---

[45] *Ibid.,* p. 259.
[46] *Ibid.,* p. 262.
[47] *Ibid.,* p. 264.
[48] *Ibid.,* p. 265.
[49] Menéndez y Pelayo, *Historia de las ideas estéticas,* V, 328.
[50] *Ibid.,* p. 335.

20   *The Exequias and the Oración Apologética*

learning, his profound thought, and his enormous reading.[51] In fact, he states that no one in Spain at the time was capable of writing anything equal to the *Exequias*.[52]

Sotelo's judgment of the work was much the same. He sums up his criticism as follows:

> . . . encontraríais en ella críticas sólidas y juiciosas sobre el mérito de nuestros escritores más célebres, invectivas severas, y vehementes contra los propagadores del mal gusto, erudición inmensa y exquisita en la historia literaria de nuestra nación, rasgos admirables de elocuencia y poesía en sus diversos géneros, facilidad en la narración, artificio en la disposición, novedad en el desenlace, amenidad en las descripciones, oportunidad en los episodios, propiedad en los caracteres, pureza y elegancia en el estilo, agudeza, gracia, jocosidad y todas las bellezas proprias de este género de escritos.[53]

Montolíu speaks of it as a work in which Forner's satirical genius reaches its height.[54] The following comments show further this author's critical opinion:

> . . . un magnífico monumento de la crítica y ningún otro escritor del siglo XVIII puede codearse con él por la sólidez de sus juicios y por el poder de su visión sintética de toda le literatura española. . . . Tuvo Forner la más profunda intuición de espíritu propio y original de la lengua castellana. . . . En esta obra Forner pone el mismo ardor y la misma vehemencia en el panegírico que en la diatriba. Es un espíritu rígido y dogmático; ejerce la crítica literaria con la severidad de un tribunal, supremo de justicia; y sus juicios son categóricos, sin apelación. . . . Esta rigidez catoniana es lo que le aleja de los tiempos modernos, en que la crítica literaria reclama ante todo compresión y ductilidad de inteli-

---

[51] This encyclopedic character shows how typical the *Exequias* was of the times.

[52] *Ibid.*, p. 336. Menéndez y Pelayo esteemed the work so highly that he recommended that it be published separately *(ibid.,* p. 328, n.); see also this study, p. 13, n. 2.

[53] Sotelo, *op. cit.*, p. 291.

[54] *Op. cit.*, p. 696.

The Exequias and the Oración Apologética 21

gencia y no puede dejar de cobijarse al amparo de un discreto interrogante. Su espíritu dogmático y esencialmente pendenciero se refleja plenamente en su estilo generalmente sentencioso y categórico, construido con la recia estructura de un discurso forense, elocuente y persuasivo más que cálido y arrebatado; es un estilo de muy escasas tonalidades que a despecho de su castiza corrección y profusa abundancia llega a hastiar al lector por su exasperante monotonía.[55]

The fact that Sainz y Rodríguez published the *Exequias* separately and incorporated it in the "clásicos castellanos" proves the value he placed on the work. In the introduction to his edition, this author writes:

La escasez de obras en prosa de valor artístico durante nuestro siglo XVIII, justifica sobradamente su inclusión en una serie de clásicos castellanos; es además esta obra, precioso documento histórico a través del cual nos podemos asomar un poco a la intimidad de aquel hervidero de polémicas y apasionadas rencillas literarias y de carácter personal que fué nuestra literatura en la época en que floreció Forner.[56]

Having presented the general background of the *Exequias*, its purpose, and some critical comments made upon it, we pass now to a similar consideration of the *Oración apologética*.

The *Oración apologética por la España y su mérito literario*,[57] which appeared in 1786, was Forner's answer to the Frenchman, Masson, who had asked in his article, "Espagne," "Que doit-on à l'Espagne? Et depuis deux siècles, depuis quatre, depuis dix, qu'a-t-elle fait pour l'Europe?"[58]

---

[55] *Ibid.*, pp. 700-701.

[56] *Op. cit.*, p. 9.

[57] In the introduction to the work, Forner calls attention to the fact that the title is not long, thus taking a little thrust at his enemies for the long titles they were using. He writes, "No hay, a fé, gran necesidad de que aumente yo el número de los que con portadas, y prefaciones magníficas nos incitan a leer sandeces estupendas" *(Oración apologética, p. iv)*.

[58] "Espagne," *Encyclopédie méthodique,* I (Paris: 1782), p. 565. For the background of this article and the story of the polemic which it produced, see Appendix I of this study.

22   The Exequias and the Oración Apologética

Being the sworn enemy of the Encyclodedists,[59] Forner was pleased, no doubt, when he was invited by Floridablanca, the Minister, to write the official protest against the insults offered by Masson.[60] According to the author's statement in the preface of his *Oración apologética,* however, the work which he offered was not new, for, at the suggestion of some of his friends, he simply presented for publication a work which he had written previously with the intention of exercising his skill in Castilian eloquence.[61]

The opening sentence of the *Oración apologética* sets up clearly and concisely the fundamental proposition which Forner wished to defend: "La gloria científica de una nación no se debe medir por sus adelantamientos en los cosas superfluas y perjudiciales."[62] From this sentence, it is evident that he sets forth his opposition to what he believed was the norm by which Spain's calumniators measured the progress of a nation. The standard of the Encyclopedists was the "science des choses utiles," a philosophy which tended toward the welfare and happiness of man in the materialistic sense,[63] but it was not in agreement with Forner's

---

[59] Menéndez y Pelayo, *Historia de los heterodoxes españoles,* III, 334.

[60] In the words of the Baron de Bourgoing, this matter had become "une espèce d'affaire d'état." (Quoted by Luigi Sorrento, *Francia e Spagna nel settecento: Battaglie e sorgenti di idee,* Milano: Vita e Pensiero, 1928, p. 245). The invitation extended to Forner and the remuneration of 6,000 reals gives proof of the government's faith in Forner and his doctrine, despite the fact that the royal decree forbidding him to publish anything without the sanction of the government had been issued in 1785, only a year before. Further evidence of government support was shown in 1788, when he was assigned the censorship of the *Historia universal,* written by the Jesuit, Tomás Borrego, for which he was likewise granted a pension of 6,000 reals (Sainz y Rodríguez, *op. cit.,* p. 12).

[61] Forner also explains in the preface to his work that his first intention was to publish a translation of Denina's discourse and accompany it with critical notes that would give proofs for the truths asserted by Denina and would enhance the glory of Spain. Dissuaded from this by a friend, however, he decided to reprint Denina's work in French along with his *Oración* (*Oración apologética,* pp. i-iii). According to Fernández y González, the friend designated was the learned Campomanes (*Historia de la crítica literaria en España desde Luzán hasta nuestros días con la exclusión de los autores que aun viven,* Madrid: Gómez Fuentenebro, 1867, p. 40).

[62] *Oración apologética,* p. 1.

[63] Sorrento, *op. cit.,* p. 234.

The Exequias and the Oración Apologética 23

standard of appraisal. His judgment, like that of most Spaniards, was based on the principle that only those sciences which lead to human happiness in the ethical, spiritual, and Christian senses, are of value, and merit praise for those who cultivate them.[64]

Forner's work was an oratorical defense of Spain's contribution to Europe, in which he contends that no nation can dispute the progress of his country in the attainment of what the Spaniards regarded as truly useful. In the preface to the work, Forner states clearly his manner of treating the subject. The work was not a "biblioteca";[65] nor was it a critical history. It was not his intention to make an exhaustive defense of the knowledge and culture of Spain or to burden the work with critical investigations, quotations, and testimonies. Nor did he wish the work to be regarded as a satire in the contemporary sense of the term—a declamation directed by an ardent, enthusiastic Spaniard against the foreigners who were maligning his country and his countrymen. The work was intended only as demonstration of the origin of the calumnies which were being directed against Spain.[66] His treatment of the matter was that of an orator. Making use of the truths which had been proved over and over again in the extensive works of the apologists who had preceded him, he aimed to direct them toward the proof of his fundamental hypothesis.[67]

Forner divides the work into two parts. At the end he adds a section containing valuable critical notes.[68] In the first part he deals with those things which contribute to true scientific merit, pointing out at the same time the injustice of the common accusations by which the enemies of Spain seek to discredit her and her culture. At the beginning of the second part, he states that since he was living in the philosophic age,[69] he would make use

---

[64] Menéndez y Pelayo, *Historia de los heterodoxos españoles*, III, 333; see also L. Sorrento, *op. cit.*, p. 235.

[65] *Oración apologética*, pp. iv, 76.

[66] *Ibid.*, p. 10.

[67] *Ibid.*, pp. iii-iv.

[68] These notes give evidence of the author's scholarship and his vast knowledge of Spain's literary and scientific past. Cotarelo y Mori asserts that this section containing the notes is the best part of the work (*op. cit.*, p. 316).

[69] Forner seldom misses an opportunity for a thrust at the "philosophic age."

24 The Exequias and the Oración Apologética

of ·a philosophical treatment of his subject, thus offering Spain's calumniators the opportunity of· seeing the views of Vives and Bacon republished in the "Península Escolástica"[70] and used· as standards for judging the literary merit of Spain.[71] In his enumeration of the many notable benefits that Europe had received from Spain it is obvious that Forner is making a direct reply to Masson. Among Spain's contributions, Forner points to her wise legislation, which existed even from the time of the Middle Ages; her systems of national and international law; her discovery of the New World and the spread of Christianity to the farthest limits of the world; her printing of the first Polyglot Bible and the first· Greek text of the New Testament; her philosophical and theological contributions through Vives and Cano; her advances made in the science of medicine through Laguna, Mercado, and others; her invaluable literary works which could be a source of great enlightenment and a means of breaking down ignorance, defective reasoning, unsound and biased judgments, ·vain theories and systems, conceit, and insubordination on the part of many of the author's sophistic contemporaries who made profession of oracular powers.[72]

The appearance of the Oración apologética caused a great furor, increasing the number of polemics. Foridablanca's appointment of Forner for the work had created sufficient jealousy among his already too numerous enemies; but the printing of the work at government expense and the recognition of the merits of the author in terms of a remuneration of 6,000 reals plus the returns from the sale of the work annoyed the galicistas exceedingly.[73] They brought forth attacks not only on Forner, but on the minister as well. Bernardo Iriarte accused Floridablanca of stirring up aversion for the French.[74] He accused him, too, of protecting and encouraging apologetic writers by engaging the

---

[70] An epithet frequently applied to Spain by her enemies.

[71] Oración apologética, pp. 75-76.

[72] The encyclopedic character of this work also shows how typical it was of the times.

[73] Cotarelo y Mori, op. cit., p. 315.

[74] Cotarelo y Mori remarks that Floridablanca never had been very "afrancesado" and that he and the government supported the Gallophobe party (op. cit., p. 314).

The Exequias and the Oración Apologética   25

biting, indiscreet pen of the public defamer, Juan Pablo Forner, to compose "una voluminosa, impertinente y fastidiosa *Apología.*"[75] The diatribes against Forner were directed both against his person and his work. The invectives were all characterized by a marked superficiality, as Sainz y Rodríguez points out and exemplifies with the following quintet of Huerta:

> Ya salió la Apología
> del grande orador Forner;
> salió lo que yo decía:
> descaro, bachillería,
> no hacer harina y moler.[76]

Criticisms of Forner were also carried in the columns of the newspapers of the day, especially, in *El Censor* and *El Apologista Universal*. P. Centano devoted thirty-two pages of one issue of the latter periodical to calling Forner a charlatan.[77] At another time, a contributor to the same paper, wrote: "He recibido la ridícula Apología de Forner . . . para decir verdad, no la entiendo, ni creo hay en el mundo quien la entienda, excepto el mismo Forner."[78] In 1787 *El Censor* published a burlesque, entitled *Oración apologética por el África y su mérito literario,* the opening sentence of which was the initial sentence of Forner's *Oración apologética.*[79]

The *Cartas de un español residente en París,* the last important book of this polemic,[80] apparently contained many petty criticisms.

---

[75] Iriarte, as quoted by Cotarelo y Mori, *op. cit.,* p. 316, n.

[76] Huerta, as quoted by Sainz y Rodríguez, *Las polémicas sobre la cultura española* (Madrid: Fortanet, 1919), p. 35.

[77] Cotarelo y Mori, *op. cit.,* p. 320.

[78] *El Apologista Universal,* as quoted by Cotarelo y Mori, *op. cit.,* p. 321, n.

[79] Cotarelo y Mori, *op. cit.,* p. 320.

[80] Sainz y Rodríguez, *Las polémicas sobre la cultura española,* p. 35. Sainz y Rodríguez states that the *Cartas de un español residente en París* is generally attributed to an Antonio Borrego, but he thinks it was inspired, at least, by Domingo Iriarte, the brother of the fabulist (Sainz y Rodríguez, "Introducción," *Exequias,* p. 26). Cotarelo y Mori says that many thought the work was written by Tomás de Iriarte in the name of his brother,

26 The Exequias and the Oración Apologética

Examples of these are seen in Carta IX, in which the author speaks of the dishonesty of Forner in calling Montesquieu, "al gran Montesquieu, escritor de leyes en epigramas y fastidiosamente ponderado."[81] Again, he speaks of Forner's boastfulness in saying that Descartes was "indubitablemente menos que Aristóteles."[82] Similarly, he takes exception to what Forner wrote of Cervantes and Don Quijote; and in Forner's tribute to Vives, which all critics have praised, he sees only simple truths written by a pseudo-Spaniard.[83]

Such was the general critical attitude of Forner's contemporaries toward him and his *Oración apologética*. Later criticism consists, generally, in the repetition of these eighteenth century comments joined to an account of the polemics which were the outgrowth of the publication of the work. A few scholars, however, add an occasional personal opinion.

Menéndez y Pelayo, in addition to reviewing the history and content of the work, remarks that Forner directed his defense along lines that were somewhat new and proved his proposition marvelously and with genuine eloquence.[84] Commenting on the content of the work, he writes:

> La cuestion del mérito literario de España, entonces como ahora, ocultaba diferencias más hondas, diferencias de doctrina, y era mucho más de lo que parece en la corteza. No es dado a ojos materialistas alcanzar el mérito de una civilización toda cristiana, desde la raíz hasta las hojas.[85]

Domingo, but that Forner attributed the *Cartas* to Antonio Borrego, the brother of Tomás Borrego, who was the author of the *Historia universal*, which was strongly censured by Forner *(op. cit.,* p. 321) ; cf. this study, p. 6. In referring to the *Enciclopedia universal ilustrada*, XX, 685, for biographical data concerning Escartín, whom Forner rails against on account of his commercialism in his literary pursuits, I found that the *Cartas de un español residente en París* is attributed to Escartín; see Escartín, Appendix II, p. 141.

[81] *Carta IX* of the *Cartas de un español residente en París,* as referred to by Cotarelo y Mori, *op. cit.,* p. 322.

[82] *Ibid.*

[83] *Ibid.*

[84] *Historia de los heterodoxos españoles,* III, 333.

[85] *Ibid.,* p. 335.

The Exequias and the Oración Apologética 27

Sainz y Rodríguez writes the following comments on the work:

> Forner, con su *Oración apologética por la España y su mérito literario,* es el representante genuino de estas polémicas en el siglo XVIII . . .[86] Puso en la polémica . . . el habitual ardor y violencia de su espíritu, no desmayando, a pesar del casi absoluto aislamiento en que se vió . . .[87]
>
> La *Apología* es una pieza retórica escrita con el nervio y la elocuencia habituales en su autor, pero que a veces peca de declamatoria y fastidiosamente correcta. Las notas eruditísimas, muestran el profundo conocimiento que tenía Forner de nuestro pasado científico y literario, y las dos páginas que dedica a Luis Vives, llenas de entusiasmo, son quizá el trozo más profundo de crítica dedicado a un filósofo nacional en todo el siglo XVIII.
>
> Con gran tino escribe Forner contra aquel ambiente de generalidades superficiales, contra aquel afán de escribir todos *de omni re scibili,* y acertadamente atribuye muchas de las diatribas de entonces contra España, no al apasionamiento, sino a la ignorancia de los hechos.[88]

Antonio Rubio remarks that in the *Oración apologética* Forner showed himself, in preparation and in character, capable of vindicating the intellectual history of Spain against the charges which were cast upon her in the name of the "esprit européen."[89]

Cotarelo y Mori has little that is favorable to say about the work. He notes that Forner does not proceed as an "erudito" but as a "retórico";[90] that he sins by tautology; and that at times he is an excessive declaimer. The critic admits, however, that there are passages in the work where Forner shows himself to be truly eloquent, especially, in his tribute to Vives. He also acknowledges Forner's successful manner of treating the judgments which

---

[86] *Las polémicas sobre la cultura española,* p. 27.

[87] *Ibid.,* p. 29.

[88] *Ibid.,* pp. 33-34.

[89] Antonio Rubio, *La crítica del galicismo en España, 1726-1832* (Mexico: Universidad Nacional de México, 1937), p. 89.

[90] *Op. cit.,* p. 316. Forner himself stated the equivalent of this comment in the introduction to his work; see this study, p. 23.

28 The Exequias and the Oración Apologética

were passed on Spain by foreigners. The section containing the notes is in his opinion, the best part of the work.[91]

Although Robert Pellissier had stated in his work that Forner should have no place in his study since he could not be looked upon as a "fair representative of the spirit of loyal opposition to the neo-classic attitude of mind,"[92] a judgment on the *Oración apologética* somehow got into his work. According to him the *Oración* was for Forner "one more opportunity to cry out against science and the rest of Europe";[93] it was "not literary but religious and moral."[94] Pellissier, in his comments, quotes a few passages from the apology, but with the explanation that he does so with the sole purpose of showing that as the neo-classic movement developed it changed its original course. The remarks which the critic makes, however, seem to explain that, after all, Forner's work was typical of the times and that it was by reason of current trends that the work was religious and moral rather than literary. The following statements of Pellissier are very clear in this regard:

> ... the time had come when the movement in the course of its evolution had passed out of the literary field, in which it had started, to extend to nearly all the other fields of intellectual activity as well as to matters of religion. By gradually leaving the discussion of the good and bad points of the three unities it had taken the road followed by the French "philosophes." By slow degrees it had become the weapon of those who wished to reform the state and the church. If we quote from Forner's apology it is only because we are thus enabled to illustrate the last stages in the evolution which we have just mentioned.[95]

As the critical comments thus far cited have referred specifically to Forner's *Exequias* and the *Oración apologética* the following

---

[91] *Op. cit.,* p. 316.
[92] *Op. cit.,* p. 114.
[93] *Ibid.,* p. 149.
[94] *Ibid.*
[95] *Op. cit.,* p. 149.

The Exequias and the Oración Apologética 29

general remarks give further evidence of the fact that Forner is regarded by the later scholars as an outstanding figure in the field of literary criticism. Continuing Menéndez y Pelayo's comments, we note that he looks upon Forner as the embodiment of the most intelligent and violent reaction against the French Encyclopedic movement[96] and the most tireless polemist of eighteenth century Spain.[97] He considers Forner, however, to be more outstanding in the field of historical and philosophical criticism than in the realm "propiamente literaria."[98] Continuing his comment, he writes:

> Listo dijo de él con profunda verdad que tenía el entendimiento más apto para comprender las verdades que las bellezas. Aquel hombre, tan independiente en otras cosas, nunca pudo romper el yugo de la retórica, y juzgaba las obras artísticas más por preceptos externos que por una fruición personal y reposada, la cual sólo en muy pequeño grado podemos concederle. Aunque misogalo, carecía del arranque estético de Lessing, y veneraba la autoridad de los franceses en el teatro, después de haberla negado en la filosofía y en todo lo restante. La misma aspereza de sus polémicas, la trivialidad de los motivos de muchas de ellas, la saña con que persigue a escritorzuelos adocenados, que ni en bien ni en mal podían influir en la corriente de las ideas, los rasgos de chocarrería estudiantil o frailuna con que matiza sus folletos, denuncian en él cierta falta de gusto y de tacto, de la cual nunca pudo curarse totalmente.[99]

Montolíu y Togores speaks of Forner and of Feijóo as the most important representatives of the eighteenth century critical spirit, superior to all other writers of the period.[100] González-Blanco presents him as the precursor of modern satiric criticism; as one of those men who love the truth, are sure of it and desire to

---

[96] *Historia de las ideas estéticas*, V, 333. J. R. Spell makes similar comments in his work, *Rousseau in the Spanish World before 1833* (Austin, Texas: University of Texas, 1938), pp. 95-99.

[97] *Historia de las ideas estéticas*, V, 323.

[98] *Ibid.*, p. 334.

[99] *Ibid.*, pp. 334-335.

[100] *Op. cit.*, pp. 695, 700.

30   *The Exequias and the Oración Apologética*

spread it at any cost.[101] Sorrento styles Forner "il nobile difensore della Spagna."[102]

Among the dissenting opinions, we note again those of Cotarelo y Mori, Robert Pellissier, and Antonio Rubio. Cotarelo y Mori, agreeing with Lista's opinion, considers Forner wanting in imagination and sentiment, better able to conceive truth than beauty. Although he states that Forner is capable only of the bitterest satire;[103] yet, he recognizes Forner's ability, as is seen from the following comments:

> Llevóse a la tumba probablemente los más sazonados frutos de su ingenio: en el campo puramente literario sólo dejó una obra en verdad notable, que, como era de esperar, es una sátira;[104] lo demás son bosquejos y ensayos, vislumbres o destellos de una grande inteligencia malo- grada por sus debilidades de hombre.[105]

Robert Pellissier speaks of him as "a writer who produced nothing of lasting value;"[106] and Antonio Rubio regards Forner as incapable of a just appreciation of "the golden age of bagatelle" because of his intellectual vigor.[107]

While the chief purpose of this chapter has been to present in a general way the critical nature and purpose of the *Exequias* and the *Oración apologética,* it has also shown the place accorded to Forner in the field of literary criticism, by both modern scholars and those who were contemporary with him.

As has been seen from the foregoing discussion, the *Exequias* is an allegorical invention, a "sátira menipea." It had for its purpose, as the author himself pointed out, the manifestation of the sources of good taste in the literature of Spain and the condemnation of its corruptors. Likewise according to the author's

---

[101] "Ensayo sobre un crítico español del siglo XVIII," *Nuestro Tiempo,* XVIII, 165.

[102] *Op. cit.,* p. 273.

[103] *Op. cit.,* p. 223.

[104] He refers here, of course, to the *Exequias.*

[105] *Op. cit.,* p. 398.

[106] *Op. cit.,* p. 175; see also this study, p. 5, n. 18 and p. 28.

[107] *Op. cit.,* pp. 89-90.

The Exequias and the Oración Apologética   31

exposition, the *Oración apologética* is an oratorical defense of Spain's culture and her contribution to Europe, in which the author contended that no nation could dispute the progress of his country in the attainment of the truly useful—the useful in the sense of the ethical, spiritual and Christian.

In both works, as a critic of ideas, he directs his criticism against the so-called progress of the eighteenth century under the hegemony of France. He shows himself not only a bitter enemy of the ideas of the French *philosophes* and of the invasion of the Encyclopedic movement in Spain, but also an unrelenting opponent of the Spaniards who were being won over to the French system of thought. In both works he defends the ancient culture of Spain, her language, her wisdom, her learning, her literature, her philosophy, her religion, her progress.

As has been noted, Forner came in for his share of adverse criticism at the hands of his contemporaries. This, after all, should be expected, and especially, in the eighteenth century when the two groups in Spain, the *afrancesados* and the *casticistas* were so bitterly combatting one another. While the contemporary comments set forth in this study have been largely those of Forner's adversaries, it must not be concluded that he had no other friends besides Sotelo and Floridablanca, whose kindly feeling and favorable comments have been indicated.

The criticism of Forner and his work which has been offered by modern scholars is on the whole quite favorable. While Antonio Rubio, Cotarelo y Mori, and Robert Pellissier offer unfavorable comments, such scholars as Menéndez y Pelayo, Sainz y Rodríguez, González-Blanco, Cueto, Montolíu, and Sorrento acclaim Forner as one of the outstanding figures in the field of literary criticism in eighteenth century Spain.

With this general discussion of the *Exequias* and the *Oración apologética* and of the critical comments on Forner's ability as a literary critic, we pass now to a consideration of Forner's views on philosophy and science as set forth in these two works, since he was primarily a critic of ideas.

CHAPTER III

PHILOSOPHY, RELIGION, AND SCIENCE

Like other eighteenth century writers, Forner was primarily interested in ideas rather than in aesthetic principles. The eighteenth century, it will be recalled, has been styled the "age of ideas," "the age of enlightenment," the "age of reason," "the philosophic age."

It was a time when France was impressing the whole of Europe with her intellectual hegemony.[1] Throughout the eighteenth century Paris was regarded as the intellectual capital of Europe. The French language was then recognized as the language of culture and diplomacy, and the arts and manners of Paris were slavishly imitated in all the courts of Europe.[2] The French, who had set themselves up as the leaders of European enlightenment and as beacons of progress, were primarily concerned with philosophical, social, and scientific questions, which they felt it their duty to pass on to the rest of Europe. Consequently, the aesthetic aspect of literature was put in the background and "literary men used their art mainly as a vehicle for philosophical and political propaganda."[3]

Beneath this propaganda, which the writers[4] claimed was devoted to political and social reforms,[5] there was a skeptical philosophy[6] and a hatred of any form of authority and tradition.

---

[1] L. Sorrento, *Italiani e Spagnuoli contro l'egemonia intelletuale Francese nel settecento* (Milano: Società editrice, s. d.), p. 37.

[2] G. Bruun, *The Enlightened Despots* (New York: Holt, 1929), pp. 2-3.

[3] K. T. Butler, *A History of French Literature* (London: Methuen, 1923), I, 307.

[4] The promoters of these doctrines were commonly known as *philosophes*. Later they were called *Encyclopédistes (ibid., p. 364).

[5] "Like all astute reformers they pretended that their program offered no new departure but a return to first principles" (Bruun, *op. cit.*, p. 18).

[6] Many of the literary men, among them Voltaire, reflected in their writings the form of skepticism known as deism, which was prevalent in the middle and upper classes of Europe at the time. Not all of the *philosophes*

32

Philosophy, Religion, and Science 33

With this new philosophical development, "philosophy" became the password of the day and practically all the intellectuals of the time were eager to be called philosophers. At that time there were two prevailing systems of thought which might be called the natural and the supernatural.[7] Naturally, these systems affected the interested parties in varying degrees; but, generally speaking, the philosophic thinkers of the time were divided into two groups, the orthodox and the *philosophes*. The division between these groups was by no means a passive thing. In fact, it was so pronounced that nearly all the literature of the period was of a controversial nature, or at least, productive of controversy.

The *philosophes* saw in reason and natural law the antidote for all the social ills of the time; and in education or "enlightenment" the restorer of man's happiness.[8] As is to be expected, the orthodox thinkers supported the traditional philosophy. They had faith in reason, but in reason guided by revelation and faith. While they recognized natural law and natural virtue, they regarded supernatural law, supernatural virtue, and a supernatural or revealed religion as essential to man.[9]

The ideas of the eighteenth century philosophic movement in France were really not new. The whole movement was based on an anthropocentric humanism which began with the Renaissance. This Renaissance humanism steadily grew and broadened its scope until it reached the peak of its development in eighteenth century France. As will be recalled, the entire century was notably marked by extreme intellectual individualism, rationalism, scepticism,

---

were atheists and materialists (Bruun, *op. cit.*, p. 8). They were all rationalists, however, in the sense that "by reasoning they meant regulating thought by observed facts, or by sensation and feeling" (R. Palmer, *Catholics and Unbelievers in Eighteenth Century France*, Princeton: Princeton University, 1939, p. 204).

[7] *Ibid.*, p. 4.

[8] As G. Bruun points out, the defect of the optimistic philosophy of the rationalist lay in its first premise. "It assumed tacitly that the emotions of the heart, the workings of the mind, the relations of society, and the business of the government, could be analyzed by the same methods and the same ease as the physical sciences" (*op. cit.*, p. 6).

[9] Palmer notes that the orthodox thinkers "could not hope to be brilliantly original" because "as conservatives they were all condemned to repeat what had been heard before" (*op. cit.*, p. 222).

34   *Philosophy, Religion, and Science*

materialism, anti-traditionalism, freedom unto license, humanitarianism, and anti-religious attitudes. The majority of the free-thinkers of the time associated natural science with a new metaphysics. They substituted the natural for the supernatural,[10] and science for theology. They considered the universe of matter and mind to be directed and controlled by an inevitable *natural law*. With them *human reason* was practically deified, and "speedy *progress* and ultimate *perfectibility* of the human race" were to be the result of obedience to the natural law.[11]

Having placed the blame for the deplorable conditions of society upon traditional institutions like the Church and the State, the reformers set out to rebuild the world, and to destroy,[12] if necessary, whatever interfered with their program.[13] With the realization that the institutions which they wished to reform or abolish were "hallowed by tradition,"[14] they set about first to break down

---

[10] As Palmer points out, there was, even by the seventeenth century, a tendency to regard the natural as "the intelligible and rational order of things," and the supernatural as "the unintelligible and the arbitrary" (*op. cit.,* p. 34). While God was still thought of as the mind or force behind both the natural and the supernatural, he was more closely associated with the supernatural. Since the supernatural was regarded as "unintelligible and arbitrary" God was becoming "mysterious and ineffable" (*ibid.).*

[11] Carlton Hayes, *A Political and Cultural History of Modern Europe* (New York: Macmillan, 1932), I, 511-512.

[12] Their destruction was always under the pretense of reform. Forner thinks some pity might be shown toward them if they had not added malignity to their delirium and imposture to their ignorance (*Oración apologética,* pp. 9-10). It was his opinion that the false philosophers who trampled upon the most sacred principles of religion and society should be punished in the same manner as the thief or the rebel (*ibid.,* p. 20).

[13] Bruun, *op. cit.,* p. 9. While the *philosophes* were opposed to any form of organized Christianity, yet it is a generally known fact that they regarded the Roman Catholic Church as the greatest obstacle to their endeavors and the strongest force they had to meet. Opposed to their doctrine of the perfectibility of man was the Church's doctrine of original sin and the necessity of redemption. Opposed to their teaching that science led to certainty was the Church's teaching that the revelation and the Fathers were the sources of highest truth; and opposed to their "reasonable" explanation of all matters was the Church's "supernatural" explanation (*ibid.,* pp. 9-10).

[14] *Ibid.,* p. 17.

Philosophy, Religion, and Science 35

the reverence which surrounded them. Whenever any irregularities or misdemeanors were observed in connection with the Church or State, they proceeded to make public scandal of them and to ridicule the persons concerned. Satire and ridicule became the chief weapons of the *philosophes* against the existing régime.[15]

(Because the social philosophy of the eighteenth century writers was in many respects anti-Christian, and because the old Spain with its traditional culture and its Christian philosophy still existed,[16] French Encyclopedism did not make the same inroads into Spain as it did in other countries. There were many in Spain, by far the majority, who, alert to the pernicious elements of the movement, feared its influence.[17]

The Gallophobes then regarded it as their duty to combat the movement. Their counter attack produced a didactic literature worthy of note, a body of controversial works, which according to Menéndez y Pelayo, was superior in content, if not in form to those written elsewhere at the time.[18] While the style of these books makes them difficult to read, a fact which deprives them of the popularity they would otherwise merit, there is contained in them a corrective measure or an answer to every objection raised by the false philosophers against the Christian traditionalism which

---

[15] *Ibid.* G. R. Havens points out that Voltaire used the drama and every other form of literature as a vehicle for satire and criticism of what he considered abuses *(Selections from Voltaire,* New York: Century, 1925, p. 10). Voltaire's "petits pâtés" and his "rogatons" went all over Europe. Through his pamphlets he became the first journalist to work through the "journalists' court of appeal, public opinion" *(ibid.,* pp. 330-331).

[16] Menéndez y Pelayo, *Historia de los heterodoxos españoles,* III, 307. It did enter Spain, however, and it would have done so in spite of the presence of the French rule in Spain at that time. Both Menéndez y Pelayo *(Historia de las ideas estéticas,* V, 129-130) and Montolíu *(op. cit.,* pp. 657-658) point out that since the movement was common to all Europe it would have penetrated into Spain even if political reasons had not seemed to favor it. Montolíu also adds that the hegemony of France was definitely due to the superiority of her intellectual culture and that the French rule in Spain at the time was a concomitant phenomenon rather than a cause of the ingress of the movement *(ibid.,* pp. 657-658).

[17] Jefferson R. Spell shows in his recent study that the infiltration of French ideas in Spain was considered a real menace by many Spaniards *(op. cit.,* pp. 95-98).

[18] *Historia de los heterodoxos españoles,* III, 307.

36 *Philosophy, Religion, and Science*

they so bitterly opposed. The Spanish apologists met their enemies in every field, whether in the realm of physical science, social science, scholastic theology, metaphysics, theodicy, natural law, cosmology, Biblical exegesis, or history.[19]

Forner was among those who directed the strongest resistance against the doctrines of the *Encyclopédistes*. According to Menéndez y Pelayo, he was a bitter opponent of the ideas of the eighteenth century, which he called the "siglo de ensayos, siglo de diccionarios, siglo de impiedad, siglo hablador, siglo charlatán, siglo ostentador," instead of giving it the customary pompous titles of "siglo de la razón, siglo de las luces y siglo de la filosofía."[20]

Forner shows in his writings that he had no sympathy with the spirit of his times. He speaks of the misfortune of being born in an age which hardly recognizes "rectitud" in its manner of thinking and judging, and yet gives itself the magnificent title of philosophic. He calls it an age of oracles, an age of ultramontane sophists, who by their boldness and vain verbosity had influenced and won over the common writers to their capricious manner of speaking. He bemoans the fact that worthwhile learning and the knowledge of antiquity were so depreciated in his time that they were found only in unreliable dictionaries. He regrets that institutions—empires, laws, religions, rites, dogmas, doctrines, customs, styles—in a word, everything that before was held in reverence, should be treated with such disrespect in the sophistic declamations of the so-called philosophers. He rails against them for their conceit in disapproving of everything that did not fit in with their imaginary worlds and the whims of their delirium.[21] He describes their conceit in the following manner:

> No hay gobierno sabio, si ellos no le establecen; política útil, si ellos no la dictan; república feliz, si ellos no la dirigen; religión santa y verdadera, si ellos, que son los maestros de la vanidad, no la fundan y determinan.[22]

---

[19] *Ibid.*

[20] Forner as quoted by Menéndez y Pelayo, *ibid.*, pp. 331-332.

[21] *Oración apologética*, pp. 7-8.

[22] *Ibid.*, p. 9.

Philosophy, Religion, and Science 37

Forner's denunciation of the philosophers of his day is very pronounced. The *philosophes*, he remarks, applied the term philosophy to "extravagancias desenfrenadas del entendimiento."[23] In his opinion, the followers of "el extravagante Voltaire" were "sofistas malignos, ignorantes de los mismos principios de la filosofía," which they boasted of possessing in a high degree.[24] They seemed to think that they were philosophers, simply because they exercised themselves in reflection, as if this ability were given only to those who called themselves philosophers.[25]

The "ilustración" of his time, Forner points out, consisted for the most part in doubts and controversies, and the period abounding in sects, systems, and opinions, possessed more nonsense than was ever written before.[26] The *philosophes* scarcely recognized any "rectitud" in their manner of thinking and judging.[27] They were defenders not of liberty, but of license in thought.[28] Their liberty consisted in the abuse of reason, which was turned to the adulation of evil, the authorization of vice, and the defense of abominations.[29] Priding themselves on their originality,[30] it was their desire to think in any manner, provided they did not think as the rest of men;[31] it was their ambition to fill volumes with their novelties.[32]

---

[23] *Exequias*, p. 187.

[24] *Oración apologética*, p. 18.

[25] *Exequias*, p. 93.

[26] *Oración apologética*, pp. 71-72.

[27] *Ibid.*, p. 7.

[28] *Ibid.*, pp. 151-154.

[29] *Ibid.*, p. 21. Helvetius, he points out, placed the incentive of heroism in obscene sensuality, and banished virtue *(ibid.*, p. 22). The destructive methods of the *philosophes* calls forth a few comments from the author on philosophy in pagan times. He notes that before philosophy, as such, came into being, the great society of nations was formed; and men who had no more philosophy than the inspiration of natural light introduced culture and virtue into these societies. By constructive, not destructive methods, they directed things along the best course *(ibid.*, p. 30). The early republics of Sparta and Rome knew sufficient philosophy for the worthy practice of human and civil virtues *(ibid.*, p. viii).

[30] *Exequias*, p. 92.

[31] *Oración apologética*, pp. 22-23.

[32] *Exequias*, pp. 92-93.

38 *Philosophy, Religion, and Science*

Forner's ideas of philosophy are very different from those held by the *philosophes*. His definition of philosophy, which he puts in the mouth of the censor of books in Parnassus, though not a scientific one, contains his ideas of practical philosophy, and shows his opposition to the views of the *Encyclopédistes*.

> La filosofía, señor don *Ridículo*, es la ciencia de la verdad y de la virtud. Y como la verdad es difícil de hallar, y la virtud no es fácil de practicar, la filosofía enseña a examinar y meditar mucho y a hablar poco; a obrar bien antes de reprender en otros las malas obras. La filosofía es la perfección del entendimiento, y el insolente, el impostor, el jactancioso, el charlatán, no serán nunca filósofos hasta que hayan logrado persuadir al mundo que la insolencia, la impostura, la jactancia y el charlatanismo son los instrumentos que perfeccionan la mente humana. Lo filosofía es la perfección de la voluntad, y el maligno, el detractor, el envidioso, el delator, el malsín y el enemigo capital de las tareas o felicidades ajenas no pueden pasar por filósofos sino entre sí mismos, y aun por eso son ellos los que se aplican a sí mismos este venerable renombre, desacreditado miserablemente por el abuso que han hecho de él tales sabandijas. La filosofía es la modestia, la decencia, la desconfianza, el decoro, la propiedad, el examen profundo de las cosas, la larga y escrupulosa experiencia, la restitud de raciocinio; todo esto y muchísimo más es la filosofía.[33]

Forner defends the practical philosophy of the Spaniards against those who accused Spain of knowing no philosophy, of possessing no philosophers,[34] and of having no liberty of thought.[35] Spain, he says, has been regarded by some as "una de las regiones del

---

[33] *Ibid.*, p. 175.

[34] *Ibid.*, p. 187.

[35] *Oración apologética*, p. 18. Voltaire, he points out, had written that the Spaniards had to have the permission of a friar in order to read and to think (*ibid.*). According to Forner, those who wrote about Spain did not want facts; and while they themselves posed as philosophers and set up their declamations in a metaphysical style which contained a few words that referred to philosophy, they knew no more about philosophy than the "lenguaje impropio y afectado" (*ibid.*, p. 11).

Philosophy, Religion, and Science 39

interior del África";[36] but it is his belief that Spain is the only nation besides Greece that has had such a high esteem of the dignity of philosophy.[37]

Forner concedes that his nation did not have any one who could increase the catalog of celebrated dreamers. She did not have a Descartes or a Newton[38] or any of those Naturalists who were filling great volumes in France with the mysteries of Mother Nature.[39] There never went out from the Iberian Peninsula systems such as Optimism, Preestablished Harmony, Fatality, or any of those moral or metaphysical systems by which the sophists wished to bring about a change in the whole universe.[40] There never went out from Spain a Doctor Irrefragable,[41] a leader of the Realists or of the Nominalists. Spain was never taken up with the subtleties of the Roscelins, Almarics, Porretanos, Dinants, or Abelards.[42]

Instead of systems and systematizers, Spain has had excellent practical philosophers and just legislators,[43] who preferred to work for the benefit of mankind rather than give themselves over to the idle occupation of building imaginary worlds. She has

---

[37] *Ibid.*

[38] *Oración apologética,* p. 12.

[39] *Ibid.,* p. 35.

[40] *Ibid.,* pp. 12-13.

[41] Forner explains that none of Spain's learned men strove to acquire the magnificent titles by which the sophists tried to distinguish themselves. He admits that Alfonso X had the title "sabio," but that this title, which was given to him by a school, was used in the same manner as one would speak of the "great Newton" or the "great Descartes" *(ibid.,* p. 170).

[42] *Ibid.,* pp. 56-57.

[43] In pointing out the fact that in Spain there were laws which obliged the people not only to do the right thing, but also to think rightly he quotes from the laws established by Ferdinand and Isabella in 1502, and from those of Philip IV established in 1627 *(ibid.,* p. 151). To Forner, there is more philosophy in these laws than in all the splendid verbosity of the defenders of license in thought. The author goes on to show that the statutes of civil societies have as their end the happiness of the individuals that compose it, and therefore, the supreme power has not only the right to enforce laws that will regulate the use of human liberty, but also the duty to punish the abuse of it when such abuse interferes with the common order and happiness *(ibid.;* p. 152).

[36] *Exequias,* p. 222.

40   *Philosophy, Religion, and Science*

had men who knew the vanity of arbitrary opinions. She had men who gave useful[44] doctrines to the people and pointed out the direct paths of knowledge according to the needs of weak mortality.[45]

The Spanish writers of the past, he points out, recognized no other aim in their investigations than that of truth and the idea of being useful to their fellowmen. They maintained the dignity of the human understanding and brought glory rather than discredit to the human reason. In the following passage, he emphasizes the utility of their writings:

> . . . y sin que en las opiniones de conjetura peligren los fundamentos de la verdad, de la justicia, o de la religión, exentos de errores peligrosos logramos una ciencia útil en la mayor parte, y en la que no lo es, segura a lo menos de consecuencias perjudiciales.[46]

In further evidence of the fact that Spain's interest had been in a practical philosophy and not in systems based on subtleties and sophistries, he cites her attitude toward Scholasticism and Arabic philosophy. It is Forner's contention that those who would make Spain the mother of cavillings and the obstinate patron of Scholasticism[47] will find that Scholasticism was engendered and

---

[44] Forner, with his strong ideas about utility, but in the Christian sense, asks of what use to humanity are the Ideas of Plato, the Materialism of the Stoics, the Qualities of the Peripatetics, the Atoms of Epicurus, and all the improbable whims of eminent men who were born to teach their fellowmen, but instead, accustom them to the sterile occupation of dreaming (*ibid.*, p. 3). To his mind, utility and solidity, which are the poles of wisdom, are not to be found in the imaginary world of a Cartesian either (*ibid.*, pp. 66-67).

[45] *Ibid.*, pp. 12-13.

[46] *Ibid.*, pp. 23-24.

[47] In tracing a brief history of Scholasticism of the middle ages the author divides it into three periods. The first begins at the end of the eleventh century with Roscelin, the chief of the Nominalists, and Peter Lombard, designated as the chief of the scholastics of that period. The second period, which covered the entire thirteenth century, he points out, had many great men, beginning with St. Albert, the Great. Albert's disciple, Saint Thomas, he says, made this period famous, while men like Saint Bonaventure, Duns Scotus, Pedro Hispano, Roger Bacon and others of minor fame supported it. The third period, which was very corrupt, he begins with William Durand, who deserted the Thomistic School (*ibid.*, p. 169).

Philosophy, Religion, and Science · 41

nourished at Paris,[48] Bologna, Oxford, Padua, Ferrara, and Naples.[49] He notes that during the early epochs of Scholasticism, from the eleventh to the thirteenth centuries, Spain produced very few Scholastics.[50] The first traces of Scholasticism in her studies, which were effected by communication with Bologna and Paris, were really not noticed in Spain until the middle of the thirteenth century. Because of the troubles occasioned by Scholasticism in Paris, Alfonso VIII did not permit Scholastic Theology to be included in the curriculum of the University of Salamanca.[51] Spain never adopted Scholasticism until long after the rest of Europe and she did so then only because she saw that it was necessary for the preservation of the unity of religion. On this point he writes:

> . . . era ya indispensable necesidad derrotar con la Teología escolástica a los que confundiendo los abusos de ésta con los fundamentos de la religión, con pretexto de desterrar el Escolasticismo, destruían el dogma, y desunían la Iglesia.[52]

---

[48] Forner notes that the University of Paris was the great theatre of scholastic disputations, where sophistries were introduced into religion and all the sciences (*ibid.*, p. 51), even medicine (*ibid.*, p. 176), and mathematics (*ibid.*, p. 163). In the notes he gives references to source material for information on the school and the abuses there (*ibid.*, pp. 159-162). He points out that in the eighteenth century sophistry had even entered the courts so that the triumph of justice was not too secure (*Exequias*, p. 202).

[49] *Oración apologética*, p. 57.

[50] According to Forner, the first Scholastics in Spain were more learned or more useful than those in other countries. Among these were Pedro Hispano, Ramón Lull, and Arnoldus de Villanueva (*ibid.*, p. 170). It is his opinion that the good which is in Scholasticism was acquired in Spain, and the bad in it, elsewhere. The Spaniards were the ones who purged it and adorned it with good taste and beautiful literature. Neither Italy, France, Germany, or England ever justly denied the great difference that there was between their Scholastics and those of Spain. Among the great Spanish Scholastics of the sixteenth century he names Victoria, Cano, Bañez, Soto, Castro, Suárez, Valencia, Maldonado (*ibid.*, p. 65).

[51] *Ibid.*, p. 170.

[52] *Ibid.*, p. 64. It seems quite evident from Forner's comments on Scholasticism that in his own mind he confused the system with the sophistries and abuses which came to be associated with it. As a follower of Vives, he probably knew a great deal about the abuses. In spite of his rather disparaging

42 Philosophy, Religion, and Science

Referring to Spain's contact with the Arabic subtleties he points out that when she tried to regain her Empire from the Mohammedans, she took from her enemy only what enlightened the understanding and was helpful in life. She never meddled with their religion, nor was she taken up with their subtleties.[53] Unlike other peoples who took from the Arabic learning only the bad, and perverted it still more by their sophistries, Spain tried to better the source of the evils by reducing Dialectics[54] to its proper

---

comments regarding Scholasticism, he apparently was not too unkindly toward its fundamental tenets. He expresses his belief that prejudice on the part of those who themselves desired to be called philosophers prompted many of the accusations made against the Scholastics (ibid., p. 65). He shows his indignation too at the hatred which is borne toward the name "Scholasticism," and toward the association of the system with Spain; and he points out that time and circumstances may replace this hatred with a great esteem for the school (ibid., pp. 68-69).

[53] Ibid., p. 56.

[54] Forner contends that the Spaniards reason and do not imagine in Metaphysics, even though foreigners condemn their logic because it is not an accumulation of common observations intermingled with remnants of all the arts (ibid., pp. 15-16). To Forner's mind, the eighteenth century orators did not possess the rudiments of logic. He blames the philosophic sects for the corruption of this science, pointing out that, in the beginning, logic was the armor of reason and that when philosophy was divided into sects, it became the patron of vanities and the instrument for obscuring truth rather than discovering it (ibid., p. 92). He explains too that it was either through opposition to "los estilos de la antigüedad" or out of hatred for the Scholastics, who always included the "Arte tópica" in their teaching, that the moderns abandoned the art and considered it useless or of little avail in the investigation of truth (ibid., p. 216). Contrary to those of his day who depreciated the artificial aids of reasoning, Forner exalts the importance and value of the analytic arts and the "tópica" of Aristotle. These arts, he says, were replaced by "una confusa miscelanea, con nombre de lógica, en que de todo se trate menos de facilitar el recto uso de las operaciones mentales" (Exequias, p. 191). He praises Aristotle's ingenuity and remarks that Bacon's Novum Organum, which received so much acclaim from his contemporaries, would probably never have existed had not the Stagyrite invented the art and use of the "tópicas" (ibid., pp. 191-192). Again, in recognition of the need of these helps in reasoning, and of the Spaniard's appreciation of their value, he points to Melchor Cano, who fifty-seven years before Bacon, made use of the "tópica" (Oración apologética, p. 217).

Philosophy, Religion, and Science 43

use and by leading the philosophers back to the right path.[55] The Spaniards always tried to strike at the root of the subtleties[56] and to show the true end of Dialectics, which he defines in the following manner:

> . . . el fin de la Dialéctica no debía ser el de entretener cuestiones de ninguna utilidad ni significación, sino el de llevar como por la mano al entendimiento para que sin extravíos halle la verdad en las ciencias.[57]

It is Forner's conviction that there can be no true philosophy without a true knowledge of the nature of man, for as he says, "el ser hombre es todo lo que constituye al hombre."[58] He sees in man a dual nature as is seen from the following excerpt:

> Vese dueño por una parte de una potencia inteligente, que le hace mirar con desdén la sujeción a su porción grosera y material; y halla por otra, que esta misma porción le obliga a acomodarse a las urgencias de la vida, proporcionando su espíritu a lo que piden de necesidad las leyes de su conservación y existencia. En esta correspondencia y servicio recíproco de la materia hacia la racionalidad, de ésta hacia la materia, estriba el ser del hombre; y en la recta práctica de estas leyes se funda principalmente el cumplimiento del orden que constituye la peculiar naturaleza del animal dotado de razón.[59]

His concept of the dual nature of man and the importance which he attaches to the recognition of both the body and the soul of man are likewise noted in his comment that man is not born solely to contemplate his duties to his Creator, but also to fulfill his duties toward himself and his neighbor.

---

[55] *Ibid.,* p. 56.

[56] According to Forner, it was a Spaniard, Pedro Hispano, "el antiguo," who in the thirteenth century, attempted to make war on the root of the subtleties; and another Pedro Hispano of the fourteenth century, who continued the reform. In the sixteenth century, Pedro Ciruelo restored the work of these two men on dialectics *(ibid.,* pp. 63, 178-82).

[57] *Ibid.,* p. 63-64.

[58] *Ibid.,* p. 81.

[59] *Ibid.,* p. 77.

44   *Philosophy, Religion, and Science*

Forner maintains that all the philosophers, ancient and modern, who have not recognized the dual nature of man have failed in their efforts to develop man.[60] In proof of this statement he cites a number of examples. Contrasting the theories of Plato with those of his own time, the author shows how both systems disregarded man's nature in its entirety. Plato in his effort to make "sabios" placed too much emphasis on the intellect and consequently failed to develop man; and the moderns, by giving too free rein to the animal instincts of man, have placed man near the brutes.[61]

The author also notes, that on the other hand, there had been philosophers who disregarded the body and made man consist in spirit alone.[62] They taught only the practice of virtue without considering the fact that the body furnishes the occasion for the exercise of virtue. To Forner, frugality, liberality, charity, fortitude, modesty, and justice would be meaningless words and not virtues if men were to live as pure spirits.[63] In like manner, the Neo-Platonics also failed because they taught that the contemplation of divine things constituted the essence of the human being.[64]

To Forner's mind, the Spanish mystics offered a system which was in keeping with man's nature. As is seen from the following comment, they recognized man as an integral being and they discerned his purpose in life:

> En ellos no hay más que un sistema, que es de amar las criaturas a su Hacedor, y amarse ellas entre sí, de modo que nunca se hagan mal, y siempre se hagan todo el bien que puedan. . . .[65]

Along with the mystics, Forner realizes that there is in man a certain order placed in him by God, and without which he would

---

[60] *Ibid.*, p. 82.

[61] *Ibid.*, p. 82.

[62] Forner believes that man would not be man without the body; and that it is in keeping with the order which God established in man that rationality be present in the body in order to guide its inclinations according to the designs of God (*ibid.*, pp. 80-81).

[63] *Ibid.*, p. 80.

[64] *Ibid.*, p. 81.

[65] *Exequias*, p. 215.

Philosophy, Religion, and Science 45

be the most despicable creature in the universe.[66] Believing, as he does, that man exists as man only when he uses his faculties to maintain the order of his being,[67] he regards as impious mockers of God's goodness those sophists who believe that man is a vague, lubricous being, adapted to any constitution.[68]

Since man has a free will, he can direct it towards ends other than those intended by God; but it is Forner's belief that when man acts in this way he does so only for pleasure and self-gratification and not out of necessity, as the blind defenders of blind necessity would have people believe.[69] He adds too that man in so acting misuses his rationality.[70] and abuses his liberty, thereby bringing about his own corruption and that of society,[71] since he is a social being.[72]

It is Forner's contention that when man uses his rationality as he should and when he recognizes the weakness of his rational nature which is joined to a fragile, corruptible body,[73] he will adjust his understanding to the proper consideration of his duties toward himself and his neighbor. The result then of his observations will be a religion and a political state that are not mere fabrications[74] of the intellect, which was created to arrive at truth.[75]

Forner holds that for a proper understanding of man it is necessary to have a knowledge of man's relation to God, and of God's relation to man and the universe.[76] Hence, the need of religion must be acknowledged. While he recognizes the existence of a

---

[66] *Oración apologética,* p. 78.

[67] *Ibid.,* p. 79.

[68] *Ibid.,* p. 77-78.

[69] *Ibid.,* p. 85.

[70] *Ibid.,* p. 79.

[71] *Ibid.,* p. 85

[72] That man is a social being is indicated, as Forner points out, by the instrument of speech and the innate inclination of man to recognize society and the necessity of laws to preserve it *(ibid.,* p. 84).

[73] *Ibid.,* pp. 78-79.

[74] *Ibid.,* p. 78.

[75] *Exequias,* p. 20.

[76] *Oración apologética,* p. 100.

46 — Philosophy, Religion, and Science

natural religion,[77] he does not consider it sufficient for man. He sees the need also of a revealed religion—the religion of Christ.[78]

To Forner, religion is not only the most important study for man, but it is his most urgent obligation.[79] The truly great man, the one who really serves and helps mankind, is the one who confirms his fellowman in the will of his Maker and who shows him the necessity of revelation and the foundation upon which it rests so that he may give to God fitting adoration and do His will as he should.[80]

That Forner regarded revealed religion as a most significant factor in man's life,[81] is evident from the following tribute which he pays to it:

> ¡O divina, o amable religión! asilo cierto de la mortal angustia! ¡suave freno de la maldad! ¡consuelo, esperanza de la virtud! ¡infalible instrumento de la felicidad del hombre; ¡apoyo, columna de la justicia! ¡adorable tributo con que la criatura racional paga a Dios en costumbres puras, en demostraciones inocentes, el inestimable don de su creación y existencia! Cuando participándote a los mortales desde el mismo trono de la Divinidad, y ofreciéndoles los medios de hacer al hombre amigo del hombre, te ves pospuesta en la consideración de los que se llaman Filósofos a ocupaciones abatidas, torpes, despreciables, a cuando menos superfluas y de ningún momento; compadécelos: los sentimientos de todo el orbe no residen en ánimos de ceguedad tan desesperada.[82]

Forner's love of revealed religion, as also his opposition to the antireligious attitude of the *philosophes,* are likewise shown when

---

[77] *Ibid.,* p. 131. In this, then, he is in agreement with Montesquieu, Voltaire, Rousseau and others. Of course, the idea of natural religion was not new in the eighteenth century. Again, Forner remarks that man without religion is nothing more than a wild animal that lives in the forest *(ibid.).* Voltaire and other *philosophes* had made similar comments.

[78] *Ibid.*

[79] *Ibid.,* p. 67.

[80] *Ibid.,* pp. 67, 102.

[81] *Ibid.,* p. 67.

[82] *Ibid.,* p. 130-131.

Philosophy, Religion, and Science   47

he writes the following, in praise of the works of the great Spanish mystics:

> Esos libros enseñan al hombre a humillarse y a reconocerse por átomo despreciable ante la presencia de la Divinidad, y esto es lo que no quiere, no la filosofía, sino la arrogancia de ciertos charlatanes, que se llaman filósofos porque llenan de desvergüenzas al género humano; esos libros, en un estilo grave, majestuoso, adornado con galas propias de la santidad del objeto, y animado con pasiones afectuosas, pero varoniles, enseñan a adorar al Omnipotente en espíritu de verdad y justicia; enseñan al hombre la beneficencia inefable de su Criador, que hizo inseparable entre sí la felicidad humana y el cumplimiento de las leyes divinas; y si sus documentos fuesen tan obedicidos en la tierra . . . yo os prometo que no habría necesidad en el mundo de filósofos, ni aun de legisladores.[83]

Since Forner had such an esteem for revealed religion and recognized it as necessary to society, he could not fail to be disturbed by the attitude which many of the *philosophes* held toward it. He condemns the scoffing attitude of the *philosophes* toward revealed religion,[84] pointing out that because they thought they saw something of a shadow of improbability in the established religion, they proceeded to set themselves up as apostles of dogmas which were repugnant and contradictory. He groups with criminals those sophists and writers who were filled with the desire and the ambition to pervert everything and to trample upon the most sacred principles of religion and society.[85] He notes

---

[83] *Exequias*, p. 215.

[84] Forner calls attention to the scoffing attitude of the *philosophes* many times. In Parnassus, during the procession, he remarks to Arcadio that certain philosophers would have a good laugh if they saw the theologian's doctoral cap resting on the works of Luis de Granada, Luis de León, and St. Teresa *(ibid.,* p. 214). Again, he remarks that these same *philosophes* would consider it a matter of fanaticism rather than an honor for Spain to have directed the first general Council of the Church; and again, that they would depreciate Hosius, the oracle of the faith at Nicea, while they made holy the name of Voltaire, the obstinate scoffer at religion *(Oración apologética*, p. 130).

[85] *Ibid.,* p. 20.

48 *Philosophy, Religion, and Science*

that what they called discoveries are really aberrations of reason, and what they called rational knowledge of the Divinity is an open corruption of reason. They substituted, he says, for the God of Moses, the God of Spinoza; for the morals of Christ, rebellion against morals. They looked for examples among savages to belittle the credit of universal sentiments of conscience; and they gave the name of religion to the absence of it. Their ideas of God and their duties toward Him were vague, obscure, uncertain, at times, absurd. They were always formed with the intention of satisfying the leisure of a number of cavillers and never with the intention of meeting the needs of active civil life.[86] Although the insults of impious incredulity, he says, did not frighten him or weaken his faith in Christianity,[87] he suggests that the defamers of religion should moderate a little the precipitation with which they condemned everything. He asks them to reflect whether it is less meritorious to work for the security of a religion which manifests in itself the distinct characteristics of divinity and truth than it is to work for its destruction and ruin.[88] Again he asks if anything of any use can come to a society that combats the religion, which, among all religions, contains "la moral más pura y benéfica."[89] It was his belief that the man who is eager to free himself from positive law and revealed religion, on the grounds that he is an intelligent being, capable in himself of practicing virtue, is decidedly an evil person.[90] He shows how in the history of time, man abused his liberty, and by following his inclinations to do what he ought not to do corrupted the ideas of religion. He shows how, instead of recognizing God, man paid homage to men and false gods. He calls attention to the very way in which man's ambition, his self-interest, and his turning away from God brought about his own corruption, effected the conspiracy of man against man, and engendered wars,

---

[86] *Ibid.*, pp. 33-34.
[87] *Ibid.*, p. 88.
[88] *Ibid.*, pp. 129-130.
[89] *Ibid.*, p. 153.
[90] *Ibid.*, pp. 88-89.

Philosophy, Religion, and Science 49

usurpations, disorder, disunion, and the destruction of society;[91] and finally, he points out how civil law and revealed Religion were offered by prudence and Providence[92] as the first antidotes for all the disorders which man has brought about.[93]

Possibly in an effort to meet the *philosophes* on their own grounds, Forner applies the term philosophy to religion, though its application is certainly not accurate in a scientific sense.

> También ésta es filosofía, y harto más sublime, harto más santa, harto más necesaria que los repugnantes sistemas de los sofistas.[94]

Philosophy, he maintains should aid religion, instead of destroying it.[95] In fact, as he points out, that is its office.

> El oficio de la Filosofía debía ser, auxiliando la santidad de los ritos, desterrar de ellos la superstición,[96] y cuando ve que los hombres son llevados al culto por una irresistible inclinación de su naturaleza,[97] examinar, no cuales

[91] *Ibid.,* p. 85. This was a common foreboding on the part of the orthodox thinkers of the time. Cf. Palmer, *op. cit.,* p. 222.

[92] This statement gives evidence of Forner's belief in Providence, as does also his reference to God as the "supremo Arbitro del universo" *(Exequias,* p. 215), or the "próvido y liberal Criador" *(Oración apologética,* p. 16), or his mention of "los designios del Omnipotente" *(ibid.,* p. 3), or "la beneficiencia inefable de su Criador, que hizo inseparable entre sí la felicidad humana y el cumplimiento de las leyes divinas *(Exequias,* p. 215). For the majority of the *philosophes,* there was no such thing as a directing providence (Palmer, *op. cit.,* p. 197). They upheld the idea of Progress rather than Providence *(ibid.,* p. 173). Those who believed in the new cosmology or the mechanistic view of the universe could hardly believe that the earth could receive any special attention from its Creator *(ibid.,* p. 110).

[93] *Oración apologética,* p. 88.

[94] *Ibid.,* p. 132.

[95] It is obvious that Forner refers here to the disrespectful attitude of many of the *philosophes* toward the Catholic religion, particularly Voltaire.

[96] Forner concedes that superstition should be destroyed; but he does not make superstition synonymous with the Christian religion, as many of the philosophers did.

[97] He grants that there is such thing as natural religion. Cf. this study p. 46, n. 77.

50   *Philosophy, Religion, and Science*

religiones son más acomodadas a làs diferencias de los climas y Estados[98] sino cual es entre todas más acomodada a las leyes de la racionalidad, más digna del hombre y del Dios que debe adorarse, más conforme a aquel orden a que están destinadas las criaturas que gozan de razón ¿Desmerecería algo el esplendor de estos talentos amantes de la singularidad, porque persuadiesen a los hombres, que pues no saben vivir sin culto, adopten el más puro, entre los que existen?[99]

Forner points with pride to the fact that Spain has always esteemed religion, however much she has been considered a barbarous, uncultured, unprogressive nation "en que se ha consumido más tiempo, más atención, y más papel en hablar de Dios y de sus inefables fines."[100]   It was her honor, he remarks, to have directed the first general council of the Church.[101]   The sacred studies, he states, flourished at the University of Alcalá from its very beginning.[102]   The Spanish philosopher, Raymundo Sabunde, he points out, exposed the principles of Natural Religion and proved the necessity of Revelation.[103]   In Spain, both natural and revealed religion were reduced to methodic science.[104]   Her theologians who were without the titles of "Sutiles" or "Irrefragables" never mingled delirious dialectics with theological matters;[105] but in their works, which are an honor to the Spanish language,[106] they maintained a stable belief by explaining and interpreting dogma and tradition, affirmed by the Scriptures.[107]   They never supported a hypocritical tyranny, disguising under the pious

---

[98] He undoubtedly refers to some of the ideas advanced by Montesquieu and Voltaire.

[99] *Oración apologética,* pp. 34-35.   Apparently, he refers here to the Christian religion.

[100] *Ibid.,* p. 16.

[101] *Ibid.,* p. 130.

[102] *Ibid.,* p. 140.

[103] *Ibid.,* pp. 137-138.

[104] *Ibid.,* p. 95.

[105] *Ibid.,* p. 61.

[106] *Exequias,* p. 214.

[107] *Oración apologética,* p. 61.

Philosophy, Religion, and Science   51

veil of religion the most barbarous and sacrilegious sentiment.[108] In regard to the study of the science of morals in Spain, he writes,

> La Moral, la divina ciencia del hombre, la doctrina de su orden, de su fin, de su felicidad, la que une a la más noble de las criaturas con su próvido y liberal Criador, no ha sido entre nosotros todavía contaminada con aquellas · legislaciones absurdas que hacen al hombre o brutal, o impío, o ridículo, y atribuyen a barbarie la prudencia de no querer hacernos bestiales, impíos o ridículos.[109]

True to their past respect and reverence for revealed religion, the Spaniards in the eighteenth century, as the author points out, in spite of the anti-religious vogue of the time, had no thought of tearing down and casting out the sacred things of life. They · had no thought of taking out of the human heart the natural sentiments of virtue, of extinguishing the conscience, of praising the culpable inclinations of nature, and of seeking defenses of vice, impiety, and sedition.[110] Commenting further on the eighteenth century attitude toward religion, Forner writes:

> Confieso sin dificultad, que para unas gentes que consideren la religión y moral como objetos de indiferencia; que gusten de razonar de todo por los principios de su corrupción o antojo; elogiar el lujo, y reírse de la virtud; franquear las puertas al desorden, y maldecir de la autoridad de los tronos; llamarse Filósofos, y obrar y pensar como Sibaritas; confieso, digo, que para tales sabios será con razón gravísimo demérito haber consumido grandes fatigas y meditaciones en confirmar y explicar las austeras verdades del Evangelio; en demostrar a los hombres la seguridad de una religión que los guía a la

---

[108] *Ibid.,* pp. xiv-xv.

[109] *Ibid.,* p. 16. Again he writes, "La Moral, unida a la religión mantiene al hombre en la perfecta constitución de su naturaleza" .(*ibid.,* p. 95).

[110] *Ibid.,* p. 19. Forner makes a very general statement here which is not entirely correct. It is true that some of the *philosophes* regarded man as essentially good, thus overlooking the idea of original sin, which, of course, · Forner believed in. It is also true that the *philosophes* built their whole religious system around the idea of natural virtue and conscience as man's guide.

52 Philosophy, Religion, and Science

paz, a la beneficencià, al amor recíproco; y en sostener este único y alto instrumento de la felicidad humana, como sagrada áncora a que se acojan cuando quieran resolverse a obrar según las leyes y constitución de su ser.[111]

The new kind of learning which Forner states was being communicated to the Spaniards from beyond the Pryenees was by no means in keeping with his idea of knowledge.[112] His was a theocentric conception of humanism, as is seen by the following definition which he gives:

> No es saber el saber opiniones, o el inventar sueños abstractos para sujetar a un capricho las leyes de ambas naturalezas física y espiritual, en lugar de observar las de una y otra en sus efectos, según los designios del Omnipotente.[113]

The legitimate "ciencia" of man, he says, ought to consist in knowing what he is and what he owes to his soul and to his body.[114] He develops this idea further as follows:

> Mantener el justo medio que entre dos extremos señala el juicio, es con propriedad enseñar sus oficios a la naturaleza humana; es distinguir la preferencia que han de lograr en su estimación unas aplicaciones respecto de otras. Considerada toda en sí del modo que existe en la tierra, sus conocimientos y estudios deben ser apreciados por la mayor o menor utilidad de sus fines; como si dijésemos, por la mayor o menor conexión con los destinos de la criatura racional. Cuanto ésta medita, hace, inventa, ordena, todo lo dirige o a *perfeccionarse,* o a *socorrerse,* o a *recrearse*: no salen de estos límites las duras y laboriosas investigaciones del entendimiento, los maravillosos efectos de la industria humana, sus innumerables invenciones, su jamás cansada actividad. Reconoce el hombre un supremo Dador y árbitro de su existencia; nota en sí la irresistible propensión a la gratitud; considera la gran-

---

[111] *Ibid.,* p. 69.
[112] *Oración* apologética, p. 159.
[113] *Ibid.,* pp. 2-3.
[114] *Ibid.,* p. 82.

Philosophy, Religion, and Science

deza del beneficio; conoce el poder de quien le recibe; y héla aquí empleada al instante su meditación en descubrir la voluntad de su Criador, para no extraviarse en el cumplimiento de las demostraciones que le son debidas.[115]

The false reasoning and the vain caprice, which, Forner maintains, dominated the eighteenth century, is not "sabiduría." It was regarded as such only by those who looked for vanity in learning and by those who thought in any manner provided they did not think as the rest of men.[116] To him, these men were the corrupters of learning rather than promoters of it; and of the infinite number of men who exhausted themselves in this corruption there were few who, although recognizing and lamenting their misconduct, admitted the vanity and bad use of their knowledge.[117]

To Forner, utility and solidity, the poles of wisdom,[118] were very much lacking in the eighteenth century. It was his belief that the learning of the time was empty and without reason, even though the period was styled the "Age of Reason."[119]

Forner's general attitude toward the encyclopedic learning then in vogue is perhaps best exemplified in the *Exequias* where he satirizes the learning and the learned. On his imaginary visit to Parnassus, those who make display of their learning are spoken of as "hipócritas de la sabiduría,"[120] charlatans who make a show of trifles and depreciate the really learned.[121] Having acquired what he calls a "ciencia de pepitoria," they talk about what they read, not about what they think; and thus they pass for "estupendos sabios" among those whose reasons and intellects are darkened and rusty,[122] as also among those who are incapable of understanding anything profound.[123]

---

[115] *Ibid.*, pp. 82-83.

[116] *Ibid.*, p. 22. This comment was made in speaking of Rousseau, Helvetius, Bayle, and Voltaire.

[117] *Ibid.*, pp. 93-94.

[118] *Ibid.*, p. 66.

[119] *Exequias*, p. 94.

[120] *Ibid.*, p. 96.

[121] *Ibid.*, p. 113.

[122] *Ibid.*, p. 97.

[123] *Ibid.*, p. 114.

54   *Philosophy, Religion, and Science*

Before these "sabios" are transformed by Apollo into frogs,[124] Forner presents some of them as "locos en la mansión de la sabiduría." He has Villegas give the warning that some may be found in such a state of frenzy that they imagine that they not only know more than Apollo, but are capable of correcting his books.[125]

The satire on the Academicians, which gives not only an idea of the author's opposition toward the learning of his time but also a splendid cue to his ability in satirical writing, is handled by having different "sabios" appear before Apollo, and in accord with the conceit of the times, boast of their remarkable abilities. The first introduces himself as a poet worthy of being classed with the sublime poets and just as deserving as Garcilaso of a place in the mansion.[126] Another boasts of being a better philosopher than Cornelius Nepos, a better historian than Horace, and a better satirist than Dictys the Cretan.[127] Another boasts that he was born in Paris; that his Doctor's cap cost him 12,000 reals; and with pride he acclaims that his academic course included the following: "ocho años de gramática, uno de filosofía, tres de Facultad mayor, cuatro actos mayores, seis menores y cinco mil patadas que me han costado, y tengo bien contadas una sobre otra."[128]

Another sabio presents his titles to Apollo and makes his boast:

> Soy académico de las Bellas Letras, de la Lengua, de las Antigüedades; y si no he publicado cosa alguna sobre estas materias, ha sido porque mi designio no era aprender ni buen gusto, ni a hablar, ni antiguallas, sino cargarme de títulos, porque convenía así a mis pretensiones. En lo demás, tan académico soy como cualquiera, y ¡voto a

---

[124] *Ibid.,* p. 103.

[125] *Ibid.,* p. 136.

[126] *Ibid.,* pp. 97-98. For the enumeration which he made of his abilities see this study, pp. 96-97.

[127] Dares the Phrygian and Dictys the Cretan, it will be recalled, are the supposed authors of two works on the Trojan War that were popular in the Middle Ages and came to be the standard sources of the medieval treatment of the legends surrounding that war *(Exequias,* pp. 98-99).

[128] *Ibid.,* p. 100.

Philosophy, Religion, and Science   55

῾ tantos! que si Apolo no me recibe, he de quejarme a mis academias para que no le reciban a él en ellas.[129]

The condemnation of one of the academicians by the fiscal in the allegory is also a splendid example of Forner's inimical attitude toward the learning of his day and of his cleverness in satirizing it.

> ¡Bellacos! ¿pensáis que tratáis aquí con aquellos babiecas que, porque os oyen bachillerear y hacer pompa de esos títulos, que son en vosotros de mojiganga, os engullen por hombres, no siendo vosotros más que pollinos con campanillas? Los méritos no han de acreditarse en la relación, sino en el entendimiento, y la ambición os hace ser majaderos, que escribís toda vuestra capacidad en un medio pliego de papel, dando a entender que no os queda de los estudios otra ciencia que la de decir que habéis estudiado. Pues el otro bribón, que se nos vende por muy académico, como si él y sus semejantes no fuesen las mazas de sus congregaciones, que van siempre a la cola de lo que dicen otros y dando que reir a los prudentes y sabios, ocasionan la mofa y burla con que hieren algunos al común de los cuerpos. Seó académico, las academias no hacen al hombre, sino los hombres a las academias; y con todo eso, cuando este pobrete se despidió de la vida, le elogiarían con una magnífica oración, en que no pudiendo representarle como historiador, no como orador, no como poeta, ni como crítico, porque nada de esto supo, con ser académico, de todo esto diría de elogiante que su héroe tuvo un empleo en tal cosa que manejó con grande puntualidad, y tal, y sí señor; y se quedaría muy satisfecho de su trabajo, y aun solicitaría que se imprimiese el panegírico. . . »[180]

It is obvious, then, from the comments made by Forner on the learning of the times that he did not consider the learning of the *Encyclopédistes* and their followers as real knowledge. Instead of reason, he sees in it superfluities, sophistries, disorders, and inventions of the intellect, which are destructive to man and society. In fact, he is inclined to conclude, after hearing Cervantes' re-

---

[129] *Ibid.*, pp. 100-101.
[130] *Ibid.*, pp. 101-102.

56 Philosophy, Religion, and Science

marks on the "sabios" who were converted into frogs, that the acquisition of knowledge may be a dangerous occupation and its effects doubtful, for, as he says, "no basta la profundidad del saber ni la abundancia de las noticias, si no asiste el juicio con sana rectitud a la formación de las obras."[131]

Since he looked upon Spain as possessing the "sana rectitud" and a true idea of knowledge, he was opposed to the entrance of the Encyclopedic ideas into his country. Spain, he points out, placed the merit of her knowledge in knowing what things ought to be and how they ought to be; not in dramas made to combat "la religión pública"; not in courses of education disposed to destroy society; not in Dictionaries, that deliberately confused truth and authorized sophistry; and not in slanderous "discursillos frenéticos."[132]

It was Forner's opinion that a nation which has given to the world more restorers and just appraisers of the most important sciences is more learned than those nations[133] which have produced a great number of superfluities in the field of knowledge.[134] A learned nation, he maintains, is one which, through her naval and military art, has turned over to Europe a real world filled with riches, instead of an arid dream world. It is a nation that has given the best legislators to actual political states, instead of reasonings upon the laws. A learned nation is one that has produced, in place of impious sophists, the most judicious supporters of the only religion that teaches men to be just;[135] it is a nation that has given reformers and restorers of the sciences, instead of scientific vanities. It is one that has tried to treat matters of importance without superfluity. A learned nation is one that has been able to become glorious in the universe no less by its learning and

---

[131] *Ibid.*, p. 94.

[132] *Oración apologética*, p. 103. It is probable that he is alluding here to Voltaire and Rousseau.

[133] It seems quite evident that he refers here to France and Italy since the greater number of attacks on Spain's culture came from those two countries. In the comments which follow, the contrast appears to be made between Spain and France.

[134] *Oración apologética*, p. 94.

[135] Forner seems to lose sight of the fact that the idea of justice is also included in natural religion.

Philosophy, Religion, and Science 57

knowledge than by its conquests, in spite of continued invasions, wars, usurpations, and tyrannic dominations.[136]

While Forner does not logically apply to Spain his definition of a "nación sabia," yet scattered throughout the *Oración apologética* are statements which show that Spain measured up to his standards. In regard to the first point in his definition of a "nación sabia," the author asserts that Spain was the first to navigate the world. She made the gifts of Nature common and brought mankind together.[137] She taught to both the new world and the old the art of conquering, or military art, which he defines as "el escudo de la legislación, el defensivo de las sociedades civiles, ya protegiendo los intereses de cada una, y vengando las infracciones de la fé pública."

Spain also measures up to his second norm for judging a learned nation, for from the earliest times, she had produced wise and prudent legislators.[138] The significance and the value which the author places upon prudent legislation is seen in the following statement:

> . . . si la prudencia legislativa es compañera indisoluble de la sabiduría, y sólo el que une la ilustración del entendimiento a la pureza del corazón, acierta a producir la felicidad en un estado con el sacrosanto instrumento de las leyes.[139]

Juridical studies, the author affirms, made great progress at the University of Salamanca in the thirteenth century,[140] and flour-

---

[136] *Ibid.*, pp. 74-75. Undoubtedly, Forner feels that the norms which he establishes for judging a "nación sabia" are in keeping with the ideas of Vives and Bacon, who were to him the models of wisdom and the only men really capable of appraising a nation. They would consider, he says, as cultured and learned, only those nations which were not ignorant of any of the useful truths. They would evaluate the creative arts also by the rules of truth and utility; and they would not consider the scientific value of a nation to be increased by anything that belonged to arbitrary system (*ibid.*, pp. 6-7).

[137] *Ibid.*, pp. 96-97.

[138] *Ibid.*, p. 96. He quotes from the statutes of the University of Salamanca to give proof of the fact that "la arte militar" was contained in the mathematics course at the University in the very earliest days (*ibid.*, p. 183).

[139] *Ibid.*, p. 126.

[140] *Ibid.*, p. 171.

58 — Philosophy, Religion, and Science

ished likewise in the School of Alcalá.[141] Legislation in Rome, which was the weakest in the world for a long time, was corrected by the Spaniard, Trajan.[142] Roman law, which was common in all Europe even after the destruction of the Empire, was the work of a Spaniard.[143] Spain, which had maritime law before others had legislation for the land, also gave this law to Europe.[144] As for the laws in Spain in his own time, Forner considered them the best in existence.[145] He also thought that it was possible for them to remain so, provided the lawmakers of his country did not imitate the "enlightened" jurisconsults of the past and present, who, in their effort to appear learned, contradicted themselves by their fastidious entanglements, subtleties, and extravagances and put the laws in such form that they themselves were unable to understand them.[146]

We have already seen that in the matter of religion, Spain also met his standard. As to the fourth requisite of a "nación sabia," that of giving to the world reformers and restorers of the sciences, no nation had done more than Spain. The accusations of ignorance brought against her, he asserts, were due not to her lack of scientific progress but rather to the ignorance and false ideas on the part of foreign writers.[147] Instead of considering the ends of the sciences,[148] their benefits, and their utility, those writers measured the scientific glory of a nation by its advance-

---

[141] *Ibid.*, p. 140.

[142] *Ibid.*, pp. 125-126.

[143] *Ibid.*, pp. 95-96, 127-128.

[144] *Ibid.*, p. 97.

[145] *Ibid.*, p. 96. Forner's esteem for the legislative works of his country is manifested in a special manner in the display in Parnassus, where he had scepters and crowns as symbols of legislation and power resting on what he considered the most celebrated legislative collections, of his nation: the *Fuero Juzgo*, the *Fuero Real*, the *Siete Partidas*, the *Ordenamiento de Alcalá*, the *Fuero Viejo*, the *Pragmáticas* of the Catholic Rulers, and the two *Recopilaciones de Castilla e Indias* placed upon the *Políticas* of Bobadilla and Solórzano (*Exequias*, pp. 216-217).

[146] *Ibid.*, pp. 89-90.

[147] *Oración apologética*, p. 15.

[148] *Ibid.*, p. 2.

Philosophy, Religion, and Science

ment in things superfluous and harmful,[149] by the amount of pomp with which the sciences were treated,[150] by the production of a great number of "fábulas filosóficas,"[151] and by the number of volumes which consisted for the most part, of doubts and controversies,[152] opinions and vain systems.[153] Forner's satirical vein is well exemplified in the following passage:

> . . . los enormes cuerpos de estos magníficos colosos que se llaman ciencias ¿ se compondrían hoy por la mayor parte de sombras y apariencias vanas, bultos portentosamente grandes y espléndidos cuando se ven de lejos, pero livianos, faltos de solidez y nieblas obscuras cuando se examina con la mano su consistencia?[154]

Although admitting the difficulty of his task in trying to persuade the Massons, the Tiraboschis, and Bettinellis, of Spain's true use of the sciences even in the Middle Ages,[155] Forner nevertheless traces Spain's interest in the sciences from earliest times. In view of the fact that other nations were talking so much about their useless inventions, he thought he should speak of Spain's contributions to science, for he deemed his country worthy of some recognition since she had been the channel of instruction in the Natural Sciences of the Arabs.[156]

Forner points out that in the eleventh century the famous schools in Spain were dominated by the Arabs,[157] who brought with them the sciences of the East and added them to the universal culture already in Spain.[158] It was from Arabic Spain that the knowledge of Mathematics, Astronomy, Medicine, Botany, Chemistry, and the elements of the Natural Sciences went out to

---

[149] *Ibid.,* p. 142.
[150] *Ibid.,* pp. 70-71.
[151] *Ibid.,* p. 13.
[152] *Ibid.,* p. 71.
[153] *Ibid.,* pp. 91-92.
[154] *Ibid.,* p. 2.
[155] *Ibid.,* p. 55.
[156] *Ibid.,* p. 169.
[157] *Ibid.,* p. 46.
[158] *Ibid.,* p. 135.

60   *Philosophy, Religion, and Science*

Europe.[159] From among the Saracens, Spain gave the ablest
doctors, geometricians, algebrists, chemists, astronomers, poets,
and historians. From among the Christians, she gave men who
competed in these arts with their tyrannical oppressors. Since
the Christians joined to these studies that of religion which was
treated with the ancient decorum, Spain became the only place
where the sciences were what they should be.[160]

Realizing that Spain had much to offer to them in the field
of science, England, France, Germany, and Italy sent learned men
to Spain as well as to Arabia, to acquire the methods and the
knowledge that they lacked.[161] The fact that Spain attracted so
many foreign doctors offers proof that she was not in need of
humanistic learning,[162] as the other countries were.

A complete course in Mathematics[163] was established at the
University of Salamanca by Alfonso, el Sabio, in the thirteenth
century. It was still flourishing at the beginning of the sixteenth
century, when Pedro Ciruelo and other Spanish professors went
to Paris to teach the subject in the proper way[164] since the scholastics, according to Forner, were treating it with the same semi-
barbarous metaphysics that they used in everything.[165]

Copernicus and Ptolemy, Forner states, were taught in the
Mathematics course at the University of Salamanca, the only university in Europe where the system of Copernicus was read pub-

---

[159] *Ibid.*, p. 48.
[160] *Ibid.*, pp. 60-61.
[161] *Ibid.*, pp. 134, 157-158.
[162] *Ibid.*, p. 138.
[163] Forner states that what was written on Mathematics was found in
Arabic books *(ibid.,* p. 157) and that Algebra was regarded as an invention of the Arabs. He gives sources for the accepted opinion that Arith-
metic came also from the Arabs *(ibid.,* p. 162). He gives two reasons in
proof of the fact that Geometry was likewise communicated to Europe by
the same people: first, among the Romans, there wasn't any outstanding
geometrician who could teach the subject, and as Greek was not known
at the beginning of the Middle Ages, no one could learn Euclid, Archimedes,
etc.; and second, the first translations of Euclid in Europe were made from
the Arabs *(ibid.,* p. 163).
[164] *Ibid.*, pp. 165-166.
[165] *Ibid.*, p. 163.

Philosophy, Religion, and Science 61

licly.[166] Although remarkable aids were offered at Salamanca, the science of Astronomy did not make great progress in Spain because of the unfavorable attitude toward Astrology,[167] yet, it is his belief that while the Arabs established astronomical observatories and taught much to Europe,[168] the Spaniards were undoubtedly responsible for the restoration of the subject,[169] especially in their contribution of astronomical instruments.[170]

The Natural Sciences, a province more characteristically Arabic than Greek, were dispersed from the School of Alcalá.[171] Medicine, according to Forner, owed much to the Arabs of Spain.[172] When Botany had been reduced to an art, the Spanish Arabs taught Europe what they knew of the science and how to establish public supplies of medicine.[173] Medicine made great progress in the University of Salamanca in the thirteenth century.[174]

In the sixteenth century, Spain had three outstanding medical men. Monardes was particularly interested in the medicinal virtues of plants.[175] He observed the riches of the New World in a manner different from that of the business men in his day, for he examined closely its plants, stones, and fruits, and wrote a medicinal history of the Indies.[176] While Heredia was making his studies of Angina, from which Europe profited greatly, Mercado was making his findings on pernicious fevers.[177]

---

[166] *Ibid.*, p. 183.

[167] *Ibid.*, p. 184.

[168] *Ibid.*, p. 134.

[169] *Ibid.*, pp. 163-164. He gives sources for his opinion.

[170] *Ibid.*, p. 158. He also gives sources for this statement.

[171] Forner gives sources for his statement that what was written on Natural Sciences was founded in Arabic books *(Oración apologética,* pp. 157-158).

[172] *Ibid.*, pp. 134-35.

[173] *Ibid.*, pp. 134, 136. Alchemy which was born among the Egyptians was, Forner says, first applied to Medicine by the Arabs who taught it also to Europe *(ibid.,* p. 168).

[174] *Ibid.*, p. 170. In having the works of Averroes and Avicenna translated into Latin, it was the chief aim of Alfonso, el Sabio, to make Mathematics and Medicine flourish *(ibid.).*

[175] *Ibid.*, p. 135.

[176] *Ibid.*, pp. 148, 135.

[177] *Ibid.*, pp. 147, 220-223.

62   *Philosophy, Religion, and Science*

Many treatises on "sólida medicina" were born, Forner asserts, in Spain, but they were greatly perverted when they returned from the European schools. The interpretations which the others had added were so expansive that they took up more space than the texts themselves.[178]   Although Spain was blamed for the corruption of these treatises, Monardes shows in his works that Spain was not responsible for it.[179]

To affirm that the Spaniards had no knowledge of chemistry because they did not take part in the crusades is, according to Forner, a ridiculous affirmation to any one who has any knowledge of the learning of the Spanish Arabs, of the spread of their books through Europe,[180] and of the establishment of chemical laboratories in Europe because of them.[181]

In the field of physics, Forner maintains that the Spaniards were likewise not so ignorant as they had been accused of being, and that as much was known in Spain about Physics as was known in France or England.[182]   He writes in this regard:

> También acá sabemos el arte de forzar los elementos a que obren, y juntar el cálculo a la observación. También sabe España desmenuzar los cuerpos, examinar sus partes, medir sus períodos, y seguir el callado curso de la Naturaleza en el admirable artificio de sus efectos y transmutaciones. Pero no por eso cree que su ciencia física pase mucho más allá de la superficie de las cosas; ni entiende que de las causas físicas puedan saberse más, que las que son efecto de otras causas que negó a la comprehensión del hombre el Dios que le crió, más para que obedeciese sus decretos, que para que escudriñase sus designios. Las leyes del movimiento no me explican qué es movimiento.[183]

---

[178] *Ibid.*, p. 62.

[179] *Ibid.*, pp. 176-177.

[180] *Ibid.*, p. 159. Greek antiquity left nothing, he says, on the teaching of chemistry *(ibid.* 158). Daniel de Clere, the author mentions, attributes the true use of chemistry to Avicenna; and Freind, to Rhasis *(ibid.*, p. 168).

[181] *Ibid.*, p. 134.

[182] *Ibid.*, p. 38.

[183] *Ibid.*, pp. 38-39.

Philosophy, Religion, and Science 63

Physics, to the Spaniard, he asserts, does not mean "el arte de sujetar la naturaleza al capricho, en vez del raciocinio a la naturaleza."[184] The great pomp and show which were connected with ignorance in other countries were not found in Spain; and because the ostentation was lacking in Spain it does not mean that she was ignorant of the physical sciences.[185] On this matter, Forner writes:

> Sin tanto esplendor ignoramos acá lo que en otros países con grande pompa y aparato; que si en la ciencia física, como en las demás, no debe contarse por parte científica lo opinable, lo incierto, lo hipotético, lo que porfiadamente se niega a la inteligencia; ignorar esto de propósito, o resolverse a no desperdiciar el vigor del juicio en averiguar cosas que ni se permiten a la comprehensión, ni pueden producir utilidad conocida no tanto es aborrecer la ciencia, como desestimar sus superfluidades. Sabe Física la nación que sabe las verdades de ella; y la justa sobriedad en abstenerse de lo inaveriguable, será solo delito entre los que llamen ciencia a la conjetura, y estimen la profusión hasta en el desperdicio del entendimiento.[186]

There are many things in science, the author affirms, which cannot be understood:

> . . . misterios que no entran en la jurisdicción, de la mecánica, o geometría, y son, con todo eso, los muelles ocultos que producen aquel concierto y correspondencia de obras en esta grande y siempre incomprehensible máquina del universo.[187]

Referring again to the matter of utility, Forner comments that although the Naturalists boasted of the utility of the large volumes

---

[184] *Ibid.*, p. 16.
[185] *Ibid.*, pp. 38, 40.
[186] *Ibid.*, p. 40.
[187] *Ibid.*, pp. 39-40.

64 *Philosophy, Religion, and Science*

which contained their opinions, he sees futility rather than utility in them.

> *¿Con tanta utilidad?* No nos deslumbremos. Sapientísimos Naturalistas, intérpretes fieles de las obras del Ente infinito; una hermosísima claridad baña el gabinete donde ahora estoy escribiendo, que me hace distinguir, los objetos que me rodean. ¿Qué viene a ser este fenómeno? Esa claridad es la luz. Bellamente: sé que se llama luz la claridad; pero ¿de dónde proceden ésta y aquélla? La luz es el fuego ... pero ¿qué es el fuego? La luz es la materia etérea: pero ¿qué viene a ser esa materia? La luz es un cuerpo sutilísimo, y rapidísimo; pero ¿de dónde le vienen la sutileza y rapidez? La luz es una materia luminosa. ... Ya lo he oído; pero esa *luminosidad,* ese esplendor, esa facultad de hacer visibles los cuerpos ¿qué es, de dónde le nace, con qué impulso obra ... ? Ciertamente no faltará aquí alguna cualidad oculta, algún elemento sutil o algún movimiento del Eter; pero entretanto yo me quedo sin saber qué es la luz.[188]

The foregoing discussion has presented Forner's reactionary views upon the philosophical, religious, and scientific tenets of the *Encyclopédistes*. In his condemnation of the new philosophers he stands out as a traditionalist, a Christian thinker, and a defender of Spain's adherence to the traditional Christian philosophy and revealed religion. He also defends the past contribution of Spain to European science and learning. Forner's discussion brings out nothing new.[189] It simply bears out again the fact that the upshot of the whole philosophic, religious, and scientific controversy of the eighteenth century revolved about the ideas of the nature of man, reason, natural law, natural virtue, supernatural law, and supernatural religion. It shows plainly that the literature of the time was developed around the struggle between the traditionalists and the anti-traditionalists, the former supporting a theocentric humanism and the latter, an anthropocentric humanism.

The points of the philosophic and scientific program which Forner surveys and assails, the points of his counteraction, as also

---

[188] *Ibid.*, p. 36.
[189] See this study, p. 33, n. 9; also p. 46, n. 77 and p. 49, n. 97.

Philosophy, Religion, and Science   65

the manner in which he presents both, show clearly that he was typical of his time, both as a man and as a critic. From the point of view of content and form, Forner's writing gives evidence of the fact that he possessed practically all the traits which he condemned in the sophists. It is obvious, of course, that Forner and the "enlightened" thinkers were widely separated on the fundamental points of the philosophic and religious issues. By extracting the essence of his comments from the verbosity of his oft-repeated statements, we find that he directs his remarks and his defense against the "whole paraphernalia of argument"[190] which was commonly advanced by the *philosophes*.

As a member of the orthodox group in Spain Forner was extremely *anti-philosophe*. He accused the *philosophes* of being ignorant of the fundamentals of philosophy. While it is generally agreed that they were ignorant of the principles of Christian philosophy and religion, yet, Forner does not prove them so, nor does he show that he himself possessed a very intelligent grasp of the subject. From his few pronouncements on essentials which can be extracted from his verbiage, it is clear that, fundamentally, his views on philosophy, religion and science were thoroughly in accord with the traditional Christian standards.

According to his own statements, he was a follower of Vives and Bacon.[191] This is evidence of the fact that his method of

---

[190] Of this, Palmer writes, "The philosophers could hardly approach any question without their whole paraphernalia of argument: nature, humanity, the enlightenment of the age, the prejudice of their opponents, the bearing of the particular question on the general perfectibility and ultimate happiness of man (*op. cit.*, p. 22).

[191] Forner shows this in his comments on Vives. See Vives, Appendix II, p.   . As Menéndez y Pelayo remarks, it was Forner's conviction that "una ciencia española," built upon the critical doctrines of Vives and the experimental ideas of Bacon, was the one by which Spain could be saved from the intellectual anarchy of the French *Encyclopédistes (Historia de las ideas estéticas*, V, 334). Bonilla y San Martín speaks of Forner as "el vivista" *(Luis Vives y la filosofía del renacimiento*, Madrid: Rubio, 1929, p. 305), and of Andrés Piquer, who directed Forner's education, as a "declarado visista" *(ibid.*, pp. 212, 126. Cf. Menéndez y Pelayo, *Historia de las ideas estéticas*, V, p. 334). Juan Luis Vives (1492-1540) was one of the most outstanding of a group of Renaissance humanists who were acquainted only with the decadent forms of scholasticism so common in their

66 *Philosophy, Religion, and Science*

attaining certitude was different from that of the traditional Scholasticism. As for his ideas on Scholasticism, his comments show that he knew it only in its degenerated forms. This fact also gives support to the idea that he was typical of his times, for pure Scholastic philosophy was seldom taught in the schools at that time. His admission that time and circumstances might bring about an esteem for the system was probably due to the fact that the names of several outstanding Spaniards had been associated with it. He appears to take pride in mentioning some of these names. For the most part, however, his comments on the subject would seem rather to encourage than discourage the side of the enlightenment in its condemnation of the system.

As an orthodox thinker, Forner held the theocentric conception of man against the anthropocentric conception advanced by the *philosophes*. Forner and most of the *philosophes* recognized the dual nature of man. The *philosophes,* however, emphasized the physical and rational side of man's nature while Forner stressed the integrity of man's being. Recognizing the doctrine of original sin, Forner considered the body to be corruptible and man's rational nature prone to error. He had faith in reason, but reason guided by a supernatural faith. Both the traditionalists and the anti-traditionalists claimed utility and truth as their end—the former, a moral utility, and truth attainable through reason and revelation; the latter, a materialistic utility, and truth attainable through reason alone. To Forner, man's ultimate end was the perfection of his being, his correspondence to God's will, and his

---

time. By reducing philosophy to dialectics, and dialectics to rhetoric, they increased the growing hostility and contempt of true scholastic doctrine (L. Miller, *A History of Philosophy,* New York: Wagner, 1927, pp. 219-220). The principal merit of Vives, whose philosophy is fundamentally Christian (Bonilla y San Martín, *op. cit.,* p. 339), lies in his effort to syncretize the various philosophies of the Renaissance *(ibid.,* p. 344). "De aquí el carácter sincrético de su enseñanza. Su metafísica es, en el fondo, enteramente aristotélica; más aun, su lógica; algún tanto su psicología; su estética, en lo fundamental, platónica; su teología con cierta simplificación, escolástica" *(ibid.,* p. 347). Bacon was a follower of Vives "por sus doctrinas acerca de la inducción y de la experiencia, por su crítica del principio de autoridad y de los demás obstáculos que al progreso de las disciplinas se oponían por su teoría sobre el valor de los sentidas como primera fuente de nuestros conocimientos" *(ibid.,* p. 246).

Philosophy, Religion, and Science 67

eternal happiness. While many of the *philosophes* recognized an after-life, they put the greater emphasis on man's happiness in this world. The chief aim of their program was to bring about man's happiness by a general perfectibility and progress, as they conceived it in their utopian world.

Both Forner and the *philosophes*, most of them, at least, were agreed that man had a free will. The latter supported the idea of arbitrary opinion and freedom to think and act as one's nature dictated, unhampered by positive law and revealed religion. Forner, on the other hand, maintained that in view of the constitution of man's nature, positive law and revealed religion were necessary for the attainment of man's end. In other words, while the *philosophes* maintained that natural law, natural virtue, and natural religion were sufficient, Forner recognized all of these but saw the need also of supernatural law, supernatural virtue, and supernatural or revealed religion.

To Forner, civil law and revealed religion were the antidotes which prudence and Providence provided for all the ills of society. While he recognized the need of reforms in the society of his day, he did not feel that they could be brought about by the destruction of the "ancien régime," as did many of the "enlightened" thinkers. Although he did not say much about reforms in government we glean that he believed that better government was possible only through a proper understanding of man's nature[192] and, on the part of each individual, a personal realization that he had certain obligations to God, to his neighbor,[193] and to himself. In regard to the other great antidote for the social ills, it was his belief that truly great men were not those who worked to destroy[194] religion and to replace it with their utopian dream

---

[192] To the intellectual conservatives, especially the defenders of religion, as Palmer notes, "law was the expression of a superhuman rightness in things, the voice of God, to which human laws and human behavior must conform" *(op. cit.,* p. 204).

[193] The *philosophes,* of course, did preach the doctrine of humanitarianism, but it was again linked with natural virtue and not with the supernatural virtue, which Forner meant when he spoke of the love of neighbor.

[194] Forner uses the word "destroy." There are those, of course, who will maintain that the *philosophes* did not want to destroy religion, but to replace it with another religion. In all events, they did want to do away with revealed religion, and when Forner speaks of their destroying religion, he means revealed religion.

68 *Philosophy, Religion, and Science*

worlds, but rather those who taught their fellow men to esteem and to avail themselves of the opportunities offered for their personal and social betterment through revealed religion, that is, the Christian religion.

From the ideas which Forner sets forth on religion, it is clear that he had no more intellectual grasp of it than he had of philosophy. This does not mean that his faith was not deep and sincere, for there is evidence that it was. It does mean, however, that his verbose and superficial treatment of the subject bears out again the fact that he was as superficial as those he condemned. By extracting again the essence of his religious ideas, we find that his principles are fundamentally sound, but that in them there is nothing beyond what the simplest Christian would, in all probability, know. He surely does not give evidence of his erudition in this regard. In fact for a scholar, he shows great ignorance in confusing philosophy with religion, and liturgy with philosophy.

In his treatment of science and learning Forner also follows the trends of the time. In tracing the literary merit of Spain he includes a history of all her human activities, even her military art.[195] Naturally, in trying to cover such a vast field, he could not give more than a surface view.

Such was the nature of the philosophical content in which Forner showed himself typical of his time. In what respects now did the manner in which he presented his discussion show him to be a typical eighteenth century writer? First of all, we note his encyclopedic tendency. This he condemned in his contemporaries, but one wonders if it would have been possible for him to have placed more ideas than he did on one page. The generalizing mania common to the period is so obvious in his statements that it needs no explanation. He generalizes almost continuously when he speaks of the philosophers. When he mentions or alludes to these writers, he includes not only the French, but also the Spaniards who were promoting the new ideas. In his attacks upon the French *philosophes,* he seldom makes a definite reference to individuals. By assembling his comments upon specific indi-

---

[195] Menéndez y Pelayo notes that this encyclopedic tendency was very common in the eighteenth century *(Historia de los heterodoxes españoles,* pp. 326-327).

Philosophy, Religion, and Science

viduals of this group, it can be inferred, however, that his criticism was directed chiefly against Bayle, Helvetius, Raynal, and more particularly, against Rousseau and Voltaire.[196] The logic which he found wanting in the writings of the *philosophes* is likewise missing in his discussion. The Aristotelian "tópica" which he so strongly recommended to his opponents would have undoubtedly improved his work and made it much easier to follow. Had his work been better planned he would not have boasted of the system of the Spanish mystics and then contradicted this some pages later by saying that Spain was never interested in systems and systematizers. Satire and even ridicule, which were so common at that time are also very noticeable in his treatment of the subject. His critical comments are, for the most part, superficial. Sometimes his criticism consists only in bemoaning the conditions of the time, in calling names, in exaggerations, in verbosity, and "charlatanismo," all of which he condemned so strongly in his enemies.

On the whole, both the content and form of Forner's writings point to the fact that he was representative of his time, both as a man and a critic. They mark him well as a traditionalist, Christian thinker, Spanish patriot, and a critic, typical of the eighteenth century.

---

[196] See his comments on these authors in Appendix II.

CHAPTER IV

ART PRINCIPLES

Although Forner's criticism was more concerned with content than with form and aesthetic principles, he makes a number of comments on the French and Spanish writers of his day, which again give evidence of his traditional stand and of his hostile attitude toward the French neo-classic movement.

There are three possible reasons why Forner took the side of the opposition in regard to this literary movement—first, he probably regarded it as merely a form of French rationalism and anti-traditionalism;[1] second, he was angry with many of the French writers who had made calumnious remarks about his country and were trying to impose their hegemony on Spain; and third, as he had been trained in the classics and, apparently, had a great interest in them, he regretted that France was abandoning them.[2] The following comments on Spanish and French writing of the time show clearly his perturbation over the Spanish acceptance of the French ideas.

Forner saw Europe in his day seething in a sort of madness, each nation trying to exalt its own literary merit and surpass that of others.[3] Following her usual custóm, Spain was still silent.[4] She had always had merit of which to speak, but she had few panegyrists, while foreigners, he remarks, were in the habit of boasting of their progress.[5] He saw France, the impetuous nation,

---

[1] As a matter of fact, "ancient classicism" had become synonymous with "traditionalism," probably because the rationalists aimed at being consistent.

[2] While the "rules" and the "unities" were never supported wholeheartedly in Spain, there had always been Aristotelian exponents, and Forner, we might say, was one of the liberal followers of the Stagyrite.

[3] *Oración apologética*, p. 4.

[4] Forner remarks that if there were stirred up in Spain some of the Europeans' "hervor," the Spaniards would not be inferior to other nations in anything. They might even find some works worthy of praise in that period as they had found them in great numbers in the past (*ibid.*, p. xvii).

[5] *Ibid.*, p. xvii.

Art Principles

spreading through Europe a vast number of books, weakening all the languages with her idiom and her taste.[6] Even Italy, out of affection for the ridiculous philosophism which characterized the French writers of the eighteenth century, had forgotten the riches of Tasso, the sublimity of Chiabrera, the purity of Annibal Caro, and strength of La Crusca.[7]

It irked Forner greatly to see France setting herself up as a model for the rest of the nations.[8] He was of the opinion that no nation had a monopoly on genius and that good taste could be learned from writers throughout the world, not from France alone.[9] He was even more sensitive to the fact that many of his own fellow countrymen were imitating French authors in servile fashion, ignoring the Spanish classics of the past, and corrupting their own beautiful language by a free and direct use of Gallic expressions.[10]

It grieved him to see the great learning of Greece and Rome depreciated and cast aside by the sophists of his time.[11] It was his belief that only the unjust judgments of a nation upon the world's debt to antiquity and an exaggerated idea of its own superiority could prompt a nation to turn away from the treasures of classical antiquity.[12] The merit of the Greeks who had established the simplest elements of the arts and sciences, he felt, could never be effaced by the emulation or the envy of the moderns.[13] The forty or fifty books preserved from antiquity could, in his opinion, easily dispute the glory of the millions of tomes that Germany, Italy, France, and England could put against them.[14]

It was Forner's contention that the literary merit of a nation was not based on the number of vain systems, sophisms, and uncertain opinions.[15] It was not based on an enormous quantity of

---

[6] *Exequias*, p. 133.
[7] *Ibid.*, p. 132-133.
[8] *Ibid.*, p. 133.
[9] *Ibid.*, p. 134.
[10] *Ibid.*, p. 133.
[11] *Oración apologética*, p. 8.
[12] *Ibid.*, pp. 37-38.
[13] *Ibid.*, p. 191.
[14] *Ibid.*, p. 6.
[15] *Ibid.*, p. 5.

72 *Art Principles*

books,[16] written on every conceivable subject;[17] nor did it depend on the size of the libraries in a nation.[18] It was his belief that literary merit depended on a literature which gave honor to the understanding and did good to mankind.[19] Most of Forner's critical comments on the literature of the time revolve about the ideas concerning the imitation of nature, imitation of models, inspiration, imagination, precepts, reason, style, language, and good taste with its elements of beauty, truth, and goodness.

The few comments which Forner makes on the imitation of nature are in keeping with the classical ideal. He remarks that the purpose of the arts of imitation is to paint the works of nature; and that the purpose of the artist is to enrich nature. On this matter he writes, "El arte, no la imitación, es el que auxilia a la naturaleza, la encamina o mejora."[20] It grieved Forner to see that the arts and artists were not esteemed in his day. As he remarked, the great historian, the eminent orator, the divine poet, the immortal genius, the emulator of nature, and the creator of new beauties were looked upon with disdain in his day or celebrated as a race born for the entertainment of the stupid.[21] He realized, however, that it was much easier to be a pragmatic news agent than an historian, a vociferous lawyer than an orator, a pedantic scholar than a poet, a copier of voluble types, than an inventor of truths and verisimilitudes.[22]

He condemns strongly the numerous translations and slavish imitations of the French writers which were made by his contemporaries.[23] He believes that the Spaniards should not be overcome by the "novedad," of the day but should turn their attention to the Spanish classics and use them as their models. He would have them heed the following advice regarding the imitation of models:

> La imitación, o por mejor decir, el estudio de las obras españolas de los siglos pasados, debe ser vuestro norte

---

[16] *Exequias*, p. 153.

[17] *Ibid.*, pp. 125, 132.

[18] *Oración apologética*, pp. 5-6.

[19] *Ibid.*, p. ix.

[20] *Exequias*, p. 169.

[21] *Ibid.*, pp. 150-151.

[22] *Ibid.*, p. 150.

[23] *Ibid.*, p. 133.

Art Principles 73

para arribar al colmo de esta empresa. Mas no sea servil esta imitación, no sea mecánica ni de pura copia. Estudiad las frases de la lengua, no las de los autores. Buscad en ellos la abundancia y propiedad, no el giro o semblante que dió cada escritor a su escrito. El vuestro, como el de todos, debe ajustarse a vuestro genio o índole. Aquél a quien domine el juicio, trabajará inútilmente en querer remedar la travesura, siempre fecunda, de *Quevedo*, o la elegancia florida de *Solís*; aquél en quien domine el ingenio, aunque lo solicite, no podrá ceñirse jamás a la severidad locónica de *Mariana* o a la naturalidad sencilla de *Zurita*. La falta de esta advertencia ha producido imitaciones muy insípidas y frialdades intolerables en las obras de éstos que, sin ser nada por naturaleza quieren serlo todo por vanidad o codicia. Sin haber recibido gracia alguna para la graciosidad, se han empeñado en seguir las huellas de los verdaderamente graciosos; y han llenado el mundo de vulgaridades sucias o de sandeces desabridas. De la imitación servil resulta también otro daño, y es, que como la habla castellana ha comparecido con dos distintos semblantes en los siglos XVI y XVII, si os atáis sólo a la locución del primero, pareceréis un tanto anticuados; si sólo a los del segundo, os privaréis de una gran parte de la abundancia de vuestra lengua.[24]

Believing, contrary to the practice of his time, that artists are born and not made by rules,[25] Forner stressed the use and need of inspiration in a work of art, maintaining that when a writer follows the dictates of his natural talent, he produces a masterpiece that is inimitable.[26] He considered the arts to be universal and their applications, infinite.[27] To him, a prudent organization and form are necessary in art,[28] but he regarded inspiration as the true preceptor.[29] Hard and fast rules, he maintained, retard the progress of the artist and deprive his work of the life and reality that it should possess.[30] The mere observance of precepts does

---

[24] *Ibid.,* pp. 134-135.
[25] *Oración apologética,* p. vi.
[26] *Exequias,* p. 162.
[27] *Ibid.,* p. 110.
[28] *Oración apologética,* p. vi.
[29] *Exequias,* pp. 127, 145, 162; *Oración apologética,* p. vi.
[30] *Ibid.,* p. 187.

74 *Art Principles*

very great harm to the progress of good taste, since that observance by itself forms only a cadaver; and regardless of how closely the artist retains the regularity of the original nature, people prefer to see a live, happy, playful monster, rather than a prostrate cadaver.[81] With a view also to showing the necessity of inspiration in art, he remarks that hands and rules are sufficient to make a statue which is very correct, but dead. He believed that the genius of the sculptor is necessary to put life in the marble since the ability of the artist proceeds from his soul rather than from his hand.[82]

It seems evident that Forner approved of rules only in so far as they place no limitations upon the use of inspiration, imagination, and reason. Anything like a "maldita exactitud" which interferes with inspiration[83] or a "sequedad simétrica" by which man thinks of improving on nature, but more often ends by spoiling inherent beauty,[84] he bans. His opposition to rules which curb the activity and spontaneity of inspiration and which impair the reason by making it serve ends which are "inútiles o perjudiciales"[85] is clearly manifested. Only one rule seemed to him to be necessary, that of giving free rein to inspiration, always guided, of course, by good taste and reason. This rule was the chief recommendation which he offered to the Spanish writers of his day. To him, even excess in inspiration, provided it was not entirely "desenfrenada e impertinente" was more tolerable than the too studied coldness and exactitude[86] so characteristic of the writing of the time. Probably with the idea of stressing its importance, he makes this rule the burden of Cervantes' counsel. ·

> «Vos, que sois joven, tened impreso siempre en la memoria este consejo de un hombre aguerrido y veterano en

---

[81] *Ibid.,* p. 187. He seems to contradict himself here in regard to the imitation of nature. Cf. this study, p. 72.

[82] *Ibid.,* p. 188.

[83] *Ibid.,* p. 145. From his brief comment on Luzán, it would seem that Forner was not opposed to the extreme classical theories of this author. See Appendix II, p. 154.

[84] *Ibid.,* pp. 139-140.

[85] *Oración apologética,* p. 92.

[86] *Ibid.,* pp. v-vi.

Art Principles · 75

la ocupación de escribir : . . . Si . . . anteponéis las glorias del entendimiento al penoso, amargo y fugaz gusto de mandar, y tenéis en más ser honor de vuestra nación en lo venidero, que rana vocinglera, después de haber sufrido los sinsabores que trae consigo el mando, despachaos generosamente y dad soltura a la inclinación de vuestro talento, llevándole, siempre por la senda del buen gusto y de la razón . . . »[87]

Since Forner regarded the arts as the daughters of the imagination,[88] he considered the imagination as a necessary factor in the lively imitation and presentation of things and one without which the inspiration cannot get along. It was the author's opinion that his contemporaries, instead of using the imagination, abused it, by making it serve to build vain, fanciful worlds and systems.[89] He speaks of the period as an age in which a troop of ultramontane sophists had introduced the new and convenient art of speaking entirely by caprice, and had influenced the servile herd of common writers to such an extent that there were scarcely any who were not unfortunate imitators of the manner established by the Rousseaus, the Voltaires, and Helvetiuses.[40]

Forner looked upon reason as a guide to man's judgment, but he points out that the efforts directed by the reason toward right ends are often frustrated by excesses which are natural to man.[41] The superficialities manifested by the writers of his time seemed to him to give evidence of a lack of reason[42] rather than the use of it. He condemned particularly the display of philosophy in the arts of imitation, branding it as sickening and ridiculous,[48] irrational and insolent.[44] It was Forner's opinion and the opinion

---

[87] *Exequias*, p. 95.
[88] *Oración apologética*, p. v.
[89] *Ibid.*, p. 9.
[40] *Ibid.*, p. 8. We note here again his confusion of ideology and art.
[41] *Ibid.*, pp. 93-94.
[42] *Ibid.*, pp. 7, 153.
[48] *Exequias*, p. 169.
[44] *Oración* apologética, p. 149. He refers here specifically to the philosophizing of the French orators; but he apparently recognized the fact that philosophy was essential to the artist, for he speaks of the true philosophic spirit of Vives perfecting the artists who imitated nature and he asks if there could have been a Rivera, a Murillo, or a Velásquez without philosophy *(ibid.)*.

76 *Art Principles*

too, as he says, of some Frenchmen just as learned as d'Alembert, that the philosophic liberty which the editor of the *Encyclopédie* promoted was not freedom of thought, but rather a miserable license of reason, pernicious to the state and to the individual,[45] since it disrupted the common order of society and destroyed the happiness of man.[46] He believed in a "sabia libertad" which would preserve the understanding from ruin and would bring about the progress of literature.[47] It was license of thought that he condemned—that type of liberty by which a man justifies himself in the teaching and publishing of whatever he pleases, regardless of the harm that may result. According to Forner, this was the type of liberty, "mísera e iniqua," in which the abuse of reason was converted to the adulation of evil, to the authorization of vice and abominations.[48] His opposition to this went to such extremes that he classed such writers with criminals[49] and maintained that the state had the right to direct and control their liberty if it interfered with the common good.[50]

Since Spain had been accused of lacking taste in her literature,[51] Forner has much to say regarding the expression "buen gusto." He points out that the phrase itself originated in Spain and that it went out from there to the other nations.[52] In order to express propriety, order, and exactitude, Spain, he says, coined and promulgated a phrase that was unknown even in fecund Greece.[53]

In the *Exequias,* after having Arcadio remark on the fact that the true practice of good taste is contained in the arts, he has

---

[45] *Ibid.,* p. 154.

[46] *Ibid.,* pp. 152-153.

[47] *Ibid.,* p. 120.

[48] *Ibid.,* p. 21.

[49] *Ibid.,* pp. 18-22.

[50] *Ibid.,* p. 153. His confusion of ideology and art is again obvious.

[51] *Ibid.,* p. 188.

[52] *Ibid.,* pp. 101, 120, 186. As authority for this statement Forner quotes from Bernardo Trevisano's introduction to his edition of Muratori's *Riflessioni sopra il buon gusto nelle scienze e nelle arti,* Part 1, p. 79 (Venezia: 1736).

[53] *Ibid.,* p. 101.

Art Principles

Cervantes speak at considerable length on propriety as the first step in culture:

> ... propiedad en las palabras, propiedad en el estilo, propiedad en el método, orden o artificio; propiedad en los ornatos, propiedad en los raciocinios, propiedad en las sentencias, propiedad en la elección de materias; sin este cuidado ... no hay, ni puede haber, obra tolerable. Donde se ignore esto, todo irá al revés, o se confundirá pedantescamente.[54]

Good taste,[55] he maintains, is easy in theory, but its practice is not always attained even by those who know the rules well.[56] As he says, it is more often named than known, and frequently it is foreign to those who think they know it.[57] He points out that while Spain is accused of lacking good taste on the grounds that she is wanting in philosophy, the foundation of good taste, he believes that good taste is lacking rather in those nations that malign others, as he shows in the following passage:

> ... los juicios malignos (y obsérvese esto) sobre el estado de otras naciones, comúnmente son hijos de cabezas ligeras que queriendo manifestar que tienen buen gusto, faltan a un documento principal de éste, que es el decoro. Sin bondad, sin verdad y sin belleza no hay buen gusto en nada.[58]

Nor does Forner hesitate to condemn the so-called good taste in the matter of language which the French imitators in his country had introduced into Spain. With Mayans as his spokesman, he declares:

> « ... detesto altamente el buen gusto que creen introducir los literatos actuales, trasladándole, no de los consejos de la razón sana y sagaz, sino de la imitación de los escritos de una lengua distinta, y que en los libros, franceses, italianos, alemanes, rusos, romanos, griegos, árabes y

---

[54] *Exequias*, p. 154.
[55] Forner says Vives dictated the rules of it (*Oración apologética*, p. xii),
[56] *Ibid.*, p. 187.
[57] *Exequias*, p. 94.
[58] *Oración apologética*, p. 188.

78 *Art Principles*

chinos, se puede aprender a pensar bien; pero a hablar con elegancia y propiedad, en ningunos, sino en los nuestros de los dos siglos anteriores.»[59]

He also has Mayans point out how ridiculous is the belief of those who think that good taste resides in foreign books and not in the nature of things, since the precepts of the arts are universal and their applications infinite.[60]

Further disapproval of the taste of his time is found in the words of Iglesias when he admits that while many poets of the time of Philip IV and Charles II wandered far from the path of good taste, he prefers their sophisms, their insolent metaphors, and their unreasonable flights to the "sequedad helada y semibárbara" of the poetasters of his own day.[61]

Showing his esteem of good taste in its true sense, and his recognition of its importance, Forner has Cervantes tell Arcadio that good taste is always to be found in the Parnassus[62] and that silence is imposed there on every subject that does not possess the essential qualities of beauty, truth,[63] and goodness, the necessary elements of good taste.[64]

While Forner does not write at any length on beauty, he does say that it is subject to the whims of men's wills and that men are inclined to consider it before truth and goodness.[65] He remarks that it is because of this natural attraction of man toward the beautiful that the "vulgo" considers the dramas of Calderón so excellent in spite of their lack of verisimilitude.[66] In speaking of poetic beauty, he shows how it is subject to the dictates of genius and points out that, contrary to the opinions of those who favor a cold, mechanical precision, beauty may be found even in the irregularities of construction or in the absence of grammatical exactitude.[67]

---

[59] *Exequias*, p. 111.
[60] *Ibid.*, p. 110.
[61] *Ibid.*, p. 146.
[62] *Ibid.*, p. 85.
[63] *Ibid.*, p. 203.
[64] *Oración apologética*, pp. 186-188.
[65] *Ibid.*, pp. 186-187.
[66] *Ibid.*, p. 187.
[67] *Exequias*, p. 145.

Art Principles 79

Since art, as Forner conceived it, is a direct imitation of representative nature and an expression of the universal, truth is naturally one of the essential characteristics of good taste. His comments on it, however, are moral rather than aesthetic. To his mind, the intellect ought to seek truth and incline the will to good,[68] an ideal which the humanists of his day did not encourage.[69] He observed with regret that studies of man and of truth held no place at that time, because of the fanatic inclination toward investigations and objects which distracted, if they did not corrupt.[70] He repeatedly points a condemning finger at the *philosophes*, who, he maintains, considered nothing of value unless it fit into their imaginary republics, their empty worlds, and the whims of their delirium.[71]

Novelty, appealing more to pleasure than to reason,[72] was according to Forner, the great business of the ostentatious, boastful philosophers of his day.[73] The vanity of these sophists, he asserts, filled them with the desire to think in any manner provided they did not think as the great majority of men.[74] Universal truth was not their concern. He denounces the dictionaries which were so much in vogue at the time on the grounds that they maliciously confused truth and authorized sophistry.[75] Forner's love of truth and his antagonistic attitude toward the French writers who, he believes, had no interest in it, are stated in his exhortation to the Spaniards to esteem the truth and to grant their accusers the infamous merit of their miserable liberty. Linking virtue with truth, he says:

> Pensemos siempre en la verdad y virtud, y trátennos en hora buena de rudos los que prefieren a la verdad el sofismo, y a la virtud los medios de justificar las acciones viciosas.[76]

---

[68] When Forner refers to *good*, he means *moral good*.

[69] *Exequias*, p. 92.

[70] *Oración apologética*, p. 102.

[71] *Ibid.*, p. 9.

[72] *Exequias*, p. 134.

[73] *Ibid.*, pp. 92-93.

[74] *Oración apologética*, pp. 22-23.

[75] *Ibid.*, p. 103. He makes no allusion here to the fact that some of this was probably due to their efforts to evade the Inquisition.

[76] *Ibid.*, p. 21.

80 *Art Principles*

While it is evident from his remarks that he considers truth essential in every literary type, he sees a very special need of it in history,[77] in the apologies of a nation's literature, and in poetry.[78] In speaking of truth and poetry, he asks if truth must be mingled with fables in order that it may be celebrated with the divine accent of poetry. Addressing truth he exclaims, "Desgraciada verdad, que tan sin culpa tuya, te ves desterrada de la más encantadora de las artes!"[79] He scorns the philosophic fables as "el escándalo de la razón,"[80] for in these, as he says, men not only deceive others, but by their vanity, debase and enslave that talent which has been given them for the purpose of discovering and contemplating the most holy and august truths.[81]

Just as he lauds Lucan as the poet of truth because of the lessons found in his writings,[82] so he praises Vives for the truths contained in his works. To him he attributes the laws of truth; he commends him for his pronouncements against the vague flights of the imagination, the laziness of mind, and the ease with which many adopt as truth what is not truth.[83] Forner believes that because of their knowledge of the value of useful truths, Vives and Bacon are the only ones capable of placing a value on the culture of a nation.[84]

For the benefit of those outside of Spain, who have so distorted the truth regarding her,[85] as also for the Spaniards of his day who have been blinded through ambition,[86] he suggests that they turn to the Spanish writers of the past who looked to truth as their chief aim,[87] a fact which, he believes, cannot be denied.

> ¿Y quién, sino la ignorancia instigada por el torpe furor de la malignidad, osará negar que han nacido, que han

---

[77] *Exequias*, pp. 177, 254-255.
[78] *Oración apologética*, p. vii.
[79] *Ibid.*, p. 114.
[80] *Ibid.*, p. 14.
[81] *Ibid.*, pp. 14-15.
[82] *Ibid.*, p. 116.
[83] *Ibid.*, p. 145.
[84] *Ibid.*, pp. 6-7.
[85] *Exequias*, pp. 93-94.
[86] *Ibid.*, p. 11.
[87] *Oración apologética*, p. 23.

Art Principles

sido educados en España la mayor parte de aquellos genios incomparables, que en todos los siglos han declamado contra las extravagancias de la razón; que han procurado restituirla al recto conocimiento de la verdad; que la han señalado sus límites, manifestando los objetos que principalmente deben interesarla, y demostrando los perversos fines a que convierte la inmortal fuerza de sus potencias?[88]

Goodness, which Forner establishes as the third essential quality of good taste, is a matter of great importance. With Cañizares as his spokesman, he expresses his regret that the theatre of his day justified the charge that it did not fulfill its office to present virtue as a good and vice as an evil.[89] He maintains that literature should promote goodness[90] and that the truly great writer is one who benefits his fellowmen.[91] In this regard, he writes:

El que me confirma en las voluntades de mi Hacedor, me demuestra la necesidad de su revelación para adorarle decorosamente, y ordena los fundamentos en que se apoya esta revelación misma; ése es el verdadero grande hombre para mí, porque es el que verdaderamente sirve y aprovecha a los hombres.[92]

As a further proof of this fundamental notion of the exalted office of literature, Forner refers to the type of book that may be found on the shelves in the Spanish libraries.

Vemos en nuestros estantes, no sin aquel encogimiento que inspira la contemplación de la dignidad del entendimiento humano, la serie de aquellos hombres eminentes que han sido en todos los siglos la gloria, y no el des-

---

[88] *Ibid.*, pp. 94-95.

[89] *Exequias*, p. 181.

[90] *Oración apologética*, p. ix.

[91] He holds that the arts of imitation are intended for the use and benefit of mankind *(ibid.,* pp. 1-2) ; that they make man think of what he is and of the wonderful powers that God has given him *(ibid.,* p. 90) ; that they extol and immortalize nations and make them respected at all times *(Exequias,* p. 180).

[92] *Oración apologética*, p. 67.

82 *Art Principles*

crédito de la razón; aquellos que han procurado mejorar, no trastornar el mundo; que no han conocido en sus investigaciones otro blanco que el de la verdad, ni en sus vigilias otra ambición que la de ser útiles a sus semejantes.[93]

He likewise assures the sacred orator that his works will become masterpieces of art if he constantly keeps his end in view, namely, the good of the people. Of this, Forner writes, "Dadme talentos aptos, que prefieran la gloria de hacer bien a los intereses del mundo, y veréis prodigios."[94]

Because Forner believes that virtue should be inspired by literature,[95] he rails against the petty writers of the eighteenth century who scoff at virtue and justice.[96] In support of the significance of virtue he refers to the esteem in which it was held even in antiquity, pointing out that the "ciencia" of the Lacedemonians was the practice of virtue; their "saber," obedience to the laws; their glory, to think and act in a virtuous manner. Nor were they considered barbarous, although they had no Academicians, Stoics, or Peripatetics.[97] He also relates how Socrates taught the citizens of Athens the art of being good and how, without any display or ostentation, he laid the foundation for the divine science of virtue.[98] Addressing himself to those nations, which he calls sybaritical, he tells them that it is their thirst for pleasure that induces them to think of the literary world in the same manner as of the civil world, and that, just as in their social life, they prefer pomp and excess to suitable modesty and decency, so too, in literature they prefer the excesses and extravagances of the understanding to judicious moderation and learned self control.[99]

---

[93] *Ibid.*, p. 23.

[94] *Ibid.*, p. 164.

[95] *Oración apologética*, p. ix.

[96] *Ibid.*, p. 102. This is one of Forner's characteristic generalizations. He does not name any specific writers.

[97] *Ibid.*, p. 3.

[98] *Ibid.*, pp. 67-68.

[99] *Ibid.*, pp. 103-104. While Forner appears very general and superficial in his remarks, his comments were undoubtedly well understood at that time because of the prevailing spirit of "libertinage," relativity in moral standards, and the irreligious character of the period.

Art Principles 83

He urges the *philosophes* to look to Spain, which is struggling for the triumph of truth and the destruction of error, since it is there that they can learn solidity, decorum, and truth.[100] He points out that Spain, even in the days of her subjugation by barbarous hordes, had men who were eminent in virtue as well as in learning;[101] and in praise as well as in defense of his country, he expresses his belief that the nation which has cultivated and continues to cultivate the type of literature that gives honor to the understanding and spreads legitimate good to mankind is, beyond doubt, a learned nation.[102]

Forner regards style as external and not the essence of literary art.[103] He places greater value on the utility of the content and considers elegance as wasted when it is used to express frivolous and harmful matter.[104] The following passage is an excellent demonstration of his satirical vein as well as of his opposition to the superficial style of many of the *philosophes,* who wrote against Spain:

> Cuatro donaires, seis sentencias pronunciadas como en la trípode, una declamación salpicada de epigramas en prosa, cierto estilo metafísico sembrado de voces alusivas a la Filosofía con que quieren ostentarse Filósofos los que tal vez no saben de ella sino aquel lenguaje impropio y afectado, se creen suficientes para que puedan compensar la ignorancia y el ningún estudio. Así lo hizo Voltaire, y así lo debe hacer la turba imitatriz.[105]

Forner condemns the style of the eighteenth-century Spanish followers of the French. He speaks of it as a vulgar, barbarous, babbling imitation either of French books or "razonamientos insulsos de entendimientos que se explican del modo que piensan, esto es, tarde y desconcertadamente."[106] He claims that barbarity

---

[100] *Ibid.,* p. 103.
[101] *Ibid.,* p. 133.
[102] *Ibid.,* p. ix.
[103] *Ibid.,* p. ix; *Exequias,* p. 88.
[104] *Oración apologética,* pp. x-xi.
[105] *Ibid.,* p. 11.
[106] *Exequias,* p. 126.

84 *Art Principles*

results when real knowledge is doubted.[107] Wit, which is used to excess in his day weakens the character of a work, especially when it is not suitable to the matter.[108]

The contrast between the style of the eighteenth century Spanish literature and that of the past is emphasized by the author's comments in the *Exequias* through Villegas' survey of the literature. The works of writers in the reigns of Ferdinand the Catholic, Charles V, and Philip II, he points out, were marked by a grave, robust, natural character; and, as he remarks, "las cláusulas caminan con una especie de reposo severo, la estructura de los períodos es lenta y noble; tal vez poco sonora, aunque muy suave e ingenua."[109] He notes that the language took on a definite splendor from the court of Philip IV and became "rápida, lozana, viva, sonora, jovial, galante, florida, deliciosa." These characteristics, he notes, were distinctly present in the writings of Quevedo, Ulloa, the Príncipe de Esquilache, Saavedra, Calderón and Solís.[110]

As for the mystic writers, Forner believes that the Spaniards could profit much from their style. Of their works, he writes as follows:

> La lástima es que los españoles, aunque aficionadísimos a esta clase de libros, no han sabido estimar cuanto debieran las riquezas que depositaron en su estilo los principales maestros de la ciencia de la religión. La sublimidad de ésta imprimió tal grandeza, tal majestad y tal abundancia de imágenes magníficas, tan copia y variedad de afectos, tal pureza, propiedad y valentía en sus voces y en sus expresiones, que en estos libros fué donde descubrió nuestra lengua su maravillosa disposición para que las cosas grandes no aparezcan pequeñas en sus frases y en la estructura de sus períodos.[111]

The miserable and lamentable[112] state of the Spanish language

---

[107] *Ibid.*, p. 94.
[108] *Ibid.*, p. 109.
[109] *Ibid.*, p. 130.
[110] *Ibid.*, pp. 130-131.
[111] *Ibid.*, p. 216.
[112] *Ibid.*, p. 45.

Art Principles

85

is a source of the greatest affliction to Forner.[113] To him it is in such a hopeless condition that in his allegory he represents himself as invited to Parnassus to deliver the funeral oration for his language, which he personifies as a beautiful, graceful matron.[114]

Through whim, neglect, and ignorance on the part of the Spaniards,[115] and, as Arcadio explains to Villegas, through French contamination, the Spanish language has lost all of its beautiful qualities[116]—its docility,[117] its poetic phrases and expression; its grace, its lively turns and constructions; its harmony, grandiloquence, abundance; and its propriety in verse and prose.[118] Because the enemies of Spain could not speak her language properly they attacked it and labelled its majestic sonorousness as ostentation.[119] Forner puts his praise of the Spanish language on the lips of Apollo, who exhorts the visitors to Parnassus to appreciate it and to preserve it.

> Poseéis ... una lengua majestuosa para las cosas grandes; concisa, para las sublimes; pomposa y sonante en extremo para las magníficas y de grande aparato; tierna, blanda y suave para las amorosas; expresiva y eficaz para las agudezas; rápida e impetuosa para las imágenes y afectos vivos y vehementes; lozana, desenvuelta y ágil para las risas, los juegos y los solaces; sencilla, cándida y noblemente rústica para los objetos campestres. Su naturalidad para las gracias y donaires, su gravedad para las cosas serias, y su amenidad para las floridas y deliciosas, son incomparables; y de esta variedad de caracteres, que no está, no, en las cosas que se dicen, sino en las palabras, locuciones y modulaciones de que está enriquecido el genio mismo de la lengua, procede aquella abundancia que tanto han ponderado y recomendado los que con mayor ingenio y estudio procuraron apurar y desentrañar la excelencias de su mecanismo.[120]

---

[113] *Ibid.*, pp. 125-126, 45-46.

[114] *Ibid.*, p. 115.

[115] *Ibid.*, p. 118.

[116] *Ibid.*, p. 146.

[117] *Ibid.*, p. 259.

[118] *Ibid.*, p. 147.

[119] *Oración apologética*, pp. 17-18.

[120] *Exequias*, p. 260.

86 *Art Principles*

While Forner admits, through Cervantes' comments to Arcadio that the language was previously weakened by the persecution of the *culteranos,* the *equivoquistas,* the *conceptistas,*[121] the Gongorists[122] and the eighteenth century preachers and novelists,[123] he attributes her death to the "caterva engalicada," which she was unable to resist; and he pictures her dying in the arms of Mayans, the last and only defender[124] of her purity.[125]

Through the words of Villegas, Forner expresses his belief that there was little remedy for the evil because of the French influence.[126] The language had become, he notes, "lánguida, afeada con nueva barbarie, corrupta y enteramente cargada de vicios propios y ajenos, que es el último extremo de corrupción a que puede llegar el uso de un idioma."[127] He has Feijóo singled out in Parnassus as the first Spaniard to gallicize the language. On this occasion the advice is given that it would be better for the ingenious not to study this author's works, although the "vulgo" might possibly read them without any great harm.[128] The author's antipathy toward Gallicisms is likewise manifested when he has the censor of books in Parnassus refuse to place in the library a certain philosophico-oratorical book, with the advice that Forner and Arcadio should take it back to Spain so that philosophers who were in need of verbiage for their "filósofo-hispano-galo-ridículo" dictionaries might have access to it.[129] A similar aversion to French terms is displayed when the author features in Parnassus a display of some modern translations of Greek authors, and has Arcadio remark that the translators in these instances turned to the primitive source of good taste in an effort to escape the uni-

---

[121] *Ibid.,* p. 115.

[122] *Ibid.,* p. 248.

[123] *Ibid.,* p. 115.

[124] *Ibid.,* pp. 114-115.

[125] *Ibid.,* p. 107.

[126] *Ibid.,* p. 132. Apparently, Forner did not realize that the *afrancesado* influence could have counteracted much of the seventeenth century exuberance.

[127] *Ibid.,* p. 132.

[128] *Ibid.,* p. 194.

[129] *Ibid.,* p. 176.

Art Principles

87

versal corruption which was loosed by the "muladares" of the *hispano-galos* who were destroying the lustre of the Spanish language.[180]

Forner believes that while some of the Gallicisms were brought into the language through the appeal of novelty,[181] much of the responsibility of the decadence rests on the Spanish authors who were ignorant of their language and literature.[182] He entertains little hope of winning over the hungry translators and ambitious charlatans,[183] as he calls them, for the squadrons of ignorance have always been invincible.[184]

Negligence toward Spain's language and literature and mercantilism on the part of the publishers are also responsible for the corruption of the language, as these men were not careful in their choice of material for publication. They seemed to think only of the popularity of the subject matter and gave practically no consideration to the excellencies of speech.[185] Although Forner attributes the present corrupted state of the Spanish language to whim, neglect, and ignorance on the part of his countrymen,[186] it is apparently difficult for him to understand how it would be possible for them to be so taken up with the French language, since to his mind, there is no comparison between the French and the Spanish. To him, the mechanism of the Spanish is infinitely more beautiful, more eloquent, more fluent, and more flexible than the very exact, harsh, monotonous French language.[187] In the *Exequias*, he has Cervantes, in his discourse on the literary frogs, emphasize the inferiority of the French when he remarks that the French poets, so eminent for their "habladuría" are also distinguished by the viciousness of their language. Of them he remarks, "Entonan un canto gangoso y obscuro, que no parece sino que

---

[180] *Ibid.*, p. 225.

[181] *Ibid.*, pp. 228-229.

[182] *Ibid.*, p. 133.

[183] *Ibid.*, pp. 133-134.

[184] *Ibid.*, p. 134.

[185] *Ibid.*, p. 227. He seems to lose sight of the fact that the idioms of Spanish are opposed to the French abstraction in language.

[186] *Ibid.*, p. 118.

[187] *Ibid.*, p. 228.

88 *Art Principles*

sale de una congregación de viejas tabacosas."[138] Forner also attributes to the French language the responsibility of weakening eighteenth century tragedy by the use of rhymed prose.[139] His criticism of the monotony of the Alexandrine verse is remarkable for its vigor and picturesqueness. He compares the rhythm to *cuatro martillazos,* which are reminders of *fraguas* or *batanes.*[140]

Over and over again Forner expresses his regret at the lack of interest. shown in his country toward the Spanish language. Through Cervantes' remarks, he observes the definite trend away from the pure Castilian. According to the great master, the poets used an inferior language;[141] the jurists even made Apollo laugh with their "latino-bárbaro" commentaries, composed to explain the laws which were written in pure Castilian;[142] and the youth, according to Arcadio, instead of being taught to master their native tongue were made to speak a barbarous and pedantic Latin, with the result that no one knew how to explain the arts and sciences in good Castilian and their own language remained sterile.[143]

As Forner traces the history of the Spanish language, he shows how it was formed on the ruins of the languages spoken by the subjugating peoples, which contributed marvellously to its abundance. Although its progress was slow in the first centuries, it acquired a nobility, a harmony, and a majesty that was remarkable.[144] Especially, did it become beautiful in the reign of Ferdinand the Catholic, when the writers tried to perfect it by availing themselves of the treasures found in the Greek and Latin poetry.[145] It was enlarged and ennobled by the right kind of translation;[146] and it was strengthened, beautified, and perfected by eminent writers before the eighteenth century.[147]

---

[138] *Ibid.,* p. 91.

[139] *Ibid.,* pp. 119-120.

[140] For his complete critical comment on the Alexandrine, see Trigueros, Appendix II, pp. 167-168.

[141] *Ibid.,* pp. 91-92.

[142] *Ibid.,* p. 89.

[143] *Ibid.,* p. 166.

[144] *Ibid.,* p. 126.

[145] *Ibid.,* p. 127.

[146] *Ibid.,* pp. 224-225.

[147] *Ibid.,* p. 126.

Art Principles

89

It is Forner's opinion that the Spanish language excels all other languages[148] in expressing worthy thoughts in a worthy manner.[149] It is the greatest and best instrument that Europe knows to express thoughts with majesty, propriety, and simplicity, grace, and energy.[150] It is, he says,

> un lenguaje sublimamente poético, una locución majestuosa, divina, que inflame el espíritu y le enajene, llenándole de una excelsa magnificencia, de un vigor robusto, de una vehemencia inquieta y arrebatada.[151]

To him there is no language that is richer, more sonorous, and of greater diversity.[152] He doubts that there was any other language spoken in his time that possessed the qualities necessary to treat pastoral poetry with proper elegance,[153] or that could really express the passions. The grandeur of its diction is such that it can dispute even that of Euripides and Sophocles.[154] In fact, because of the majesty of its diction, Spanish is the only language than can console the tragic theatre for the loss of the Greek and Latin.[155] It is the language, too, that had the glory of bringing the inhabitants of New Spain out of the barbarity which had held them in harsh and cruel slavery for centuries.[156]

Such are Forner's critique of the Spanish and French languages, his esteem for the former, and his opposition to the latter. From the point of view of criticism as we know it today, Forner's criticism of these languages seems puerile and primitive; yet, it was quite typical of the subjective, superficial, satirical criticism of his day, especially in Spain.

Forner was, by no means, alone in his attitude toward the French language. The opposition was, in fact, common at that time. The continuous controversy over the comparative merits of

---

[148] *Ibid.*, p. 120.
[149] *Ibid.*, p. 147.
[150] *Ibid.*, "Introducción," p. 46.
[151] *Ibid.*, p. 120.
[152] *Ibid.*, p. 193.
[153] *Ibid.*, p. 245.
[154] *Ibid.*, p. 119.
[155] *Ibid.*, p. 244.
[156] *Ibid.*, p. 259.

90   *Art Principles*

the French and Spanish languages was a natural outgrowth of the
attempts of some *afrancesados* to establish French neo-classicism
in Spain. There was probably no phase of the French movement that was so commonly under attack as the matter of Gallicisms.[157] The Spanish authors were, in general, opposed to the
introduction of French words and expressions[158] into the Spanish
language on the grounds that it corrupted their language and
brought dishonor to their country. Some were filled with a
puristic zeal; others with a patriotic enthusiasm. As Antonio
Rubio notes, many "were irritated by the tacit or expressed ar-
rogation of the French that the patrimony of the ancients had
been deposited in their care, as if they were the anointed custodians
of the classical culture."[159] Angered by the efforts of the French
to impose their hegemony on Spain as also by the attacks which
French writers and statesmen had made upon the Spanish culture,
the Spaniards turned to defending themselves by "recalling their
epoch of supremacy over the French and returning insult with
insult and arrogance with arrogance."[160]

Forner was one of the many Gallophobes who scathed the
French language in their defense of the Spanish. Apparently, he

---

[157] A. Rubio, *Comments on Eighteenth Century Purismo* (Philadelphia:
1935), p. 321. Among the Spanish authors who made these comparisons besides Forner, were Feijóo, Huerta, Mayans, Isla, Cadalso, Iriarte, Jovellanos, Leandro Moratín, and later, Quintana, Marchena, Capmany, Cienfuegos, and Gallardo *(ibid.,* p. 318). As Rubio points out, the Gallophobes
like Huerta, Forner, Capmany, and Gallardo found almost nothing but
faults in the French, and one was just as scathing in his criticism as the
other. Mayans, Cadalso, Moratín, and Jovellanos did not vilify the French,
however. Iriarte, as a musician, took exception to the French for singing.
Feijóo considered the articulation of the French easier than the Spanish.
Mayans declared the "French more erudite than the Spanish because it had
books which were more erudite." Padre Isla, at first, regarded the Spanish
language as sufficient in itself and equal to any other language. Several
years after writing his *Fray Gerundio,* however, he expressed his belief
that the Spanish needed a moderate amount of the "dulzura e insinuación
francesa" *(ibid.,* pp. 321-322).
[158] There was much discussion and disagreement at the time as to the
real meaning of Gallicisms and neologisms.
[159] Rubio, *Comments on Eighteenth Century Purismo,* p. 323. Cf. this
study, p. 71.
[160] Rubio, *Comments on Eighteenth Century Purismo,* p. 323.

Art Principles 91

was blind to the good qualities of the French. It is evident that he had little appreciation of its clearness, precision, and vowel harmony, as also of the fact that the language is governed by intellectual laws. It is clear that the logic and the abstraction of the French were of little interest to him, and that its terseness and the rigidity even wearied him.[161] Perhaps in this matter, Forner might be accused of a blind patriotism; yet, in this, he was again acting in accord with the spirit of the times, for this kind of national enthusiasm was characteristic of eighteenth century Europe.

From Forner's observations on aesthetic principles and from his method of presenting his views it is evident that he was not an art critic. His comments on the imitation of nature, imagination, rules, reason, good taste, beauty, truth, goodness, and style are so general, so commonplace, and so superficial that it can be readily seen that he possessed neither the knowledge nor the understanding of a professional critic. What he says regarding these matters, however, does reveal his interest in aesthetic subjects which were commonly discussed in eighteenth century Spain and France. They also reveal his strong leaning toward the traditional classical ideal. His views were not essentially different from those held by his classical predecessors and contemporaries in Spain, or by the supporters of Hellenistic classicism in France. Even his opinions regarding directed and reasonable inspiration were the same as those held by many of his French contemporaries.

Forner was definitely not a literary preceptor, for his criticism, as has been seen, is mainly negative. He satirizes and condemns the Spanish and French writers of his day, but his attack on them lacks organization, force, and directness. It is characterized by the very repetition, verbosity, exaggeration, and superficiality that he unrelentingly condemned. It must be said, however, that there is a bit of cleverness in some of his satirical comments on the French language, particularly, in those on the French Alexandrine.

It is obvious from the author's comments on aesthetics that his interest in the French neo-classic movement and his opposition

---

[161] Cf. Salvador de Madariaga, *Englishmen, Frenchmen, Spaniards*, London: Oxford, 1928, pp. 192-202.

92 *Art Principles*

to it rested almost entirely on the matters of content and language. His repeated confusion of ideology with art principles again manifests his critical concern with content rather than form. His opposition to the ingrafting of the French Encyclopedic philosophy and the French language in the literature of Spain is clearly evident in the preceding pages and will continue to show itself in the following chapter which will contain a digest of his remarks on specific literary forms and types.

CHAPTER V

LITERARY FORMS AND TYPES

As has been observed in the preceding chapter and as will be seen in the following pages, Forner favored the ancient Aristotelian literary principles, but he did not wish them to come through France. It must be remembered that Forner was a Gallophobe and that to him French neo-classicism connoted not only the idea of precepts, but also the idea of gallicisms and an anti-Christian philosophy. His opposition to the French spirit was never concealed.[1] In the matter of poetics, he undoubtedly held views similar to those contained in Mayans' *Retórica,* a work which Ticknor describes as being founded on the philosophic opinions of the Roman preceptists rather than on the modifications introduced into them by Boileau and his disciples.[2]

Forner's taste for the ancient classical doctrines is revealed particularly in the comments which he makes concerning the classical literary types of poetry, drama, and eloquence. This chapter, however, will also contain his views on history, the philosophic fables, criticism, and works of a didactic nature.

---

[1] The following quotation from an undated set of statutes which he drew up for an academy not only satirizes the Spanish Academy which reflected and promoted the French taste, but also represents an open declaration of his anti-French attitude: "El juramento único que se tomará a todo individuo será el de detestar la secta semigálica, y defender a sangre y fuego el verdadero buen gusto castellano, así en prosa como en verso. Y por lo mismo deberá obligarse a promover la afición a nuestros buenos escritores de los dos siglos XVI y XVII que serán su único norte y guía" (Statutes quoted by Cueto, "Bosquejo histórico-crítico de la poesía castellana en el siglo XVIII," *Poetas líricos del siglo XVIII,* I, CXLVII).

[2] Ticknor, as quoted by the *Enciclopedia universal ilustrada,* XXXIII, 1295. Forner's great admiration for Mayans is shown in the *Exequias.* It is interesting to note that Forner's only reference to Luzán is that of naming him in the procession with the preceptists and of remarking that his poetics was better than his poetry. *(Exequias,* p. 247.) Luzán's original work, it will be recalled, was influenced more by the ideas of the Italians and the ancients than it was by those of the French writers. Cf. Cueto, "Bosquejo histórico-crítico," p. LIX.

94   *Literary Forms and Types*

In his remarks on poetry we discover his attitude toward it as an art, its importance to men and to nations, its value as a medium of teaching, its decline in the eighteenth century, some characteristics of its decadent state, some possible reasons for it, and his esteem for the Spanish geniuses of the Golden Age.

Because Forner regarded poetry as the most charming of the arts,[3] he recognized man's need of it. He recognized its importance both for pleasure and for instruction.[4] Because he considered it the most useful of the arts, he honored it in his allegory by giving to the poets the first place in the procession. This he explains in the following lines:

> Antecedían los poetas, porque en España, así como en todas las naciones que han cultivado las potencias del ánimo, fué la poesía la que abrió el camino a los progresos de la sabiduría; y de los poetas iban en primer lugar los que habían cantado las alabanzas del Criador y las doctrinas morales; porque el hombre ha nacido primero para la virtud que para los institutos de su conveniencia y recreo; y hermanando entre sí esta primera obligación con las bellezas del ingenio, se consigue de una vez hacer a los hombres cultos y virtuosos, lo cual es propiamente procurar que florezca en ellos la constitución de su racionalidad y que no degeneren. . . .[5]

That Forner considered thought essential to poetry is evident from the advice which Arcadio gives him when he expresses his desire to write poetry.

> Darse todo a pensamientos
> Que atraigan la voluntad,
> Si son falsos o caducos,
> ¿De qué, en fin, le servirán?
> Piense bien y piense a tiempo:
> Ésta es la ley principal;
> Que para hacer versos malos
> Siempre le queda lugar.[6]

---

[3] *Oración apologética*, p. 114.

[4] *Exequias*, p. 240.

[5] *Ibid.*, pp. 239-240. Referring again to the procession of the poets, he writes, "Pasamos revista allí a aquella serie de hombres respetables, por quien es hoy glorioso España, más que por las inútiles mortandades de sus conquistas" (*Ibid.*, p. 240).

[6] *Ibid.*, p. 73.

Literary Forms and Types   95

The author's condemnation of the absence of thought in so much of the poetry written since the Golden Age is manifested in the allegory by having Cervantes remark how the Spanish poets find no difficulty in breaking forth into animated song over the least trifle, even "la caída de una piedrezuela en la laguna."[7] Referring again to the shallowness and emptiness of much of the Spanish verse in his day, Forner has one of the "sabios" in Parnassus ask, "¿Qué utilidad traen al mundo versecillos de garapiña?"[8]

He could see no reason why truth could not be contained in poetry. He recognized the merit of the "fábula verosímil" and the easy manner of instruction offered by inventing facts, yet he believed that poetry lost much when its lines were not adorned with "the lovable teaching of truth."[9] Although critics maintained that Lucan confused history with poetry, Forner held him in particular esteem because of the truth contained in his verses. Forner knew no law that excluded the narration of facts from poetry. Pointing out that Virgil sings of real facts in the sixth and eighth books of the Aeneid and of fiction in the others, he asks if Virgil ceases to be a poet in those books which treat of facts.[10]

Because the author realized the power that poetry exerts over nations, it was with deepest regret that he saw its decline in his day. To him it seemed that Nature had withdrawn her helping hand entirely from his contemporaries.[11] In the words of Arcadio, the

---

[7] *Ibid.*, p. 91. Forner does not name specific poets, but he probably had in mind some or all of the following whom Cueto mentions as outstanding in the matter of writing on trifles: Nieto Molina, Alejo de Dueñas, the Marqués de Ureña, and the Marqués de Méritos ("Bosquejo histórico-crítico," p. CLXVI).

[8] *Exequias*, p. 91.

[9] *Oración apologética*, p. 115.

[10] *Ibid.*, p. 114.

[11] *Exequias*, p. 144. He refers here particularly to the dramatic poets of the past, for he writes: "No parece sino que la naturaleza, cansada de desperdiciar ingenio en los poetas del siglo de *Lope y Calderón* . . ." Here likewise, is noticed the favorable attitude of Forner toward the Golden Age dramatists. See this study, p. 101.

96 *Literary Forms and Types*

poet of the time lacked not only the inspiration of the muse, but even the respect of his fellowmen:

> ¿Qué utilidad esperáis de esa profesión, que han dado en llamar divina los pícaros, a quienes rompería yo de buena gana la cabeza, por la bellaquería de atribuir a los poetas la comunicación con los dioses, cuando no la tienen siquiera con los hombres más miserables de la república, que en viendo a uno gritan: «*Guarda el poeta*» como si viesen algún oso o lobo suelto de la jaula?[12]

Evidence of the fact that the eighteenth century poets themselves had not the slightest notion of their own dignity, of the significance of poetry, and of the art of writing it,[13] is cleverly exemplified by Forner in the following speech of one of the poets in Parnassus, who, before being converted into a frog, boasted of his abilities and made a magnificent display of his ignorance:

> . . . yo, para servir a vuestra serenidad, hago coplas, que llamo versos; y como Garcilaso hacía versos también, no sé qué razón ha de haber para que se me arroje de donde él habita. La poesía, ¿acaso se reduce a otra cosa que a formar décimas, seguidillas, liras, octavas reales y romances de arte mayor y menor? Yo tengo en la uña al Rengifo, y sin tenerle, sé contar las sílabas y los pies con tanta facilidad còmo la mismísima *monja de Méjico*. Pues si por erudición va, según la opinión de algunos hombres descontentadizos, que creen que sin gran caudal de doctrina no puede haber buena poesía, yo he aprendido en los cafés la ciencia del mundo, que es la principal, y de las especulativas sé pronunciar física, matemáticas, *éctica, dragmática*, y sé muy bien que Virgilio compuso la *Eneidas*, Ovidio, un poema sobre el *fausto*. Cicerón fué

---

[12] *Exequias*, pp. 73-74.

[13] Cueto also bears witness to this indifference on the part of the poetasters of that time. The following is one of the most striking of his comments: "*Olivade* se proponía deliberadamente escribir versos incorrectos y descoloridos. Él mismo lo dice sin rebozo en estas palabras: 'No ha sido mi designio hacer versos correctos y brillantes, y por eso no he pedido a la poesía me prestase sus hermosos colores y sus imágenes atrevidas. Estos adornos serían extraños y nada oportunos para decorar grandes verdades'" ("Bosquejo histórico-critico," p. CLVIII).

Literary Forms and Types

> - muy buen gramático, según dicen los dómines, y entiendo medianamente los himnos del Breviario. Con que ¿qué no hay en mí que pueda haber en los poetas más sublimes?[14]

The author explains how the eighteenth century versifiers, considering the poets of the past to be inexact, introduced a "maldita exactitud" which converted poetry into a "mecanismo gramátical, como si la gramática de la poesía no fuese diversísima de la prosaica, y como si las leyes del entusiasmo y de la belleza poética no se burlasen a cada paso de las menudencias de los pedagogos."[15] To write verse in the eighteenth century meant nothing more, therefore, than the stringing together of half-French words and expressions,[16] "una prosa corrupta en el número de unos versos lánguidos, que son versos sólo porque tienen medida."[17] Tied to their petty rules, the poets of the eighteenth century could not be directed away from this manner of writing verse,[18] described by Forner as "una fría serie de malas prosas en consonantes, llamadas poemas sólo porque martillean la oreja con el golpe de la rima."[19]

From the pens of such writers came forth eclogues written in the tone of declamations; didactic verse written in the tone of eclogues;[20] comedies that made one weep; tragedies that produced

---

[14] *Exequias,* pp. 97-98.

[15] *Ibid.,* p. 145. In Forner's condemnation of the prosaicism of the period, he names only the poet, Rejón de Silva. He mentions, however, Iriarte's *El Apreton,* and alludes to his poem, *La música* and his *Fábulas literarias* (See Appendix II). In addition to these, he possibly had in mind some of the following who were noted for their prosaicism: Pablo Olivade, Francisco Gregorio de Salas, Pedro de Silva Bazán, Ignacio de Meras, José de la Olmeda, Pedro Pichó, Montengón, Pérez de Celis (Cf. Cueto, "Bosquejo histórico-crítico," pp. CLVIII-CLXIX.

[16] *Exequias,* p. 145.

[17] *Ibid.,* p. 144.

[18] *Ibid.,* p. 145.

[19] *Ibid.,* p. 143. Commenting further on the rhyme, he writes: "Antes la rima era lo de menos en los poetas. Hoy no hay poeta si se le desnuda de la rima" (*Ibid.,* p. 144).

[20] Cueto makes similar observations, remarking that poets used the eclogue to sing of almost anything: fine arts, an aristocratic wedding, death, war, etc. ("Bosquejo histórico-crítico," p. CLXIII).

98 *Literary Forms and Types*

laughter;[21] sonnets with their fourteen measured verses but nothing more; epics built upon dreams; and odes that made the unfortunate reader shiver.[22] Through their works, not only was the literature ruined, but the language lost its beauty, grace, life, energy, grandiloquence, abundance, and propriety.[23] Nothing that was written at that time was in the least representative of Spain. It was "todo, todo, no sólo sin alma, pero sin cuerpo castellano, si es lícito explicarme así."[24]

Forner attributed the sad state of Spanish poetry in the eighteenth century to several causes: the lack of encouragement given by those in power to poets and their art;[25] the idea held by many versifiers that poets could be made by rules;[26] the mercantile attitudes of many aspiring poets;[27] the bad influence of French writers;[28] the lack of popular appreciation of real poetry;[29] and the indifference or ignorance of the "vulgo," who, because of their long acquaintance with poor translations from the French, were unable to distinguish Castillian poetry from the semi-French.[30]

By having Cervantes compare the poetry of the eighteenth century with that of the Golden Age,[31] Forner continues to set forth his views on the manner of writing poetry and to show wherein

---

[21] Forner, in all probability refers here to the sentimental plays that were so popular at the time, particularly those of Comella, Valladares, and Zavala. (Cf. I. L. McClelland, *The Origins of the Romantic Movement in Spain*, Liverpool: Institute of Hispanic Studies, 1937, pp. 226-228.)

[22] *Exequias*, p. 146.

[23] *Ibid.*

[24] *Ibid.*

[25] *Ibid.*, p. 122.

[26] *Ibid.*, p. 145; *Oración apologética*, p. vi.

[27] *Exequias*, p. 78.

[28] *Ibid.*, pp. 145-146.

[29] *Ibid.*, p. 74.

[30] *Ibid.*, p. 146.

[31] Forner was interested in the regeneration of the classical poetry of sixteenth century Spain. With this idea in mind, he affiliated with two groups of "eruditos," one in Salamanca and the other in Seville. Fray Luis de León was regarded as the exemplar of the Salamancan school and Herrera as the idol of the Sevillan academy.

Literary Forms and Types

the poets of his day failed to measure up to the standard set by those of Spain's classical epoch.[32]

In the days of Philip IV, Cervantes remarks in the allegory, poetic figures and expressions were found in verse.[33] Because genius dictated to poets at that time, their poetry was filled with expressions that were suited to the images they portrayed. With their imaginations enlivened, poets then said what they ought to say, without any particular study.[34] This freedom of expression added beauty, he points out. He regrets that the poets of the eighteenth century did not appreciate the genius of the poets of the Golden Age and that they turned away from them, as he says, "con nuevo e inaudito modo de juzgar, no son buenos nuestros Poetas porque lo son realmente."[35]

In the person of Cervantes, Forner expresses his longing for the energetic buoyant poetry written by the Spanish geniuses of the past.

> ¿Dónde está aquella fecundidad de imaginación tan pródiga que, pasando los términos de lo conveniente, a modo de río que sale de madre por la abundancia del caudal, hacía a la poesía más poética de lo que debía ser? ¿Dónde está aquella locución enérgica, que en los versos sonaba divinamente, y era intolerable cuando se quería desatar en prosa, no de otro modo que acaece en todo idioma que posee lenguaje poético?[36]

While he admits that many of the poets in the time of Philip IV and Charles II strayed far from the path of good taste, he prefers the poetry of the past with all its excesses to that written in his day when all was "miseria."[37]

---

[32] The following are the names of the sixteenth century poets whom Forner deemed worthy to walk in the procession in honor of the Spanish Language: Luis de León, Fernando de Herrera, Bartolomé de Argensola, Francisco de Rioja, Francisco de Quevedo, el Principe de Esquilache, Vicente Espinel, Agustín de Tejada y Paez, Pedro Espinosa, Artemidoro (Rey de Artieda), Juan de Arguijo (*Exequias*, p. 241).

[33] *Ibid.*, p. 144.

[34] *Ibid.*, p. 145.

[35] *Oración apologética*, p. 17.

[36] *Exequias*, pp. 144-145.

[37] *Ibid.*, p. 144.

100 *Literary Forms and Types*

> . . . prefiero sus sofismas, metáforas insolentes y vuelos
> inconsiderados, a la sequedad helada y semibárbara del
> mayor número de los que poetizan hoy en España;
> porque, al fin, en los desaciertos de aquéllos veo y admiro
> la riqueza y fecundidad de mi lengua, que pudo servir de
> instrumento a frases e imágenes tan extraordinarias;
> pero en éstos no veo más que penuria, hambre de in-
> genio y lenguaje bajo y balbuciente. Los primeros se
> me representan como un campo fertilísimo, cuya fuerza
> para producir ofusca sus producciones con la excesiva
> pompa y prodigalidad de ellas. En los segundos creo ver
> un erial árido, vestido de arena y de peñascos pelados y
> en que de largo tiempo en largo trecho se deja ver un
> cardo mustio y tal cual césped de grama agostada, ca-
> bizbaja y rociada de polvo.[88]

The question of the reform of the Spanish stage was one around which much controversy revolved in the eighteenth century. All critics, nationalist and neo-classic, advanced their criticism of the theatre and their ideas of reform. Forner, too, had very definite views on these matters. In his discussion of the drama he sets forth his opinion concerning the importance of the drama as an art, its significance in the cultural development of a nation, its purpose, its decadent state in the eighteenth century, and the possibilities and means for its improvement.

It will be observed from Forner's discussion of the theatre in the *Exequias* that he shows again his leaning toward ancient classicism combined with the Spanish spirit and atmosphere. He follows the ancients in the aim that he sets for the drama—that of teaching as well as entertaining. Other Aristotelian qualities which he considers essential to the drama are a reasonable inspiration, a regulated imagination, verisimilitude, and a pure and elegant style. It will be seen, however, that he manifests in the *Exequias* a more lenient attitude toward the national classical

---

[88] *Ibid.*, pp. 146-147. Cueto remarks that the same sort of prosaic verse was turned out by those who possessed a little talent as well as by those who had none. The former used the precepts to curb the little talent they had lest they be accused of gongorism and the latter used the rules in the hope of becoming poets ("Bosquejo historico-critico," pp. LXI-CLVII).

Literary Forms and Types

drama[39] than he did in his *Sátira contra los vicios introducidos en la poesía castellana* in 1782, in his letter to Ayala in 1784,[40] and in his *Reflexiones de Tomé Cecial,* written against Huerta in 1786.[41] In his earlier pronouncements on the drama he placed greater emphasis on the value of the precepts, and although acknowledging some good qualities in the Golden Age drama, he was very free with his condemnation of the masters, especially, Lope and Calderón. In the *Exequias* he manifests a considerable change of attitude. In this work, while pointing out the defects of the old masters he stresses their good qualities and even sets Lope and Calderón up as models—models, however of inspiration and genius, capable of combining their defects with beauty. Yet, in spite of his praise of the national dramatists he still holds to his earlier idea of the need of a reasonable observance of the precepts to put balance and order into the work.[42] Forner advocates, then, as will be seen, a drama that would combine true Spanish spontaneity of inspiration and imagination exemplified in the old national dramas, with the good taste, that is, the propriety and order of the classicists.[43]

In regard to the drama as an art, Forner points out that since it is the art in which all the other arts concur for the instruction of man, it is only proper that it should be considered the chief of the arts.[44] In the *Reflexiones sobre el teatro en España* which he

---

[39] This was probably due to several factors: he was always a loyal Spaniard, a Gallophobe and not a Gallophile; the old national drama had maintained its popularity with the people throughout the century; the neo-classic drama was never accepted on the stage (McClelland, *op. cit.,* p. 187); Masson's unjust attack on Spain in 1782 had brought both nationalists and Gallicists to a greater national consciousness and to a more loyal defense of Spain's past glories *(ibid.,* pp. 101-102).

[40] "Sátira contra los vicios introducidos en la poesía castellana," Cueto, *Poetas líricos del siglo* XVIII, II, 304; "Carta de Don Juan Pablo Forner a López de Ayala," *ibid.,* p. 374.

[41] Cf. Menéndez y Pelayo, *Historia de las ideas estéticas,* V, 325-326.

[42] It will be recalled that in the letter which he wrote to Ayala in 1784 he defends his own observance of the precepts in his drama entitled *La cautiva española* ("Carta de Don Pablo Forner a Don Ignacio López de Ayala," Cueto, *Poetas líricos del siglo* XVIII, II, 374).

[43] See this study, pp. 106-107.

[44] *Exequias,* p. 181.

102   *Literary Forms and Types*

has Cañizares discover in Parnassus and read to him and his companions, Forner observes that the theatre is of such importance that it cannot be regarded with indifference by any nation that desires to raise the cultural level of its people.[45] To emphasize this fact, he points out that history attests that there has never been a cultured people whose first steps toward culture were not initiated by dramatic poetry.[46] In Greece, the immortal works of Sophocles, Euripides, and Menander were presented on the Athenian stage long before Aristotle defined the art of poetry. In Rome, Plautus and Terence opened the way for Roman culture. In Italy, Trissino, Ariosto, Machiavelli, Tasso, and other men of superior talent made famous the Age of Leo X;[47] and in France the dawn of learning and culture appeared only after the presentation of the *Cid*.[48]

From the earliest times, the purpose of the drama has been to teach and reform as well as to entertain.[49] Since the drama can be made a great means of correcting the vices of the people, the examples offered in it should be true to life. If they are not, they will be useless, vain, and even vicious in themselves, because the impossible and the unusual are not applicable to the possible and the common. In the following lines, the author states clearly his idea of what a drama should be:

> Éstos [dramas] no son, ni deben ser, más que unas parábolas puestas en acción, ejemplos naturales de la vida humana, desengaños mismos que mejoren la sociedad, pintando con verisimilitud lo que pasa en ella realmente. Deben copiarse los genios, los designios, las inclinaciones, los pensamientos, los modos de obrar y los afectos mismos que se experimentan en el trato, en los estados y en las ocupaciones de los hombres.[50]

It was Forner's opinion that the theatre had degenerated into a "deleite bárbaro y escandaloso" and an instrument of corrup-

---

[45] *Ibid.*, p. 180.

[46] *Ibid.*, p. 180.

[47] Tasso really does not belong to the Age of Leo X. He was born twenty-three years after the death of the pontiff (Cueto, *Poetas líricos del siglo XVIII*, II, 403, n. 2).

[48] *Exequias*, pp. 180-181.

[49] *Ibid.*, pp. 181, 184.

[50] *Ibid.*, pp. 184-185.

Literary Forms and Types

103

tion,[51] for which reason he believed that there was need to raise the question of the licitness of the theatre in Spain. In his opinion it would have been better for the theatre to cease to exist since it had rejected the very reason for its existence, namely that of teaching and reforming as well as entertaining. He speaks of the theatre of his time as "una región imaginaria"[52] which aimed only at making people laugh. Continuing this idea he writes:

> ... se presentan indistintamente personas de todas clases y especies a recitar largos trozos de versos campanudos, a decir delirios y bufonadas, y a ejecutar acciones que ni aun pasarían por sueños si los contase un hombre enfermo.[53]

As a result of such productions, the "vulgo" became so accustomed to the extraordinary and the unusual that it frowned upon the works of those who imitated nature.[54] People held in equal esteem, he says, "una farsa estrafalaria y una acción propia y bien conducida."[55] Men of great talent were restrained from writing in accordance with their abilities because of the competition with insignificant writers who, claiming to cater to the popular taste, supplied the stage with their farces and their "delirios."[56]

In satirizing the prevailing *comedias,* Forner calls them "monstruos del arte."[57] The following description of them, which he has Cañizares read in the allegory, gives a very comprehensive idea of the nature of the dramatic productions then in vogue in Spain:

> Se ven en nuestros dramas, pintados con el colorido más deleitable, las solicitudes más deshonestas, los engaños,

---

[51] *Ibid.,* p. 182.

[52] *Ibid.,* p. 185.

[53] *Ibid.*

[54] *Ibid.*

[55] *Ibid.,* p. 187.

[56] *Ibid.,* p. 185.

[57] *Ibid.,* p. 183. Forner probably refers here to the plays of Comella, Valladares, Zavala y Zamora, and Moncín, for their plays were the ones that drew the people to the theatres in throngs during the last part of the century (Cf. McCelland, *op. cit.,* pp. 183-193, 227 ff).

104 *Literary Forms and Types*

los artificios, las perfidias, fugas de doncellas, escalamientos de casas nobles, resistencias a la justicia, duelos y desafíos temerarios fundados en un falso y ridículo pundonor, robos autorizados, violencias intentadas y ejecutadas, bufones insolentes, criados y criadas haciendo gala y ganancia de sus tercerías infames; y todo esto, no para hacerlo odioso, como debía ser, sino para embelesar a los espectadores teniéndolos colgados de la suspensión de sus lances, hasta que al fin dos o tres casamientos honestan los atrevimientos de los galanes y desenvolturas de las damas; quedando así sin el debido escarmiento las acciones viciosas, y los oyentes instruídos en el arte de galantear, sin miramiento al honor, a la justicia, ni al respeto que se merecen las costumbres públicas.

No son menos perversas, miradas a la luz del arte y de la razón, las comedias en que se introducen reyes, príncipes y personajes heroicos. En estos monstruos del arte teatral no parece sino que nuestros escritores han puesto todo su estudio en degradar el carácter de los héroes, no presentándolos jamás sino con las costumbres de los plebeyos más desenfrenados. ¿Qué utilidad puede dar de sí la representación pública de estas ficciones, en que no se trata de exponer el peligro de las grandezas humanas, pintando los funestos errores o males a que está sujeto el poder, sino de convertir a las personas heroicas en otros tantos pisaverdes y damiselas, rondando calles, persiguiendo hermosuras, trazando estupros y adulterios despachando billetes, buscando tercerías, practicando cuanto dicta el desenfreno de la juventud a los que no conocen otra ley que su gusto? Así, no sin razón se echan menos en estas tramas mezquinas y abatidas, caracteres, costumbres, propiedad, verosimilitud, moral y las demás calidades que constituyen el verdadero mérito de los dramas. Nada de esto puede haber donde se arranca y desencaja de su juicio la naturaleza de las personas y acciones. Porque creer que los reyes, príncipes y personas de alta dignidad no deben servir en la representación para más que para lo que podían servir personas plebeyas o galancillos particulares y simples ciudadanos, sería persuadirme que los estados son todos indiferentes, y unos mismos para los efectos del teatro, y que para dirigir la trama de un amorío desatinado, tanto monta un D. Juan como un rey de Chipre. Son innumerables las comedias nuestras en que los reyes y príncipes no hacen otro papel que el que pudieran hacer un D. Luis o un D. Diego, y en que las reinas y princesas no son más

Literary Forms and Types

> - que unas Leonores y Violantes. Mudando los nombres y quitando las alusiones a la autoridad Real, estas comedias pasarán por verdaderos dramas de los que llaman de capa y espada, porque entre éstos no hay más diferencia que la de los nombres de las personas.[58]

> . . . en las comedias que se han escrito para los teatros de medio siglo acá, ya no se ven sino absurdos, delirios y disparates enormes e intolerables, en que no hay ni sombra de las bellezas de *Lope* o *Calderón,* y se ven acumulados cuantos sucesos y lances inverosímiles, violentos, prodigiosos y desatinados, se hallan esparcidos en la multitud de aquellas comedias nuestras que pasan por más cargadas de despropósitos.[59]

We note in the above passage Forner's appreciation of the old national dramatists, particularly Lope and Calderón.[60] In another place, he speaks of these dramatists as "la raza de los ingenios eminentes, que a sus vicios juntaban bellezas originales."[61] In the following passage he again expresses his admiration and his reasons for it:

> Ingenios muy grandes, cuales lo fueron casi todos los dramáticos de los siglos anteriores, descargándose de todas las rigideces del arte, y extraviándose del camino recto de la imitación, alma de la poesía, escribieron dramas que, en medio de su desarreglo, contenían es-

---

[58] *Exequias,* pp. 182-184.

[59] *Ibid.,* p. 186.

[60] Cf. this study, p. 101. Forner presents Lope and Calderón as leading the procession of dramatists who appeared in the following order, Mira de Amescua, Guillén de Castro, Vélez de Guevara, Montalván, Rojas, Moreto, Solís, Hoz, Zamora and those who wrote dramas from the time of Lope to Cañizares. Bartolomé de Torres Naharro, Lope de Rueda, and the older dramatists followed this group; and they in turn were followed by the tragic poets, Fernán Pérez de Oliva, Jerónimo Bermúdez, Cristóbal de Virués, Juan de la Cueva, Tanco de Fregenal, and "el continuador de Celestina" (*Exequias,* pp. 242-243). Valmar, in his edition calls attention to the fact that the names of Tirso and Alarcón are not mentioned. (*Ibid.,* p. 242, note.) Tirso and Alarcón were hardly more than names, however, at that time. Their dramas were not rediscovered until some years later (Cf. McClelland, *op. cit.,* pp. 129-130, 167).

[61] *Exequias,* pp. 186-187.

106 Literary Forms and Types

> cenas, situaciones y lances excelentes. Su estilo, cuando
> no querían remontarse, era elegante, puro, halagüeno,
> suave, rápido, armonioso; muchas veces pintaron ad-
> mirablemente caracteres y costumbres muy vivas y muy
> proprias; hay comedias suyas que no deben nada a las
> más célebres de las extranjeras.[62]

Nevertheless, in spite of his praise of the Golden Age dramatists, Forner shows clearly that he advocates the use of some
rules. He does this in his allegory by picturing Cañizares in Parnassus in a fit of passion. When asked to account for his anger,
he explains how he realized shortly after his arrival in Parnassus
that his dramas were not what they should have been, in spite of
the praise they received not only in Spain but throughout Europe.
Upon comparing his dramas with those of "la docta antigüedad
y con la puntualidad de los preceptos que sirven para evitar los
delitos en la composición,"[63] he realized, he says, that he had failed
in the purpose for which he was born, that of increasing the small
number of good plays. The Conde in Parnassus tried to comfort
him by praising his great genius and by attributing the defects in
his dramas to the times in which he lived, but Cañizares would not
be consoled. He relates that he was so angry with himself for
having written such *comedias* that he had torn a number of them
to pieces.[64] When he has read the *Reflexiones sobre el teatro,*
Cervantes encourages him by telling that although he did create
some "monstruos," they were full of life and that the people preferred his "vivísima irregularidad" to the "regularidad cadavérica"
of those who boasted of being reformers.[65] Cañizares replies,
however, that no one should be obstinate in maintaining that the
bad is good. Then he adds the following remark:

> Voy a seguir en el examen de mis comedias, y creed que
> no me desdeñaré en corregir o borrar en ellas cuanto me
> parezca ajeno de la perfección que pide este género de
> obras.[66]

---

[62] *Ibid.*, p. 186.
[63] *Ibid.*, p. 179.
[64] *Ibid.*, pp. 178-180.
[65] *Ibid.*, p. 188.
[66] *Ibid.*, p. 188.

Literary Forms and Types 107

After his reading of the *Reflexiones,* Cañizares asks Cervantes his opinion of the drama. The following reply of the great master combined with the comments of Cañizares, noted above, was undoubtedly intended by Forner as the epitome of his views concerning the drama:

> Paréceme . . . que si nos atenemos a los dramas que con título de nuevos han parecido estos últimos años sobre los teatros de España, es menester creer que allí se tiene en igual estimación una farsa estrafalaria y una acción propia y bien conducida. Mientras no aparezca un talento tan grande como el de *Calderón,* que juntado la regularidad a las bellezas de la imaginación, se apodere de la opinión pública y ponga en descrédito los absurdos, las cosas permanecerán en el mismo estado de depravación y ruina; porque el arte por sí no basta para producir obras excelentes, y al contrario, hacen grandísimo perjuicio a los progresos del buen gusto aquellos entendimientos secos, lánguidos y fríos, que no pueden dar de sí más que la observancia de los preceptos; porque esa observancia por sí sola no forma más que cadáveres, y el pueblo quiere más ver un monstruo vivo, alegre y juguetón, que un cadáver pálido y postrado, por más que conserve la regularidad correspondiente a su naturaleza.[67]

It is evident from the above comments that the ideal drama which Forner advocated was not an exact replica of the old national drama, neither was it one of the cold, mechanical neo-classic dramas drawn up entirely by rules, nor one of the absurd combinations that had developed during the century. The ideal drama for Forner was, as has been shown, a prudent combination of the freedom, the spontaneity, and the best qualities of the Golden Age drama with a reasonable observance of the classical precepts, which would produce a drama of good taste. The author makes it clear, however, through the speech of Cervantes that this ideal drama is possible only at the hands of a genius.[68]

---

[67] *Ibid.,* p. 187. Forner emphasizes here his own disapproval of the strictly neo-classic dramas and their failure with the people.

[68] I. L. McClelland speaks of a growing interest in this type of drama (Cf. "Tirso de Molina and the Eighteenth Century," *Bulletin of Hispanic Studies,* XVIII, 182-192).

Evidence of the fact that Forner and Moratín held similar views on the

108   *Literary Forms and Types*

Forner manifests his regret at the decline of Spanish tragedy by presenting the writers of tragedy walking in the procession in tears,[69] with Fernán Pérez de Oliva, the leader, explaining the cause of the sad spectacle.[70]

> «Con lágrimas de sangre, dijo, debierais vos llorar sobre vuestra patria, al ver que no pasamos de seis los poetas trágicos que ha educado en los tres siglos de su mayor esplendor. Mengua es que la escuela de los reyes y de los próceres haya sufrido el abandono lamentable que se deja ver en los que vamos aquí. ¿Qué diréis de una nación avara de lecciones y de escarmientos para aquellos en quienes son peligrosos los vicios y los atentados? Nuestros bosquejos sirvieron sólo para indicar que la lengua española podía sola por sí consolar al teatro trágico de la pérdida que hizo en la extinción de los idiomas romano y griego; porque en sola ella cabe la majestad de dicción que demanda la magnificencia de los dioses de la tierra. Pero ¡oh dolor! de nuestros conatos triunfó la monstruosidad de ingenios licenciosos, y las composiciones en que más resplandece el encanto de la poesía son, no sólo mal vistas, pero despreciables en el depravado juicio de nuestra ridícula posteridad.[71]

The weakness of the tragedy Forner describes in the *Exequias* when he pictures it at the side of the unconscious matron, the Spanish Language:

> . . . yacía descaecida y débil en las angustias de un estilo prosaico, sin nervio, sin vehemencia, sin aquel grande idioma de las pasiones grandes, único y peculiar de nuestra lengua entre las modernas, cuando en medio de

---

drama is found in a letter from Moratín to Forner, in which he asks Forner to examine his *Comedia nueva* and point out its good and bad points (Cueto, "Bosquejo histórico-crítico," p. CLXXVI, n. 1). Similar evidence is noted in an open letter which Forner published in *El Correo*, in which he defends the *Comedia nueva* against several hostile attacks (Sainz y Rodríguez, "Introducción," *Exequias*, p. 31).

[69] *Exequias*, p. 243.

[70] The six tragic poets named in the procession were Fernán Pérez de Oliva, Jerónimo Bermúdez, Cristóbal de Virués, Juan de la Cueva, Tanco de Fregenal, and "el continuador de Celestina." (*Ibid.*, p. 243.) It will be noticed that not a single eighteenth century poet is included.

[71] *Ibid.*, p. 244.

Literary Forms and Types · 109

los desarreglos del arte levantaba el vuelo y se elevaba
con ardor, siempre enérgico, siempre sublime, a disputar
la grandeza de la locución a los Eurípides y a los
Sófocles.[72]

The author particularly regretted that the tragedy was no longer
written in poetry. He considered poetic expression essential to
tragedy, "como miembro muy principal del poema épico."[73]

In the following passage, he condemns the prosaic imitations
of the French and the corrupted language that is used in place of
the pure Spanish which, he says, vies with the Greek in magnificence and power:

> . . . con dificultad me contenía en los límites del comedimiento al considerar que una perversa envidia de imitar
> lo que no es envidiable por ningún término, nos ha reducido a arrojar del todo el estilo poético de la tragedia,
> nada más que porque en Francia, cuya lengua carece de
> aquel estilo, las disponen en prosa rimada, siendo ésta su
> única poesía. ¿Cuándo acabaremos de conocer que nos
> defraudamos de nuestras riquezas por comprar con risible
> descrédito la pobreza de los extraños? ¿Acaso el arte
> trágica consiste sólo en las unidades y en los caracteres,
> y en no dejar las escenas vacías y en sacar las personas
> al teatro con motivo sensible? Bueno, y aun necesario,
> es todo esto; pero si a ello podemos juntar nosotros, en
> competencia de la pompa griega un lenguaje sublimemente poético, una locución majestuosa, divina, que
> inflame el espíritu y le enajene, llenándole de una excelsa
> magnificencia, de un vigor robusto, de una vehemencia
> inquieta y arrebatada, ¿qué miseria es la nuestra en desposeernos de aquello en que ninguna nación se acerca a
> competirnos?[74]

Consistent with his interest in the classical heritage, Forner also
regrets the abandonment of the art of forensic eloquence in his
country. Because lawyers saw no necessity for using it, they even
depreciated its value and made fun of it.[75]

---

[72] *Ibid.*, p. 119.
[73] *Ibid.*, p. 119.
[74] *Ibid.*, pp. 119-120.
[75] *Ibid.*, pp. 195-196.

110 *Literary Forms and Types*

In the discussion carried on in Parnassus regarding the significance of oratory and its decline, Arcadio points out that it was in Rome that the "raza de los oradores" ceased with the change from the republic to the despotic monarchy,[76] at which time the jurisconsults were satisfied with "la seca sutileza de sus interpretaciones, descuidando enteramente las galas del estilo, la inversión de los argumentos, su artificio, su disposición, la moción de los afectos; en una palabra la belleza y fuerza del decir."[77] When the barbarians of the north took possession of the Roman Empire, there was no eloquence to be found in the tribunals; and from that time barbarity of language and the worst possible taste were joined to the "sequedad del decir."[78] When the vulgar languages arose, those vices continued in proportion as the nations adopted the teaching of the barbarians. Unfortunately, in Spain, the idea prevailed that simple legal study was sufficient for the practice of law.[79]

By representing Pliny as an opponent of Muratori in the lively exchange of ideas regarding oratory, Forner contrasts ancient and modern eloquence, showing the advantages of the former over the latter.

> En una palabra, nuestra elocuencia no era más que una dialéctica usada con ornato, y el modo de abogar de los modernos no es más que el uso de una autoridad intrusa, ilegítima, bastarda, expresada con desaliño por no decir con grosería. En mi tiempo defendían los oradores las buenas y las malas causas, como las defienden también ahora los abogados; porque del conflicto entre lo justo y lo injusto resultan los pleitos; pero afirmo que era más seguro el triunfo de la justicia con las armas de nuestra elocuencia, que lo es con la espantosa perplejidad de las opiniones y cavilaciones de los jurisconsultos.[80]

---

[76] *Ibid.*, p. 197. Forner also writes, "la majestad y gracia de la elocuencia aumentada por un idioma latino-bárbaro, moría ahogada entre las lamentables ruinas de la esclava Grecia abitada Roma (*Oración apologética*, p. 53).

[77] *Exequias*, p. 197.

[78] *Ibid.*, pp. 197-198.

[79] *Ibid.*, p. 198.

[80] *Ibid.*, pp. 201-202.

Literary Forms and Types   111

While the forensic orators had little or no interest in the adornments of eloquence,[81] the preachers, the *culteranistas* of the seventeenth century and the *galicistas* of the eighteenth, turned to a false eloquence, which was marked by exaggeration, extravagance, affectation, novelty, unreality, and gallicisms.[82] Concerned only with display and an artificial externality, the preachers lost sight of the dignity of their office and of the object of their sermons.[83] He criticizes their sermons in the following manner:

> . . . según mi modo de pensar, la religión no se descontentaría de que no abundase el número de los que hacen tráfico en los templos con una elocuencia que no influye en la mejora de las costumbres, e influye muchísimo en el descrédito de las letras. Dadme talentos aptos, que prefieran la gloria de hacer bien los intereses del mundo, y veréis prodigios.[84]

With Cervantes as his spokesman, Forner rails against the orators who were making their sermons ridiculous by their absurd imitations of the French and particularly by their use of gallicisms. His satirical spirit is evident in the following pronouncement:

> ¿Que espíritu infernal ha metido en la cabeza a algunos de vuestros predicadores hacer hablar al Espíritu Santo

---

[81] Forner refers to Cicero's views on the relationship between oratory and poetry, and to the need of moderation in the stylistic adornment in both. Concerning this he writes, ". . . como dice Cicerón, y sin que él lo diga lo enseña la misma inspiración natural, que la Oratoria y la Poesía tienen estrecho parentesco entre sí en lo que toca a los ornatos del estilo y al aire extraordinario con que visten ambas artes los argumentos que se encaminan a la persuasión" (*Oración apologética*, p. v). Forner believes that orators, like the poets, are born and not made (*ibid.*, p. vi). For the author's definition of Spanish eloquence as found in the early historian, see this study, p. 115.

[82] *Exequias*, pp. 256, 115.

[83] *Oración apologética*, pp. vi-vii. In his condemnation of the overemphasis on externals, he writes, "Y ciertamente si la elocuencia no es más que una modificación, o, digámoslo así, un afeite de los pensamientos; siendo éstos frívolos o sofísticos, ¿qué mérito le queda al ornato?" (*ibid.*, pp. vi-vii).

[84] *Exequias*, p. 164.

112   *Literary Forms and Types*

> en lenguaje semifrancés? Predican la moda, no la virtud;
> y siendo así, ¿con qué cara osan reprender la inconstante
> profanidad de la gente mundana? Estos infelices,
> estando obligados a reformar el siglo, se dejan llevar de
> la corriente de la corrupción; y aplicándose al oficio de
> persuadir, persuaden, ya que no puedan la verdad, la in-
> capacidad propia.[85]

The difficulty of these preachers lay in their servile imitation of
authors whom they regarded as models. Lacking the proper
penetration and study necessary to distinguish and to adapt the
artificial beauties of others to their purposes, they were blinded
by a superficiality which ruined their work.

> Creen que mejoran el gusto de la predicación, y cor-
> rompen, con la majestad y pureza de la lengua, la ver-
> dadera idea del arte de persuadir, el cual no se funda en
> copias serviles o imitaciones mecánicas, sino en la aptitud
> y disposición del talento, en el estudio y ejercicio del bien
> hablar, en el íntimo conocimiento del hombre, en la ciencia
> de mover las pasiones que lo arrebatan a la parte que más
> conduce, en la grande habilidad de trastornar el interior
> humano y obligarle a amar lo que antes aborrecía o
> aborrecer lo que antes amaba; y finalmente, en ser sabio
> en lo que es debido, circunstancia que creen tener todos
> y se ve en muy pocos.[86]

> ... la imitación no consistirá en desflorar la superficie de
> las oraciones ajenas, trasladando de ellas una imagen
> aérea, semejante a las que decía *Epicuro* que se evaporan
> de los cuerpos, sino en tomar la eficacia en el probar del
> uno, la destreza del proponer en el otro, de éste la
> elocuencia y gallardía, de aquél la grata y robusta ma-
> jestad, y a este tenor, sin atarse a lo que cada uno tuvo
> que decir en la ocasión, decir en la suya lo que convenga
> y como convenga.[87]

The author's description of the sacred orators in the procession
sets forth his conception of what sacred oratory should be and

---

[85] *Ibid.*, p. 155. Forner, however, does not refrain from praising Bossuet,
Massillon, and Bourdaloue.

[86] *Ibid.*, pp 155-156.

[87] *Ibid.*, pp. 164-165.

Literary Forms and Types   113

also presents the contrast between the Spanish orators of the past and those of his day, whose defects had been so well satirized by Padre Isla.

> *Juan de Ávila, Luis de León, Luis de Granada, Bautista de Lanuza, Fonseca, Alfonso de Cabrera,* caminando con majestuosidad y austera gravedad, retrataban en la misma compostura exterior el sagrado genio de su elocuencia. Sólo el verlos era una acusación muda para las disoluciones del mundo. Pintado en sus semblantes el celo que brotó por sus labios en las solemnidades religiosas, decía él por sí que aquellos hombres no subieron al púlpito para darse en espectáculo, sino para confundir los vicios y dilatar el santo imperio de la virtud. No en ellos verdores y lozanías immodestas no discreciones y retruecanillos de estrado, no follaje estéril, a propósito sólo para causar estrépito como en inútil salva, no sutilezas caviladas con artificio, no estilo afeminado y teatral, no frases simétricas y colocadas con afectación pueril, no metáforas, no alegorías, no figuras hacinadas con estudio insolente para embelesar necios y negociar su aplauso con la horrenda profanación de la enseñanza del Altísimo. En ellos habló la elocuencia con divina expresión por la conformidad grande que supieron acomodar entre la alteza de sus asuntos y la manera de persuadirlos.[88]

History, too, according to Forner, had become a lost art. In the days when Spaniards read the classical historians of Greece and Rome, history possessed a remarkable dignity and majesty. In earlier times history was the one field where the Spanish language displayed its riches. It was the only one of the literary arts that maintained "la castidad del idioma sana, incontaminada, limpia."[89] All of the historians of Spain,[90] even the minor ones, strove to present truth in a language marked by a purity, clarity, propriety, and variety unknown before.[91]

---

[88] *Ibid.,* pp. 249-250.

[89] *Ibid.,* p. 256.

[90] Forner mentions, in particular, the historians Mariana, Zurita, Morales, Mendoza, Solís, Muñoz, Fuenmayor, Sigüenza, and Saavedra *(ibid.,* pp. 255-256).

[91] *Ibid.,* pp. 256-257.

114   *Literary Forms and Types*

In the eighteenth century, the old idea of history was changed. According to Forner, the term was applied to "un fárrago enorme de noticias mal digeridas, una mezcolanza monstruosa de asuntos inconexos, una eterna obra de investigaciones pesadísimas sobre puntos de ninguna importancia al linaje humano."[92] In his allegory he describes the lamentable state in which he saw history in Parnassus: .

> . . . afeada su magnificencia y revolcándose con flojo y despreciable desaliño, sin arte, sin decoro, sin dignidad, en la inmundicia de la barbarie y de la torpeza, mendigando frases de las extrañas, pobre de sentencias, tarda y amortiguada en el discurso, escasa en la prudencia civil y desenlazada en sus miembros, sin más artificio que el de un capricho inexperto y vulgar, y sin más cultura que la que ocasiona un ansia desatinada y sórdida de afear con estilo bajo los grandes hechos.[93]

The author puts on the lips of the historian Mariana the following definition of history, which he gives to Ferreras who came to seek his advice and help:

> La historia, . . . no consiste en referir hechos desenlazados, sino en retratar hombres, naciones y siglos. Las acciones de los hombres públicos están íntimamente enlazadas con el estado de los pueblos y de su república, y ved aquí el oficio de la historia, poner patentes estos enlaces y manifestar de qué modo el mayor número de los mortales es feliz o infeliz por el modo de obrar del menor número. A este grande objeto deben acompañar los lineamentos y coloridos correspondientes.[94]

The following is Forner's description of a true historian:

> . . . el que escribe sin los intereses del odio, del amor, del partido: los demás pueden llamarse esclavos de sus preocupaciones, y plumas más propias para el escarmiento que para la enseñanza.[95]

---

[92] *Ibid.,* p. 152.
[93] *Ibid.,* p. 119.
[94] *Ibid.,* p. 177.
[95] *Oración apologética,* pp. 142-143.

Literary Forms and Types 115

In praise of the earlier history written in Spain, the author points out that the historians from the time of Florián de Ocampo displayed a real eloquence in their writing, a Spanish eloquence which he characterizes as follows:

> . . . la elocuencia española, aquella que consiste en la propiedad de las palabras, en la gravedad de sentencias, en lo escogido de las locuciones, en la llanura y armonía de los períodos, en la viveza y fuerza de las imágenes, en el decoro y facilidad de la narración, en la naturalidad de los adornos, y por último, en no decir sino lo que se debe y como se debe.[96]

In Parnassus Forner groups the novelists of his time with the preachers and the other "semigalos" to whom he attributes the death of the Spanish language.[97] He considers the "cuentistas" more ridiculous and more worthy of being converted into frogs than the pedants and "mostrencos" because, as he says, they might have been useful to their country and might have brought honor to it, but through ambition and vainglory they became mere charlatans.[98] That Forner was not an admirer of pure fiction is apparent from his comments on the French "ficciones."

> Las ficciones nacen ordinariamente después que se ha agotado el descubrimiento de las verdades; y una nación, en poseyendo éstas, debe reputar aquéllas como una superfluidad mental que adorna, pero no sirve.[99]

He points out, too, that the stories which are supposed to paint situations and circumstances that can be verified as true to life are not authorized because of the matter contained in them.[100] The so-called philosophical fables so common in France, he vigorously condemns as follows:

> Las ficciones que van fundadas en la verosimilitud han sido siempre el escándalo de la razón. Acrecientan y

---

[96] *Exequias*, p. 257.
[97] *Ibid.*, pp. 114-115.
[98] *Ibid.*, p. 102.
[99] *Oración apologética*, p. 4.
[100] *Ibid.*, pp. 13-14.

116 *Literary Forms and Types*

añaden peso al número de los engaños; el capricho coherente y bien enlazado toma en ellas la máscara de la verdad, y hace pasar por dogmas de la experiencia las que son conjeturas de la fantasía; tal vez pervierten las ideas más comunes y recibidas, y por la ambición de aparecer con singularidad desnudan al hombre de su mismo ser, trasladándole a regiones, imperios y estados imaginarios, dignos sólo de habitarse por quien los funda; suscitan parcialidades, cuyos partidarios, sacrificando al vergonzoso ministerio de propugnar ficciones ajenas aquel talento émulo de la divinidad que se les concedió para levantarse por sí al descubrimiento y contemplación de las verdades más santas y más augustas, le envilecen y hacen esclavo de la vanidad con injuria de la dignidad eminente de su naturaleza. En suma los sistemas de la filosofía, fábulas tan dañosas a los adelantamientos de las ciencias como las antiguas sibaríticas a la pureza de las costumbres, ninguna otra utilidad dan de sí sino la de admirar la extraordinaria habilidad de algunos hombres para ordenar naturalezas y universos inútiles, y aquellas apariencias admirables con que hacen pasar por interpretaciones de las obras de Dios las que son en el fondo adivinaciones tan poco seguras como las de los Arúspices o Agoreros.[101]

Although he presents a group of novelists in the procession, he names only the leader of the band, Cervantes. He praises their contributions to the literature, with the remark that "las riquezas que aumentaron a nuestra lengua en el estilo bucólico, en el moral, en el narrativo, en el descriptivo, en el jocoso, riquezas abundantísimas y muy dignas de muy particular estudio."[102]

It is Forner's opinion that criticism, like all the arts, had also gone out of bounds at the hands of men.[103] Acknowledging both constructive and destructive types of criticism, he points out that the latter should be used primarily with a view to perfecting a

---

[101] *Ibid.*, pp. 14-15.

[102] *Exequias*, p. 257.

[103] Forner thought that there were too many censors. He writes, "En cada libro hallamos un oráculo: en cada escritor un censor inexorable de los hombres, de las opiniones, de las costumbres, de las naciones, de los estados, del universo" (*Oración apologética*, pp. 8-9).

Literary Forms and Types

117

work.[104] This ideal is seldom found in practice, he observes, for critics who are looking for defects have little difficulty in finding them.[105] He regrets too the attitude of superiority which so many of the critics in his day assumed, as is seen in the following passage:

> La primera intención del crítico es siempre desacreditar la obra ajena, para deprimir el mérito ajeno; la segunda, dar a entender al público que él sabe más que aquellos cuyas obras merecen estimación universal, pues prueba, a su parecer, que no valen nada. Con estos fines suelen mezclarse muy de ordinario pasiones y designios más indecentes: la envidia, el odio, la venganza, y de aquí las calumnias, los dicterios, la infame maledicencia y todos los vicios que abortan la destemplanza y malignidad de ánimos perversos.[106]

Further comments on eighteenth century criticism are found in Arcadio's remarks to Cervantes:

> En España, y especialmente en la corte, no es buena ni mala una obra porque ella lo sea en sí, sino por la casualidad de que la critiquen o no. La mayor parte de los juicios son de reata; para ellos, el último que escribe es el que tiene razón. Los que, sin principios, leen por pura curiosidad no pueden juzgar de otro modo, bien lo sabéis; porque en saliendo de hechos donde son palpables las demostraciones en lo que toca a raciocinios, propiedad y excelencias del arte, caminan siempre a obscuras; y ved aquí por qué se toleran en el teatro, y aun se aplauden muchas veces, los despropósitos más groseros y ridículos, y por qué en la infinita variedad de juicios que se hacen de cada obra, son poquísimos los que atinan a la primera, e innumerables los que van mudando de parecer según corre el viento de la crítica.[107]

---

[104] *Exequias*, p. 137.

[105] Cervantes, he points out, spoke in praise of his time (*Exequias*, p. 183); and foreigners boasted of what they had (*Oración Apologética*, p. xvii).

[106] *Exequias*, pp. 137-38.

[107] *Ibid.*, pp. 148-49.

118 *Literary Forms and Types*

Calling these critics "homicidas de créditos,"[108] he recommends two ways for a conscientious writer to deal with them—first, to ignore them and proceed with useful study; second, to make them appear ridiculous to the cultured and prudent. In this manner, he believes it possible for the writer to correct the abuses of the critics and to increase his own renown at their expense, because "la buena sátira no menos inmortaliza los talentos que cualquiera otro género de composición ingeniosa."[109]

It is his opinion that "las críticas de obras ajenas" are bound to die a short time after their publication.[110] Even if such studies are the work of geniuses, they all meet with the same lot. If the work criticized is a poor work, both the critical study and the work itself are soon forgotten; if the work is a good one, the critical matter affords conversation and entertainment in the idler's lounges for twelve days, and then the critical study is relegated to the attic and the work of merit passes on tranquilly to posterity.

> . . . la crítica es siempre la vencida en estas batallas. Verdad es que los críticos suelen infinitas veces tener en poco esta reflexión, aun cuando la prevean; porque a fuer de soldados rasos, tratan sólo de matar el crédito del contrario, sin cuidarse de la gloria póstuma ni dárseles un comino de que sus nombres suenen, o no, entre los venideros.[111]

Speaking of the apologists of a nation, Forner observes that they are frequently held in derision by those who regard themselves as universal reformers. As for himself, however, he never regretted taking up the cause of his country against those who defamed her. His genuine patriotism and his gratitude to

---

[108] *Ibid.*, p. 142.

[109] *Ibid.*, pp. 142-143. It is Forner's opinion that the journalists of his time probably thwarted much good work by giving vent to personal feelings and to partiality (*Exequias*, p. 113). Because of their unfavorable criticism of Mayans, Forner has Cervantes condemn the three editors of the *Diario de los literatos de España* (*ibid.*, pp. 111-112).

[110] In the allegory, Forner depicts a pile of dry critical works ready to furnish fuel for the funeral pyre (*ibid.*, p. 141).

[111] *Ibid.*, p. 142.

Literary Forms and Types 119

his forefathers prompted him always to defend his country, as he points out:

> Harto más glorioso es erigir ilustres monumentos a la memoria de los grandes hombres de cuya mano hemos recibido los documentos de la verdad y de la virtud, que pasar el tiempo en la triste y obscura ocupación de reprehender lo que otros hacen, pudiendo emplearle más provechosamente, y con menos disgusto en dar buenos ejemplos para la enseñanza.[112]

He notes that apologies of a national literature can do great harm if they are not based on truth. He believes too that an apology which has for its purpose the authorization of error and deceit is so much the more abominable, the more excellent it is in its development.[113] Referring in all probability to the type of defense which should be made against the French calumniators, he writes:

> La defensa no debe recaer sobre los abusos que en grande número reinan, ya de un modo, ya de otro, en todas naciones y países. Tal vez nuestros acusadores nos culpan justamente en algunas cosas; y entonces, si faltan a la urbanidad y al decoro en las expresiones con que nos reprehenden, la mejor Apología es hacer ridícula su desvergüenza, y procurar aprovecharnos a la sordina de la substancia de las acusaciones.[114]

The "bibliotecas críticas" and the "diccionarios" Forner considers to be of little value. In regard to the former, he remarks that while they embrace a great deal, the criticism contained in them is generally unreliable, because the writers lack the time to read everything and consequently cannot pass a fair judgment on everything.[115] As for the "diccionarios," they are "excelentes en equivocar," although they have been set up as authoritative sources,

---

[112] *Oración apologética*, p. xvi.
[113] *Ibid.*, p. vii.
[114] *Ibid.*, p. vii.
[115] *Ibid.*, p. 212.

120 *Literary Forms and Types*

superior even to antiquity.[116] The information contained in them is frequently misplaced, distorted, and the connection of systems is often lost or broken.[117]

In his comments on the eighteenth century literature, Forner makes direct references to few writers. Of the 150 or more Spanish writers whom he mentions in the *Exequias* and the *Oración apologética,* there are only about twenty who belonged to the eighteenth century. Among the poets whom he mentions or to whom he alludes are Iglesias, Meléndez Valdés, Iriarte, Rejón de Silva, and Trigueros.[118] In the allegory, he shows a particular esteem for Iglesias. He seeks his counsel on the manner of writing poetry; he makes him his companion on his visit to Parnassus; and he assures Cervantes that Iglesias belonged to the "good sect," that is, to the group of writers who were not imitating the French and corrupting the Spanish language with gallicisms. He speaks of Meléndez Valdés as "tierno Batilo." He pictures this poet and himself as called upon to avenge the death of the Spanish Language, at whose side they kneel in Parnassus. As regards Iriarte, Forner remarks ironically on his *Apretón* and makes satirical allusions to his poem, *La música* and his *Fábulas literarias.* He mentions Rejón de Silva by name and makes a satirical allusion to his poem *La pintura.* His comments on *La Riada* of Trigueros, though brief, are marked by a biting satire, as also are his comments on this author's poem entitled, *El poeta filósofo.* The latter work he designates as a wick for the funeral pyre. Forner's criticism of the Alexandrine used by Trigueros shows great critical power on the part of the author.

The only dramatists of the period that are mentioned by Forner are Cañizares, Zamora, and Valladares. He naturally praises the first two since they perpetuated the national drama. Cañizares, as we have seen, played an important part in the allegory. Valladares is mentioned when Forner satirizes the mercantilism of so many writers of his day.

In the field of history, the author pays tribute to Juan de Ferreras by placing him in the procession; and he shows his dis-

---

[116] *Exequias,* p. 86.

[117] *Oración apologética,* p. 8.

[118] See Appendix II for page references to specific authors.

Literary Forms and Types 121

dain for the *Historia* of the Mohedanos brothers by referring to the patience required to read it.

Among the other writers of the period named or alluded to are Mayans, Luzán, Padre Isla, Feijóo, López de Ayala, Nipho, Escartín, Sempere y Guarinos, Martínez Salafranca, Manuel de Huerta, and Leopoldo Jerónimo Puig. Of these, Forner praises highly the work of Mayans, representing him as the last and only defender of the Spanish language. As for Luzán, the author makes no further comment than to remark that he was in the procession with the preceptists and that his poetics were superior to his poetry. While there are some things in the *Fray Gerundio* which Forner does not exactly approve, he concedes the first place among the burlesque writers to Padre Isla. Feijóo and his *Teatro crítico* do not meet with much consideration at the hands of Forner. He condemns Feijóo's Latin, his lack of order, and above all, his use of gallicisms. In fact, he accuses Feijóo of being the first Spaniard to gallicize Spanish. López de Ayala likewise meets with little consideration from Forner. This may have been due largely to the fact that Ayala when in the office of censor did not approve of Forner's *Cautiva española.* In the *Exequias,* he refers with disdain to Ayala's pamphlet entitled the *Carta crítica del Bachiller Gil Porras a los RR. PP. Mohedanos sobre la Historia literaria que publican.* Nipho is indirectly referred to several times in the *Exequias* in connection with the author's satirical comments on those writers who look upon writing as a money-making business. Escartín is also placed with these writers and meets with the same scorn. Forner speaks of Sempere y Guarinos and his "infausta Biblioteca." His attitude toward this man and his work is probably the result of the article which Sempere wrote in his *Biblioteca* on Trigueros, whose writing Forner had criticized. Forner refers to the works of Martínez Salafranca, Manuel de Huerta, and Leopoldo Jerónimo Puig, editors of the *Diario de los literatos.* While accusing them of making partial and unjust appraisals of certain writers, particularly Mayans, he finds some good in their works.[119]

---

[119] Standard critical sources give evidence that the authors who were favored by Forner were, in general, held in similar esteem by his contemporaries, and nearly all the others mentioned were the source or the subject of many of the prevailing polemics.

Literary Forms and Types

From a study of the comments made by Forner concerning these authors it cannot be said that he approved of certain authors because they belonged to the so-called nationalist group and that he condemned others because they belonged to the so-called neo-classic or *afrancesado* group. He probably had as much difficulty as we have now in trying to determine which writers were distinctly nationalistic and which ones were distinctly neo-classic or *afrancesado*.[120] As far as we can determine there seems to be a considerable overlapping in the terms, for there were nationalists who supported a reasonable observance of the precepts and there were neo-classicists who supported the Spanish literature of the Golden Age. There were some who were nationalistic in one phase of the literature and neo-classic in another; but apparently all claimed to be working for the improvement of the national literature.

We can, however, make the following inferences from Forner's appraisal of the aforementioned writers. He approved of those who imitated the good qualities of the Spanish writers of the classical epoch; those who followed or recommended a reasonable observance of the ancient classical principles of good taste; those who strove for purity of language and style; those, in particular, who avoided gallicisms; and those who avoided prosaicism in

---

[120] It is interesting to observe that several of the members of the Salamancan and Sevillan schools were, or became, *afrancesados*. While many of them began as Hellenists they were gradually influenced by the French literary canons, the French language, and the French philosophy. For example, Forner's friend, Meléndez Valdés, who is generally regarded as the greatest Spanish lyric poet of the century, was for a time hailed as a nationalist, then as a neo-classicist, again as a nationalist, and finally he was definitely linked with the neo-classicists or *afrancesados* (W. E. Colford, *Juan Meléndez Valdés,* New York: Hispanic Institute, 1942, pp. 48-49, 341-342).

This proved to be the case also with Forner's friend, Estala. His affiliation with the *afrancesados* became so strong that toward the end of his life he joined the ranks of the *Encyclopédistes (Enciclopedia universal ilustrada,* XXII, 626). There were others too, like Moratín who were *afrancesados*. Yet Forner was a friend of them all. Apparently they were attracted to one another solely by their common interest in the regeneration of the national poetry.

Literary Forms and Types 123

their verse. He disapproved of those who went to extremes in the use of the precepts; those who sinned against good taste by a cold, dry, mechanical style; those who introduced gallicisms in the Spanish language; those who paid tribute to poets who wrote in any of these ways; and those who were interested in writing as a mercantile project.

A general summary now of Forner's comments on the various literary forms and types will help to give a succinct conception of his literary views. The observations made in this chapter bear, as has been seen, the same general marks as those set forth in the preceding chapter. We note again that Forner's criticism is not that of a literary preceptor or a professional literary critic. Although he does not enter into real aesthetic issues, he does have some specific ideas regarding literary principles; and although his critical views may not be original and are expressed more often negatively than positively,[121] they are none the less interesting.

Forner looks upon the writing of all literary types as an art. He emphasizes particularly the significant value of poetry and drama to men and to nations, since the object of these forms is not only to entertain but to teach and reform, to make men cultured and virtuous. He also stresses the instructional value of history, fiction, and works of criticism; hence, he emphasizes the need for conformity of content to truth. The form used should be in keeping with the nature of the art.

In his condemnation of the eighteenth century poetry, Forner points out the absence of thought, of truth, and of beauty; he scorns its studied use of the precepts, its prosaicism, its gallicisms. He appeals to the versifiers of his day to turn to Spain's classical epoch[122] for their models, because in the works of the sixteenth century poets they will find thought, truth, beauty of form, freedom of expression, poetic figures, and purity of language.

In his disapproval of the drama of the period, he notes many of the same defects that characterized the poetry. He condemns

---

[121] This type of criticism was common at the time. Cf. McClelland, "Tirso de Molina and the Eighteenth Century," p. 185.

[122] See this study p. 99, n. 32 for the names of the poets whom Forner recommends.

Literary Forms and Types

the inane ideas found in the *comedias,* the lack of verisimilitude, absurd and artificial plots, and shallow and often ridiculous characters. ᐟ He censures the failure of the drama to fulfill its nobler purpose of teaching and he scorns its degeneration into a mere form of vulgar entertainment. By means of his negative criticism he advocates deeper thought and verisimilitude in plots and characters. His positive recommendations for the creation of an ideal drama—the combination of classical order and regularity with the typical Spanish freedom and spontaneity found in the Golden Age drama—were, as he was aware, practically impossible except in the hands of a genius. In his support of the Golden Age dramatists, particularly, Lope and Calderón, he evidences a change of attitude, a change which is significant and totally in keeping with the historical development of the drama in Spain, and even throughout Europe.

In the matter of the tragedy, Forner's criticism is again chiefly negative. He bemoans the cold imitations of the French tragedies in rhymed prose; he deplores the corrupted language used in place of the sonorous, poetic Spanish that vies, he says, with the Greek in magnificence and power. In his opinion, Spain possessed only six worthwhile writers of tragedy, all of whom belonged to the sixteenth century classical period.[123]

Eighteenth century forensic eloquence and pulpit oratory likewise met with Forner's disapproval. In his treatment of the former he refers again to the ancients and shows the advantages of ancient oratory over the modern because of its dignity, beauty, and forcefulness. In contrasting the forensic eloquence of the time with the pulpit oratory then in vogue, he points out that while the former was bereft of all adornment, the latter consisted chiefly in externals. He condemns the sermons as absurd imitations of the French, characterized by exaggeration, extravagance, affectation, and gallicisms. For models in sacred oratory, he again turns to the sixteenth century and recommends six famous preachers and sacred writers.[124]

---

[123] *Exequias,* p. 243. See this study, p. 108, n. 79.
[124] *Exequias,* p. 242. See this study, p. 113.

Literary Forms and Types 125

In Forner's opinion, history, too, was a lost art. He looks upon the history of his day as an enormous mass of badly digested information and unconnected subjects, as an eternal work of weighty investigations upon subjects that have no importance to man. Apparently he had little esteem for the scientific methods that were then being introduced. Once more he suggests the ancients as models, recommending that the historians of his day refer to those of Rome and Greece. He also advocates the study of Mariana and the other Spanish historians of the sixteenth century.

Forner's criticism of the fiction of the period is based on its lack of verisimilitude. He rails, as we have seen, particularly against the French philosophic fables. The only Spanish exemplar that he suggests in this field is Cervantes.

It is interesting to observe that in his comments on the criticism of the time Forner employs the destructive type that he himself condemns. His satire on the lack of originality and the dependence of critics on others is particularly good and brings out many of the characteristics that were typical of the criticism of the time.[125]

It has been seen that although Forner was chiefly concerned with content he does not fail to take exception to the style of his contemporaries. Here he again manifests his hostile attitude toward the French influence in general, but in particular, toward the French language. Among his chief objections to the manner of writing by his countrymen are: the excessive use of half French words and expressions, the consequent impoverishment of the Spanish language, the influence of French translations, and the imitation of the French, especially in the matter of servile adherence to petty rules which curbed genius and inspiration and produced works which were not only barren in thought but bereft of all beauty and life in their style. Again, we notice that Forner failed to see in the French neo-classic movement any stabilizing element that might have been used to advantage in counteracting the many seventeenth century excesses which marred so much of Spain's literature and which Forner so unrelentingly condemned.

---

[125] Cf. McClelland, "Tirso de Molina and the Eighteenth Century," p. 185.

CHAPTER VI

CONCLUSION

From this study it can be concluded that Forner was not a critic in the sense of a literary preceptor or a professional critic; nor did he pose as such. The criticism contained in his two outstanding works, the *Exequias de la lengua castellana* and the *Oración apologética por la España y su mérito literario*, was advanced directly against the *afrancesados* and the Gallophiles in his own country, and indirectly against the French *Encyclopédistes*.

The purpose of his criticism was first, to oppose the infiltration, propagation, and the ingrafting of the French Encyclopedic philosophy and the French language in the literature of Spain; secondly, to defend the ancient culture of Spain, her language, wisdom, learning, philosophy, religion, and progress against the so-called progress of the eighteenth century under the hegemony of France. The author defended the ancient culture of Spain, her wisdom, learning, philosophy and religion because he saw in these the embodiment of his Christian views. He opposed the philosophy of the *Encyclopédistes* because he looked upon it as anti-Christian. Like other orthodox thinkers of his day, he saw in it the breakdown of all authority and order—civil, religious, social, and personal. He feared the outcome of its spread. Though he had nothing original or novel to offer as a remedy for the ills of the time and although he was undoubtedly considered a medievalist by the progressives of his day and was probably laughed at by the *Encyclopédistes*, he proclaimed, nevertheless, the age-old antidote—Christian principles of life and of living.

In his treatment of philosophy, religion, and science, he discusses the ideas around which the whole philosophic controversy of the eighteenth century revolved, namely, the nature of man, reason, natural law, natural virtue, supernatural law, supernatural religion, utility, and the general perfectibility and happiness of man. Although Forner's criticism appears to be chiefly destructive, it is

Conclusion 127

indirectly constructive, for while he condemns the anthropocentric and materialistic views of the *philosophes,* he would replace them with the Christian theocentric conception of man, which the orthodox thinkers held to be timelessly true.

Both Forner and the *philosophes,* we have seen, believed in the dual nature of man, the latter stressing the physical and the rational side of man, and Forner, the integrity of man's being. While the *philosophes* emphasized the perfectibility of man's physical and rational nature, Forner, recognizing the doctrine of original sin, saw the possibility of corruption in man's body and the possibility of error in his reason. Both had faith in reason, but Forner had faith only in reason guided by a supernatural faith. They both recognized the free will of man. The *philosophes* supported the idea of man's freedom to think and act in accordance with the dictates of his nature, unhampered by positive law and revealed religion. Forner, on the other hand, maintained that in view of the constitution of man's nature, positive law and revealed religion were necessary for the attainment of his ultimate end. Many of the *Encyclopédistes* recognized an after-life, but they associated man's happiness primarily with this world, as a result of his general perfectibility and his material progress. In the matter of progress, Forner attacked the materialistic, utilitarian ends of the *philosophes,* opposing to them his ideas on the truly useful, that is, in the sense of the ethical, spiritual, and Christian. Forner, holding to the Christian view, considered man's ultimate end and happiness to consist in the perfection of his being in accordance with God's designs for him and in his union with God in the life to come.

Forner's philosophy is really nothing more than that of a practical-minded Christian who recognizes the value of useful truths. It is that of a man who sees true wisdom in right thinking and right living, who puts first things first and has a place for secondary things. To him, the first source of truth is a supernatural religion, which is unattainable without revelation and faith; the second, philosophy and science, attainable through reason alone. Since his philosophy was Christian he could not possibly agree with any philosophic system, ancient or modern, built

128   *Conclusion*

upon a purely anthropocentric humanism.' In so far as he was a
supporter of any philosophical system as such, he was a Vivist.

The second purpose of Forner's criticism, we have stated, was
to oppose the ingrafting of the French language in the language
and literature of Spain. As has been observed, he joined with the
side of the Gallophobes in fighting against the spread of gallicisms,
for he saw in their propagation the dishonor of his country and
the inevitable corruption of the Spanish language. After considering the author's bitter antagonism toward the French Encyclopedic philosophy and his frequent confusion of ideology and
art, one is inclined to believe that some of his opposition to the
language might have resulted from his fear of the language as a
carrier of the French philosophic germ. Other reasons for his
opposition might have been his resentment against the French for
setting themselves up as the dispensers of an improved classicism,
and the reaction of his national pride against those Frenchmen
who had made calumniating remarks about Spain's culture and
progress.

Although Forner's criticism was directed primarily against the
spread of the Encyclopedic philosophy and gallicisms in his country, it manifests his interest in the aesthetic topics and the literary
types which were commonly discussed at the time, in Spain as
well as in France. Because Forner was not a professional literary
critic he does not enter into real aesthetic issues. Occasionally he
makes a good point, but for the most part he talks around these
matters. He makes general and commonplace statements on the
imitation of nature, imagination, the rules, reason, good taste,
beauty, truth, goodness, and style. He also generalizes when
treating the prevailing eighteenth century literary types—poetry,
drama, history, eloquence, pulpit oratory, fiction, and criticism.

The observations which he makes on these subjects reveal, however, his strongly classical tendencies. In so far as the French
neo-classicists followed the ancient classical program, he was quite
in agreement with them. He was not in accord with them, however, in the matter of strict adherence to the precepts and the
supremacy of reason. Although he stated that he believed in a
nation's availing itself of the good and useful that other nations
had to offer, the literary principles, the authors, and the works

Conclusion 129

which he recommended to his contemporaries were not those of the French, but rather those of the ancients and the best writers of Spain's Golden Age. In the fields of poetry, eloquence, and history, he cited the ancients as models and advocated, in particular, the study of the chief Spanish writers of the sixteenth century. In the drama, he supported, as we have seen, the great national dramatists of the seventeenth century; but while urging the playwrights of his day to use the masterpieces of Lope and Calderón and their followers for their models of Spanish spirit, freedom, and spontaneity, he also advocated a reasonable observance of the classical precepts to curb the excesses of inspiration and imagination found in them.

Forner's manner of presenting his criticism is disappointing. Despite the fact that he makes some good points and gives some rather clever turns to his satire, his method is not scholarly, but puerile. It is wanting in logic, organization, and force. It is characterized by a frequent confusion of ideology and art, and by many other defects which were common to his age—encyclopedic display, generalizations, exaggeration, repetition, superficiality, and verbosity.

In general, the author's comments on the writers of the past, as also on his contemporaries, are worthy of special consideration and commendation. In the *Exequias* and the *Oración apologética* he passes judgment on approximately two hundred authors, three fourths of whom are Spanish and the remaining one fourth, French, Italian, English, Greek, and Latin. His judgments, although brief, are on the whole accurate. Using the *Enciclopedia universal ilustrada* as a sort of clearing house of Spanish opinion, it has been observed that Forner's comments regarding the various authors are generally in agreement with the views held by Spanish critical authorities. In few instances is there any appreciable difference of opinion. For example, the *Enciclopedia* does not go to such excess as Forner in praise of Porcius Latro's oratorical ability. Forner designates him as "el mayor y mejor declamador de su siglo" while the *Enciclopedia* simply comments to the effect that Seneca considered his eloquence to be remarkable. In the case of Las Casas, it seems evident that Forner had no sympathy with this writer's views on the Spanish conquests.

130   *Conclusion.*

In all probability, his opposition was due in great part to his nearness to the revival of the "black legend" by Raynal. The critic who treats Las Casas in the *Enciclopedia,* being farther away from the heat of the eighteenth century controversy, takes a broader view of the history of the conquests and sees in Las Casas a calumniated apostle of human liberty who wanted to replace brutal punishment with the persuasive word. In regard to Paravicino, Forner's criticism appears to be more rigid than that found in the *Enciclopedia.* His comments likewise on the French writers, Rapin, the Comtesse de Genlis, and Masson, are also more rigid than those in the *Enciclopedia.* While in his allegory Forner has the works of Rapin and the Comtesse used as wicks for the funeral pyre, the substance of the appraisal of the latter as found in the *Enciclopedia* is that the author neither merits the praise of some nor the diatribes of others. In regard to the work of Rapin, the *Enciclopedia* quotes Goujet to the effect that his work is the best commentary in French on the poetics of Aristotle. The appraisal of Masson as made by the *Enciclopedia* contains no condemnation of the man and his work.

Such then was the nature of the criticism of Juan Pablo Forner. His knowledge, like that of the learned men of his day, was expansive, encyclopedic; but his opinions and the expression of them were marked by the same expansiveness and encyclopedism, by the same superficiality and verbosity, which he criticized in others. As a critic, therefore, he was as dependable and undependable as his contemporaries; and although his work was probably regarded by the "enlightened" of his day as the work of another outmoded orthodox traditionalist, it accomplished the author's designs, for it fanned and kept aglow the dying flame of Hispanicism, Traditionalism, and Christian Faith.

APPENDIX I

The antagonistic attitude commonly entertained by the French toward Spain in the eighteenth century was nothing new, for this hostility really dated back to the fifteenth century.[1] A somewhat more favorable spirit had prevailed during the sixteenth century and part of the seventeenth, when the value of Spain's linguistic and literary contribution was recognized and appreciated in France, especially among the nobles and the intellectual classes. Toward the end of the seventeenth century, however, the feeling of sympathy changed to hostility. The Spain of a Catholic king, the Spain of a new Scholasticism, and of a Calderón could not exercise the same influence as it had in the epoch preceding.[2] From that time, Frenchmen looked askance at Spain and were exceedingly free with their derogatory remarks, descending even to insult. On this point, the Italian Hispanist, Farinelli, writes in his *Ensayos*, "En todo el siglo XVIII, apenas encuéntrase en Francia una voz que no suene desdén contra una nación que creíase sumergida voluntariamente en la ignorancia, llena de frailes y clérigos."[3]

Saint Simon had spoken of Spain as a victim of the Inquisition;[4] the Abbé Prevost remarked that the Spaniards were not so pleasing when one knew them.[5] This antagonism continued to grow. Montesquieu in his *Lettres persanes* spoke of the ignorance of Spain, so full of friars and clerics; Voltaire in his *Essai sur les moeurs*, wrote, "on chante, on dit la messe, et on tue des hommes;" and again, "la misère grandit, mais les sérénades ne diminuent pas . . . tout le monde jouait de la guitare."[6] The philosophy of the "encyclopédistes" was concerned only with the science of things useful, useful in the material sense,[7] hence the Encyclopedic antagonism toward Spain spread. The intellectual hegemony of France was really responsible for the Franco-Hispanico-Germanico-Italian polemics of the eighteenth century.[8]

Nicolas Masson, a mediocre French writer, took up the appraisal of Spain made by the Encyclopedists and published in Paris in 1776 his *Abrégé de la*

---

[1] Sorrento, *Francia e Spagna nel settecento.*, p. 249.

[2] *Ibid.*, p. 93.

[3] Arturo Farinelli, *Ensayos*, as quoted by Sorrento in *Francia e Spagna nel settecento.*, p. 93.

[4] Sorrento, *Francia e Spagna nel settecento.*, p. 93.

[5] *Ibid.*

[6] Voltaire, *Essai sur les moeurs*, as quoted by Sorrento in *Francia e Spagna nel settecento.*, p. 94.

[7] Sorrento, *Francia e Spagna nel settecento.*, p. 234.

[8] *Ibid.*, p. 95.

131

132   *Appendix I*

Géographie de l'Espagne et du Portugal, in which he showed hostility towards the two countries.[9] In 1782, his article, "Espagne," which appeared in the *Encyclopédie Méthodique,* proved to be the ignition spark for the series of polemics that were to follow. Masson developed his discourse around such points as the commerce of Spain, the weakness and pride of the government, the inertness of the people, scholasticism, the inquisition, religion, and finally the Church, which, in the opinion of the *philosophes,* curtailed the progress of the arts and sciences.

Judging Spain in the light of utility, Masson raised his famous query, "Mais que doit-on à l'Espagne? Et depuis deux siècles, depuis quatre, depuis dix, qu'a-t-elle fait pour l'Europe?"[10] Although Cotarelo y Mori remarks that the article was insignificant[11] and probably would have been passed over had not the idea of translating the *Encyclopédie* occurred to D. Antonio Sánchez,[12] the fact remains that it did become even an affair of state.[13]

D. Antonio José de Cavanilles, a learned cleric, eminent botanist, and preceptor of the children of the Duque del Infantado, then a resident of Paris, was the first to protest against this article, with his *Observations sur l'article Espagne de la Nouvelle Encyclopédie.* This work was translated into Spanish the same year, 1784, by D. Mariano Rivera. According to Sainz y Rodríguez, the work of Cavanilles was superficial, its weakest point lying probably in the fact that the author gave too much attention to his contemporaries, especially to Tomás de Iriarte, Cordero, and Trigueros.[14]

The Abbé Carlos Denina, an outstanding Piedmontese scholar at Frederick's court, was the next to respond to Masson's article, reading his defense of Spain before the Academy of Science in Berlin on January 26, 1786. In enumerating the names of illustrious Spaniards and their contributions to progress in the various fields, Denina affirmed that Spain had done more for France from the time of Charlemagne to Cardinal Mazarin than France had done for the rest of Europe. In the same year, Denina also published an interesting series of letters addressed to different German,

---

[9] *Ibid.,* p. 91.

[10] Masson, *op. cit.,* p. 565.

[11] Cotarelo y Mori regards the matter as a "pueril. asunto," which took on proportions of a national cause. He speaks of the blind patriotism of the greater number of Spaniards, who resented the charges made against their nation and returned injury for injury. He remarks, too, that there were some enlightened Spaniards, however, who accused the blind patriots of proclaiming a progress which existed only in their minds, and of deceiving the nation by lulling the people to sleep instead of stimulating them to a greater progress *(Op. cit.,* p. 314).

[12] *Ibid.,* p. 312.

[13] Sorrento, *Francia e Spagna nel settecento,* p. 234.

[14] *Las polémicas sobre la cultura española,* p. 32.

Appendix I 133

French, and Italian gentlemen, in which he also treated of Spain's cultural contributions.[15]

The Gallophobe party in Spain gained additional strength from Denina's *Réponse*. The dissension between France and Spain was increased, too, when the editor of the *Encyclopédie* seeking to promote its sale through Spain was refused the permission. The Spanish King and his people were incensed. Letters and documents passed between the two governments; apologies were made by the French government, but matters changed very little,[16] for the Spanish government could not see why it should be an accomplice in its own dishonor.[17]

Then it was that Floridablanca, Spain's minister, thought it necessary to intervene in an official manner in the question, and we have Forner's *Oracion apologética por la España y su mérito literario.*

---

[15] Cotarelo y Mori, *op. cit.*, p. 315.

[16] Sorrento, *Francia e Spagna nel settecento.*, p. 234.

[17] Bourgoing, as referred to by Sorrento, *Francia e Spagna nel settecento.*, p. 245. Cf. Paul Mérimée, *L'influence française en Espagne au dix-huitième siècle*, Paris: Les Belles Lettres, 1936.

APPENDIX II

This Appendix contains the comments made by Forner in the *Exequias*, and the *Oración apologética* upon Spanish, French, English, Italian, Greek, and Latin authors. The comments found herein, are, for the most part, additional to those given in the dissertation itself. The comments which are not included in the Appendix may be referred to through the Index. The dates used in the Appendix, as also the alphabetical order followed, are those given in the *Enciclopedia universal ilustrada*.[1] The Latin writers born in Spain are included with the Spanish authors.

SPANISH AUTHORS

Abril, Pedro Simón de (c. 1530-?)
Translations of the Greek and Latin classics which were made by this author were included in Forner's display of translations in Parnassus.[2]
Acosta, José de (1539-1600)
Forner alludes to this author's *Historia natural y moral de las Indias*.[3]
Agustín, Antonio (1517-1586)
This scholar and bibliophile is spoken of as the "censor" of Zurita's works.[4]
Alderete, Bernardo José (1565-1645)
Forner cites the *Orígenes de la lengua castellana* as the first Spanish book to contain proof that the "idioma sabio" was common in the earliest times and that teaching and learning were likewise common.[5]
Alfonso X (1221-1284)
Forner praises Alfonso's earnestness in spreading the useful arts throughout his kingdom.[6] The monarch had the works of Averroës, Avicenna, and other Arabs translated to Latin in order that mathematics and medicine might flourish, and not because he was interested in the delirious dialectics or the metaphysics of the Saracens.[7] It was his ambition to have all the wisdom of the Orient translated to the Spanish.

---

[1] *Enciclopedia universal ilustrada europeo-americana*, 70 vols. in 72. Barcelona: Espasa-Calpe, 1907?-30.

[2] *Exequias*, pp. 224-25; for further comment see Gracián de Alderete, Appendix II, p. 145.

[3] *Exequias*, p. 231; see also Las Casas, Appendix II, p. 150.

[4] *Exequias*, p. 252.

[5] *Oración apologética*, p. 172.

[6] *Ibid.*, p. 138.

[7] *Ibid.*, p. 160.

Appendix II 135

Para este efecto, hizo traducir multitud grande de libros, que desde luego, salida apenas de su infancia, engrandecieron maravillosamente la lengua castellana, no sólo con los ornatos de las artes, pero, lo que es más, con abundancia de voces y frases científicas, que sirvieron como de barbechos para que en los tiempos más sabios se prestase sin violencia al cultivo de la sabiduría en toda su extensión.[8]

Forner declares that although Alfonso did not take part in the Crusades, and although he could not have been a disciple of Roger Bacon, he probably knew as much chemistry as Bacon, because he had the masters of it with him.[9]

The legislative works of this great Spaniard, Forner considers among the most celebrated of his country.[10]

Because of Forner's esteem for Alfonso's contribution to the development of the language, Alfonso is given the honor of placing the wreath upon the head of the dying matron, the Spanish Language.

> ... el sabio *Alfonso*
> Augusto padre de España, y de ella
> Docto legislador, culto maestro,
> Con vestido sucinto, su corona
> Ciñe en la sien a la matrona yerta.[11]

He also has the honor of being designated to carry the bier along with Alfonso XI, the Príncipe Carlos de Viana, and Juan Manuel.[12]

Alfonso XI (1311-1350)

His *Ordenamiento de Alcalá* is regarded by Forner as' one of the most celebrated legislative works of his nation.[13] This ruler is honored in the allegory by being designated to carry the bier of the Spanish Language.[14]

Antonio, Nicolás (1617-1648)

In the procession with the critical historians.[15]

Arguijo, Juan de (1564-1628)

Forner speaks of him as the "digno alumno de la escuela de *Herrera.*"[16]

---

[8] *Exequias*, p. 226.
[9] *Oración apologética*, p. 159.
[10] *Exequias*, pp. 216-17.
[11] *Ibid.*, p. 206.
[12] *Ibid.*, p. 258.
[13] *Ibid.*, p. 217.
[14] *Ibid.*, p. 258.
[15] *Ibid.*, p. 254.
[16] *Ibid.*, p. 241.

136 *Appendix II*

Bermúdez, Jerónimo (1520-1589)

Forner places him in the procession with the writers of tragedy, Fernán Pérez de Oliva, Jerónimo Bermúdez, Cristóbal de Virués, Juan de la Cueva and Tanco de Fregenal.[17]

Borja, Francisco de, El Príncipe de Esquilache (1582-1658)

In the procession with the poets was *"El Príncipe de Esquilache,* florido, galano, aliñado, pero cándido y suave; más rico en atavíos que en cosas.[18]

Boscá or Boscán Almogáver, Juan (1493-1542?)

> *Boscán, Garcilaso, Mendoza,* apartándose de la simplicidad de las coplas castellanas, y valiéndose diestramente de los tesoros de la poesía latina y griega, formaron el estilo poético, a cuya formación ayudó admirablemente la docilidad y genio mismo de la lengua, que sin repugnancia admite variedad infinita de locuciones enérgicas y hermosas en las poesía, y absolutamente para la prosa.[19]

Cabrera, Alfonso de (1546-1598)

A great sacred orator.[20]

Cabrera de Córdoba, Luis (1559-1623)

Forner places him in the procession with the historians, remarking that he was "diligente en los preceptos y no infeliz en la ejecución de ellos."[21]

Calderón de la Barca, Pedro (1600-1681)

Forner has Calderón and Lope de Vega lead the dramatists in the procession.

> *Lope* y *Calderón* guiaban la comparsa, pomposos, desenvueltos, ágiles, llenos de espíritu y de vida, y haciendo gala de la fecundidad de su imaginación, con desprecio de las puntualidades del arte.[22]

The author remarks that Calderón's writings show the splendor of the Spanish language.[23] He points out that Calderón is worthy of imitation, but that the dramatists in his time have imitated only his defects and have not manifested a shadow of the beauty found in his works.[24]

The comments which he has Cervantes make upon Calderón emphasize the great esteem in which Forner holds him. Cervantes remarks, referring to the eighteenth century dramatists:

> Mientras no aparezca un talento tan grande como el de *Calderón,* que juntando la regularidad a las bellezas de la imaginación, se

---

[17] *Ibid.,* p. 243.

[18] *Ibid.,* p. 240.

[19] *Ibid.,* p. 127.

[20] *Ibid.,* p. 249; see also Juan de Ávila, Appendix II, p. 149.

[21] *Exequias,* p. 254.

[22] *Ibid.,* p. 242.

[23] *Ibid.,* pp. 130-31.

[24] *Ibid.,* pp. 185-86.

Appendix II 137

apodere de la opinión pública, y ponga en descrédito los absurdos, las cosas permanecerán en el mismo estado de depravación y ruina.[25]

Forner believes that it is the beauty of Calderón's dramas that wins for them the admiration of the people. He writes:

El vulgo admira todavía las comedias de Calderón, sin que toda la madurez de la crítica más justa y sensata baste a hacer que no se divierta con aquellos tejidos de aventuras poco verosímiles. Esto ¿de qué nace? De que en efecto hay bellezas admirables en aquel mismo desarreglo: y como la inclinación a la belleza puede más que la inclinación a la verdad y bondad; el vulgo, sin hacer cuenta de éstas, sigue la inclinación dominante, y halla excelentes aquellos dramas. Si apareciese por ventura un cómico tan feliz, que supiese hermanar las bellezas de Calderón con las estrecheces de la verosimilitud, el vulgo le aplaudiría y admiraría también, sin meterse en sí aquello estaba o no escrito según manda el arte o la razón reducida a reglas. Satisfaríase con lo que le recrease, y dejaría libremente el autor ordenar sus dramas como mejor le pareciese.[26]

Cano, Melchor (1509-1560)
Forner credits Melchor Cano with the formation of "la ciencia Teológico-Escolástica."

Hieren a Melchor Cano las amargas quejas de su patricio sobre el lloroso estado de la Teología: dase por entendido: medita, reflexiona sobre la Tópica que debiera establecerse peculiarmente en cada ciencia, antes que Bacon contase esta Tópica entre las que faltan: reduce a sus fuentes los argumentos teológicos; los pesa, los confirma; y copiando en parte a Vives, y usando en parte de su penetración, forma la ciencia Teológico-Escolástica, ordenándola en sistema científico, y dando su complemento a la primera ciencia del racional.[27]

Forner notes that while the transition from the general to the particular was a very natural development, centuries passed after Aristotle until Cano made the discovery of it.[28] He also points out that Cano wrote on the "tópica" fifty-seven years before Bacon and that Bacon's *Novum Organum* does not compare with Cano's *Tópica teológica* in method, in elegance, perspicacity, skill, nor "crítica."[29]

---

[25] *Ibid.*, p. 187.
[26] *Oración apologética*, p. 187.
[27] *Ibid.*, pp. 146-47.
[28] *Ibid.*, p. 219.
[29] *Ibid.*, p. 218.

138 *Appendix II*

Although Forner notes that Cano copied Vivès in part,[80] he points out that Cano did not have the greatest esteem for Vives, possibly because of the fact that Vives had severely criticized the ancient commentators on Saint Augustine's *Ciudad de Dios*.[81]

Cañizares, José de (1676-1750)

Forner has Cervantes speak of this author as "el célebre *Cañizares*, el mejor escritor cómico de vuestro siglo."[82] When speaking to Cañizares in the allegory, Forner praises his works in these words:

> Vos, amigo mío, labrasteis monstruos, pero monstruous muy agradables y muy llenos de vida, y ved aquí por qué el pueblo prefiere vuestra vivísima irregularidad a la regularidad cadavérica de algunos de los que hoy se jactan de reformadores.[83]

The author's attitude toward Cañizares and his condemnation of the times is further brought out by his presenting Cañizares in Parnassus in a fearful state of anger, tearing a book to pieces. When questioned regarding his anger, he explains that his comedies had been esteemed by the "sabios" not only in Spain but throughout Europe, and that, there in Parnassus, where he has compared his works with those of antiquity, he finds himself more or less a failure as a dramatic writer. In the following remarks exchanged in the allegory between Cañizares and Cervantes, one gleans the modified sanction which Forner gives to the dramas of Cañizares.

> Confirmábanme en esta vana credulidad los continuos aplausos que han logrado constantemente en las representaciones; remachaban el clavo de mi vanidad los elogios que han merecido a algunos varones habidos y reputados por sabios, no sólo en España, pero en Europa; y al fin y al cabo, habiéndome obligado, luego que vine aquí, a cotejarlas con las de la docta antigüedad, y con la puntualidad de los preceptos que sirven para evitar los delitos en la composición, he venido a conocer, ¡pecador de mí! que, habiendo yo nacido para aumentar el escaso número de las buenas comedias, por haber vivido en una edad estragada absolutamente en el conocimiento y práctica del buen gusto, no hice más que disparatar con seso y ganar nombres de grande ingenio sí, pero de desatinado escritor—Sin embargo, le dijo el Conde, debéis consolaros con que en la labor confusa de vuestros dramas engastáis a veces ciertas escenas que harán disculpables vuestros desaciertos; porque ellas

---

[80] *Ibid.*, p. 146.
[81] *Ibid.*, p. 210.
[82] *Exequias*, p. 178.
[83] *Ibid.*, p. 188.

Appendix II

139

fueron hijas de la grandeza de vuestro ingenio, y éstos procedieron de la oscuridad y depravación del siglo en que florecisteis.[84]

Cascales, Francisco (1570-1642)

Following the didactic and epigrammatic poets in the procession, Forner places "los escritores del arte *Fernando López Pinciano, Francisco Cascales, Jusepe Antonio González de Salas y D. Ignacio de Luzán,* todos ellos mejores en sus poéticas que en sus poemas."[85]

Castillejo, Cristobal de (1494-c. 1590)

Walked in the procession with the poets.[86]

Castillo, Fernando del (1529-1595)

Made known the richness of the language.

> ...*Alejo Venegas, Fernán Pérez de Oliva, Luis de Granada, Hernando del Castillo, Antonio de Guevara, Jorge de Montemayor* y otros muchos... no tanto enriquecieron la lengua, cuanto dieron a conocer las riquezas de ella, que, abandonada en los siglos anteriores y desdeñada de los que se llaman sabios, yacía sin brillo como el diamante en la rudeza de la mina.[87]

Castillo de Bobadilla, Jerónimo (1547-e. 17th cent.)

This author's *Política para corregidores y señores de vasallos* was included in the display of legislative works. Forner speaks of it and Solórzano's *Política indiana* as the two works of pragmatic jurisprudence which deserved a place in the library of Parnassus.[88]

Castro y Bellvis, Guillén de (1569-1631)

In the procession after Lope and Calderón, walked Guillén de Castro and other dramatists.

> *Mira de Amescua, Guillén de Castro, Velez de Guevara, Montalván, Rojas, Moreto, Solís, Hoz, Zamora* y la demás turba de los que dramatizaron desde la época de *Lope* hasta la de *Cañizares,* en cuyas obras goza la lengua castellana un tesoro, riquísimo de su propiedad y variedad elocuente para todo género de estilos y asuntos.[89]

---

[84] *Ibid.,* pp. 178-79.

[85] *Ibid.,* p. 247.

[86] *Ibid.,* p. 241; see Pérez de Guzmán, Appendix II, p. 160.

[87] *Exequias,* pp. 128-29.

[88] *Ibid.,* p. 217.

[89] *Ibid.,* pp. 242-43. Sainz y Rodríguez comments that it is interesting to observe, as Valmar has, that the names of Tirso and Alarcón are not included in the enumeration of the dramatists *(ibid.,* p. 242, n.).

140 *Appendix II*

Cervantes de Saavedra, Miguel de (1547-1616)
Forner shows his great love and esteem for Cervantes by having Apollo send him to be his guide through Parnassus and by having him make many of the important comments on the writers and the literature of Spain, especially, those in praise of the Golden Age and those that condemn the Eighteenth Century.

On meeting Cervantes, Forner exclaims:

> ¿Quién podrá referir dignamente mi angustia, por una parte, con la funesta nueva, y mi gusto, por otra, con tener presente a mi embeleso, a mi recreo, a aquél en cuya pluma pusieron las Gracias sus delicias y amenidad?[40]

Again, Forner addresses him, "¡Oh, ingenio riquísimo, venturoso sólo en la posteridad, cuyas obras son hoy el mayor descrédito de los poderosos de vuestro tiempo!"[41]

The author has Villegas praise the style and works of Cervants thus:

> Cervantes...creó el estilo jocoso y dió inimitables ejemplos de narración fácil y amena, del diálogo urbano y elegante, del arduo modo de expresar con las frases la ridiculez de los hombres. Su pluma fué un pincel en cuanto escribió, y su *Quijote* es un ejemplar o idea de los estilos más agradables.[42]

According to Forner, Vives cried out against the abuse of the books of chivalry; and Cervantes listening to him, set out to destroy them by means of his *Quijote*.[43] To Forner, there is no comparison between the value of the *Quijote* and that of the philosophical tales of France and Germany, which, to his mind, have always been the "escándalo de la razón."[44]

Coloma, Carlos, Marqués de la Espina (1567-1637)
It was probably this author's translation of Tacitus which Forner included in his imaginary display of worthwhile translations.[45]

Columela, Lucius Junius Moderatus (3 or 4 B.C.-54 A.D.)
"...eminente ilustrador de la más precisa de las artes."[46]

---

[40] *Ibid.*, p. 82.

[41] *Ibid.*, p. 83.

[42] *Ibid.*, pp. 129-30.

[43] Oración apologética, p. 149.

[44] *Ibid.*, pp. 13-14.

[45] *Exequias*, pp. 224-25; for further comment see Gracián de Alderete, Appendix II, p. 145.

[46] *Oración apologética*, p. 121.

Appendix II

141

Cruz, Juana Inés de la (1651-1691 or 1695)

Forner refers to this poet by having one of the "sabios" remark:

... sé contar las sílabas y los pies con tanta facilidad como la mismísima *monja de Méjico*.[47]

Cueva de Garoza, Juan de la (1550-1609)

Placed in the procession with the writers of tragedy;[48] also pointed out as an epic poet of note.[49]

Díaz del Castillo, Bernardo or Bernal (c.1498-c.1568)

Forner shows him as the strong opponent of Raynal who in the eighteenth century revived the "black legend." He speaks of him as "el valeroso *Bernal Díaz*,"[50] "el buen *Bernal Díaz*" who declared that he would teach "al francesillo a tratar verdad y a respetar la memoria de unos hombres que murieron casi todos en la demanda de la conquista..."[51]

Díaz Tanco de Fregenal, Vasco (16th cent.)

Recognition is given to him by placing him in the procession with the writers of tragedy.[52]

Ercilla y Zúñiga, Alonso de (1533-1594)

With Juan Rufo, he led the historical poets. Forner describes him as "majestuoso, noble, vivísimo en las pinturas y descripciones, maravilloso en los afectos, y pocas veces inferior a la grandeza de la trompa."[53]

Escartín y Carrera, Francisco Antonio (18th cent.)

When speaking of the commercialization of literature, Forner writes of him as follows:

> ¡Venturoso *Escartín*, a quien *Cilenio*
> Negó su inspiración, e impunemente
> Puede vender los hongos de su genio!
>   Sin que el odio le muerda, o se ensangriente
> Contra él la envidia, cobra sosegado
> De su *Pouget* el rédito inocente.[54]

Espinel Gómez Adorno, Vicente (1550-1624)

In the procession with the poets, and described by Forner as "puro y templado, y diestrísimo en el artificio de la versificación."[55]

Feijóo y Montenegro, Benito Jerónimo (1676-1764)

---

[47] *Exequias*, p. 98.

[48] *Ibid.*, p. 243; see also Jerónimo Bermúdez, Appendix II, p. 136.

[49] *Exequias*, p. 246; see Vega Carpio, Appendix II, p. 170.

[50] *Exequias*, p. 232.

[51] *Ibid.*, p. 233.

[52] *Ibid.*, p. 243; see Jerónimo Bermúdez, Appendix II, p. 136.

[53] *Exequias*, p. 247.

[54] *Ibid.*, p. 270.

[55] *Exequias*, pp. 240-41.

142   *Appendix II*

Forner's attitude toward Feijóo is well exemplified in the following description of their meeting in Parnassus:

> Menos dócil se manifestaba en una mesa inmediata un varón despierto de acciones y entonado de frente, que revolviendo, ya un tomo, ya otro, de doce o trece que traía entre manos, con dificultad se resolvía a aligerarlos a imitación de los demás. Notólo el Conde, y díjole con franqueza de poderoso: «Acábese de resolver, reverendísimo, y reconozca que no están ya sus obras en parte donde prohiban el impugnarlas. ¿Qué detención es esa? ¿Mide este tiempo por el de sus aplausos? La posteridad docta condena ya en él muchas cosas que celebró en sus días la parcialidad. Sus dos tomos de correcciones corrigieron citas y equivocaciones en las noticias: y siendo de los escritos lo menos útil la erudición, dejó intactas las ideas falsas o diminutas de las artes y asuntos científicos en que tropezó, parte por amor a la novedad, y parte por la calidad de los tiempos.»
>
> Sonrojóse el reverendo, e inclinando la frente, atendió con más solicitud a la enmienda de sus discursos.[56]

Forner further remarks that while Feijóo had frequently attacked common truths instead of errors, Apollo had pardoned the absurdities found in his works. Commenting on the jests made by Quintilian and Herennius[57] in Parnassus, Forner refers to Feijóo's poor Latin and to the eloquence which Feijóo thought he possessed, but which the two Romans refer to as "un discurso falso, pueril."[58] His eloquence, they maintained, showed the lack of the "auxilios artificiales."[59] In the *Teatro crítico*, they condemn the frequent use of "versos octosílabos, que llevan su oración como cojeando sobre las muletas de la mensuración poética,"[60] a point on which, Forner says, Vives disagreed.

> Bien es verdad que esta reprensión pareció no sólo injusta, pero ridícula, al perspicacísimo *Juan Luis Vives,* que, poco satisfecho de este dogma retórico de la antigüedad, procuró persuadir que la introducción de los versos en la oración suelta, lejos de afearla, la hermosea y adorna.[61]

---

[56] *Ibid.,* pp. 188-89.

[57] Sainz y Rodríguez notes that Forner cites Herennius for Cicero. (*Ibid.,* p. 189, n. 20).

[58] *Ibid.,* p. 190.

[59] *Ibid.*

[60] *Ibid.,* p. 192.

[61] *Ibid.*

Appendix II

143

Forner himself would condemn the use of verse in prose, only when it produces inharmonious effects, when "hagan sonido completo o terminen la redondez de los períodos."[62] This dissonance, he finds, is very common in the *Teatro crítico*.

> La del *Teatro crítico* es frecuentísima por este defecto; se resiente además, en muchos lugares, de la hinchazón y verbosidad retumbante que estaba en uso en los tiempos de la juventud de su autor.[63]

While recognizing the utility of Feijóo's writings the author does not approve of the style because of the Gallicisms found therein. He cites Feijóo as the first Spaniard who gallicized the Spanish language, and, consequently, as an author whose style should not be imitated.[64]

Forner also disapproves of Feijóo's superficial treatment of the *Theologia Naturalis* of Ramón Sabunde, declaring that Feijóo did not read the work carefully;[65] nor does he like the manner in which Feijóo wrote of Lull's art.[66]

Fernández Navarrete, Pedro (1647-1711)

Included in the display of works on legislation and politics is the author's *Conservación de monarquías*, "expurgada de la pedantería de los textos latinos, que hacen escabroso su estilo y redundante la doctrina."[67] He likes the content of this book better than its form.[68]

Ferreras García, Juan de (1652-1735)

Forner pictures him in the procession with the historians.

> ...*Pellicer y Ferreras* fueron los más consumados en el estudio crítico aplicado a la historia, pero abandonaron enteramente las galas de la narración, y por lo mismo en la inmediación con que caminaban a los historiadores elocuentes, se daba a entender que la crítica y el ingenio deben concurrir con igual esfuerzo para construir historias dignas de este nombre.[69]

This historian is also found in the library at Parnassus, recasting his history in accordance with the suggestions of Mariana, who showed esteem for it in these words:

> Vuestra historia carece, no hay duda, de aquellas admirables calidades que aseguran la inmortalidad de los talentos; pero, aunque

---

[62] *Ibid.*, p. 193.

[63] *Ibid.*, pp. 193-94.

[64] *Ibid.*, p. 194.

[65] *Oración apologética*, p. 203.

[66] *Ibid.*, p. 200. Forner refers to the *Libro apologético* of Fray Bartolomé Fornés who wrote against Feijóo and his attitude toward Lull. *Ibid.*, p. 202.

[67] *Ibid.*, p. 219.

[68] *Ibid.*, p. 220.

[69] *Ibid.*, p. 253; see Ocampo, Appendix II, p. 159.

144 *Appendix II*

escasa en la parte del ingenio, es, no óbstante, digna de particular estimación, por la escrupulosidad, juicio y pulso con que procurasteis ajustar los hechos a la medida de la verdad, o acercarlos a los límites de la mayor verosimilitud, no pasando por ninguna de las patrañas, ni aún de las preocupaciones nacionales, de las cuales son muy raros los que aciertan a desprenderse.[70]

Figueroa, Francisco de (1536-1620)
One of the pastoral poets in the procession.

Saá de Miranda...Soto de Rojas...iban detrás de *Francisco de Figueroa* y del misterioso *Francisco de la Torre*, cuyos epigramas pastoriles serán siempre en su clase la mayor gloria de la poesía, por no haber en ninguna lengua cosa igual que pueda comparárseles, y en cuyas canciones, odas y églogas revivió el espíritu de *Mosco* y *Teócrito* y la mejor emulación dè los bucólicos antiguos, sin agravio de *Figueroa*, admirable también por la candidez y pureza de sus idilios.[71]

Fonseca, P. Cristóbal de (?-1621)
An eloquent prose writer and sacred orator in the procession.[72]
Fuenmayor, Antonio de (1569-1599)
An historian admired by Forner for his "nervio y vehemencia."[73]
Furió y Ceriol, Fadrique (1532-1592)
His *Consejo y Consejeros del Príncipe* was named in connection with the display of legislative and political works.[74] In this work Forner admires more the content than the expression.[75]
Garibay y Zamalloa, Esteban de (1533-1599)
Forner speaks of him in connection with the representative Spanish historians, calling him a "diestro compilador"[76] and giving him credit for helping to beautify and enlarge the Spanish language, "uniendo en ella la majestad, la robustez y la dulzura con increíble naturalidad."[77]
Gómez, Antonio (16th cent.)
Referred to by Forner in his comments on the status of legal study in Spain.

Por desgracia, en España ha durado constantemente la persuasión de que para abogar basta el simple estudio legal, sin más aditamento

---

[70] *Exequias*, p. 177.
[71] *Ibid.*, pp. 245-46.
[72] *Ibid.*, p. 249; see also Juan de Ávila, Appendix II, p. 149.
[73] *Exequias*, p. 255.
[74] *Iid.*, p. 219.
[75] *Ibid.*, p. 220.
[76] *Ibid.*, p. 253; for further comment, see Ocampo, Appendix II, p. 159.
[77] *Exequias*, p. 128.

Appendix II   145

ni auxilio que el que se busca en la insigne barbarie de *Pas,
Gómes* y la demás turba de la escuela pragmática. En estas fuentes
bebe la juventud que se consagra al foro las ideas de su profesión,
con la fatalidad de que cuando se entrega al estudio práctico, tiene
que olvidar la mayor parte de lo que aprendió en la universidad, lo
cual no sería acaso fortuna corta, si el nuevo estudio que se emprende
fuese de mejor condición que la doctrina que se olvida. Pero la
lástima es que en esta lucha la impertinencia cede a la barbarie....[78]

Gómez de la Huerta, Jerónimo de (?-1643)
It was probably this author's translation of Pliny which was included
by Forner in the display of translations.[79]
Góngora y Argote, Luis de (1561-1627)
Forner has him lead the epigrammatic poets, who were few in number.[80]
González de Salas, José Antonio (1588-1651)
He walked in the procession with "los escritores del arte." He was
better in poetics than in his poems.[81]
Gracián de Alderete, Diego (fl. first part of 16th cent.)
Among the small number of translations which Forner considered worthy
to appear in the display, those of Gracián were given a prominent place.

Reducíanse a un escaso número de traducciones, entre las cuales
sobresalían en lugar preeminente las de Gracián, Huerta, Manero
Pérez, Velasco, Villegas, Abril, Coloma, Pellícer, y no tanto por
su exactitud, cuanto por la soltura y propiedad con que expresaron
en castellano la sentencia de sus originales, bien así como si no
fuesen traducciones.[82]

Granada, Fray Luis de (1504-1588)
Forner's respect for this writer's works was manifested in a particular
manner by having, in the display in Parnassus, the theologian's doctoral
cap rest upon the Castillian works of the great Spanish mystics, Luis de
Granada, Luis de León and Teresa de Jesús.[83] He places this author in
the procession with the eloquent prose writers and the sacred orators,[84]

---

[78] *Ibid.,* p. 198.

[79] *Ibid.,* pp. 224-25; see Gracián de Alderete, Appendix II, p. 145.

[80] *Exequias,* p. 27; see Forner's comments on gongorism, p. 86, also
Paravicino, Appendix II, p. 159; and Tarsis, *ibid.,* p. 167.

[81] *Exequias,* p. 247; for further comment see Francisco Cascales, Appendix
II, p. 139.

[82] *Exequias,* pp. 224-25.

[83] *Ibid.,* p. 214.

[84] *Ibid.,* p. 249; pp. 128-29; see also Juan de Ávila, Appendix II, p. 149, and
Fernando del Castillo, Appendix II, p. 139.

146   *Appendix II*

and speaks of his making known the richness and beauty of the Spanish language.[85]

Guevara, Antonio de (1480?-1545)

This author is credited with having made known the richness and beauty of the Spanish language.[86]

Heredia, Pedro Miguel de (1590-1659)

Forner praises this doctor for his studies.[87]

Hernández de Oviedo y Valdés, Gonzalo (1478-1575)

Named among those who defended the Spanish conquests in the New World. In all probability, Forner has in mind this author's *Historia general y natural de las Indias* (1535).[88]

Hernández de Velasco, Gregorio (?-c.1586)

Referred to as a translator of note.[89]

Herrera, Fernando de (1536-1599)

"...grandílocuo, levantado, fogoso, fértil en imágenes sublimes y en locuciones hermosas."[90] He added majesty to the Spanish language.[91]

Hispano, Pedro (fl. 13th cent.)

Stripped the dialectics of the time of its sophisms and vanities.[92]

Hoz y Mota, Juan Claudio de la Cruz (?-1709?)

Found in the procession with the dramatists.[93]

Huarte de San Juan, Juan (between 1530 and 1535-1592?)

Some of his works are found in the display of philosophical books. He was not noted for his eloquence.[94]

Huerta y Vega, Francisco Manuel de la (1697-1752)

Forner's comments on Huerta and other editors of the *Diario de los literatos de España* show his unfriendly attitude toward them. He has Cervantes explain how they attack Mayans unjustly.

> Este anciano, nos dijo Cervantes, se queja con razón; trabajó infatigablemente en restituir las letras de España a su esplendor antiguo. Tres diaristas, de los cuales el uno dejó por testimonio de su grande ingenio dos tomejos de *Memorias literarias*, esto es dos cuerpecillos de noticias copiadas tumultuariamente; otro, una historia cuajada de fábulas y cuentos de viejas, y el tercero nada,

---

[85] *Exequias*, pp. 128-29; see Fernando del Castillo, Appendix II, p. 139.

[86] *Exequias*, pp. 128-29; see Fernando del Castillo, Appendix II, p. 139.

[87] *Oración apologética*, p. 147. Forner also quotes authorities which give proper recognition to the work of Heredia (*ibid.*, pp. 220-23).

[88] *Exequias*, p. 232; see Las Casas, Appendix II, p. 150.

[89] *Exequias*, p. 225; see Gracián de Alderete, Appendix II, p. 145.

[90] *Exequias*, p. 240.

[91] *Ibid.*, p. 129; see Luis de León, Appendix II, p. 151.

[92] *Oración apologética*, p. 182.

[93] *Exequias*, pp. 129, 242; see Guillén de Castro, Appendix II, pp. 139.

[94] *Exequias*, p. 220.

Appendix II 147

se empeñaron en desacreditarle, y si no lo consiguieron, faltó muy poco. Culpábanle por haber escrito que en España *pauci colunt literas, caeteri barbariem;* y los buenos de los diaristas, que persiguieron de muerte a todos los escritores de su tiempo; que no dejaron libro sano a ninguno, tratándolos de bárbaros, de pedantes, de rudos; que llegaron a proferir con no menor arrogancia que la que culpaban en aquel varón docto, que se avergonzarían de suscribir su nombre en cualquiera de los escritos que se habían publicado en este siglo hasta sus días, le hicieron un cargo horrible porque publicaba lo que ellos mismos publicaban. ¡Rara condición de hombres, pero ejemplo no raro del poder de este desventurado amor propio, que nos hace ver con odio en los demás aquellos mismos vicios que los demás reprenden en nosotros! Yo sé que su aplicación era digna de otra consideración en este sitio; pero, como vendieron a veces el juicio en obsequio de la parcialidad, y cargaron sus críticas de resentimientos personales, que aceleraron, sin duda, la ruina de una obra que hubiera sido utilísima manejada con más comedimiento y moderación, Apolo los ha expuesto al común escarmiento, destinándolos a maestros de esgrima en el Parnaso, y no sin bizarría en la justicia; porque de sus extractos hizo colocar en la *Biblioteca Délfica* los útiles, doctos e imparciales, remitiendo los demás al ministerio que se ha dado aquí a los malos libros.[95]

Hurtado de Mendoza, Diego (1530-1575)
Helped to enrich the Spanish language and to form the Spanish poetic style.[96] Forner speaks of his "laconismo majestuoso" in his historical writing.[97]
Ibañez de Segovia Peralta y Mendoza, Gaspar (1628-1708)
In the procession with the critical historians, Forner includes the Marqués de Mondejar.[98]
Iglesias de la Casa, José (1748-1791)
Forner apparently had great respect for Iglesias, judging from the prominent part he has him play in the allegory under the name of Arcadio. He speaks of him as "mi amigo *Arcadio,* antiguo comilitón mío en la Universidad, socarrón de primer orden, y hombre que diría una pulla en verso al mismo *Apolo* en sus doradísimas barbas."[99] When Arcadio expressed his desire to go with Forner and Cervantes, the latter declared his approval,

---

[95] *Ibid.,* pp. 111-113. Forner evidently alludes to Huerta and his *Historia de la España primitiva,* when he speaks of one author leaving a history. For the other two authors referred to in this passage, see Martínez Salafranca and Puig, Appendix II, pp. 155 and 161.

[96] *Exequias,* p. 127. See Juan Boscán, Appendix II, p. 136.

[97] *Exequias,* p. 255.

[98] *Ibid.,* p. 254.

[99] *Ibid.,* p. 72.

148 *Appendix II*

providing Arcadio belonged to the good sect, the qualifications of which he established as follows:

> Si nunca habéis traducido
> **Algún librito de Francia,**
> Copiando gálicas frases
> Con españolas palabras;
>   Si no habéis hecho tragedias
> De prosa que mal se inflama;
> En que el héroe Sismontano,
> Antes que muera, nos mata;
>   Si porque en París se encuentran
> Fábulas en abundancia,
> No enfabuláis el idioma
> Con frialdades imitadas;
>   Si de un *esprit* que está en boga
> Nunca espiritáis el habla,
> Haciendo que bogue y reme
> La majestad castellana;
>   Si no escribís taraceas
> Cual de estructura mosaica,
> Y por mostraros pantojo,
> No publicáis mezcolanzas.[100]

After hearing the qualifications, Forner lost no time in assuring Cervantes that Arcadio "era un buen español."[101] Describing the meeting of Iglesias and Apollo, Forner writes:

> Arcadio se presentó a Apolo, recomendado por nuestro guía, y fué recibido mejor que lo fuera en su patria en casa de un título recién titulado.[102]

Forner also has Arcadio give him advice on the writing of poetry;[103] and has him give his views on the works of certain writers in Spain.[104]
Iriarte, Tomás de (1750-1791)

Forner makes only an allusion to Iriarte's *Poema de la Música,* when he refers to the mercantile ends of many writers of his day.

> ... yo creo que un ente espiritual, destinado a la inmortalidad, se envilece cuando se hace vendible. Si la necesidad de vivir civil-

---

[100] *Ibid.,* pp. 84-85.
[101] *Ibid.,* pp. 84-85.
[102] *Ibid.,* p. 105.
[103] *Ibid.,* pp. 72-73.
[104] *Ibid.,* pp. 147-57.

Appendix II
149

mente ha hecho comerciante a la razón, y se venden sus producciones, como los zapatos y las lechugas, los ánimos nobles, que conocen la grandeza y dignidad de su origen, admiten el galardón, pero no le buscan; se resignan con la miseria, y la saben sufrir a vista de la opulencia injusta. Es verdad que yo no tomo las cosas tan en cerro, que crea absolutamente que aquella arte no tenga acogida. En nuestros días hemos visto algún ejemplar, que nos ha admirado y consolado.[105]

Commenting on the verse of this author, Forner writes:

> ¿De *Mevio el Apreton* y los sonetos,
> La prosa de sus versos, fría y seca,
> Buena para recetas y secretas?[106]

Isla, José Francisco de (1703-1781)

The author's opinion of Padre Isla is found in Arcadio's comment, "Hay pedazos admirables en el *Gerundio*, y a su autor no se le puede negar acaso el primer lugar entre los escritores burlescos, y uno muy distinguido entre los verdaderamente graciosos."[107]

Jáuregui y Aguilar, Juan (1583-1641)

"...flúido, lozano, frondoso, si puede decirse así, gran músico en la poesía, deleitable cuanto puede decirse."[108]

Jiménez de Cisneros, Francisco (1436-1517)

Forner praises his work in connection with the *Poliglotta Complutense*, his school at Alcalá, his integrity, and his virtue.[109]

Juan Manuel, El Infante (1282-1347)

Honored in the allegory by his appointment to carry the bier, along with Alfonso X, Alfonso XI, and el Príncipe Carlos de Viana.[110]

Juan de Ávila (Beato) (1499-1569)

Forner places this author in the procession with the "prosistas elocuentes" who were distributed in different classes with the sacred orators and ascetics. Of this group of authors, he writes:

> *Juan de Avila, Luis de León, Luis de Granada, Bautista de Lanuza, Fonseca, Alfonso de Cabrera,* caminando con majestuosidad y austera gravedad, retrataban en la misma compostura exterior el

---

[105] *Ibid.,* pp. 79-80; Saínz y Rodríguez comments in a note that Forner alludes here to the *Poema de la Música (ibid.,* n. 28). Forner also makes a satirical allusion to Iriarte's *Fábulas literarias (ibid.,* p. 102).

[106] *Ibid.,* p. 285.

[107] *Ibid.,* p. 224; see Juan de Ávila, Appendix II, above, and Paravicino, Appendix II, p. 159.

[108] *Exequias,* p. 241.

[109] *Oración apologética,* pp. 139-40.

[110] *Exequias,* p. 258.

150   *Appendix II*

sagrado genio de su elocuencia. Sólo el verlos era una acusación muda para las disoluciones del mundo. Pintado en sus semblantes el celo que brotó por sus labios en las solemnidades religiosas, decía él por sí que aquellos hombres no subieron al púlpito para darse en espectáculo, sino para confundir los vicios y dilatar el santo imperio de la virtud. No en ellos verdores y lozanías inmodestas, no discreciones y retruecanillos de estrado, no follaje estéril, a propósito sólo para causar estrépito como en inútil salva, no sutilezas caviladas con artificio, no estilo afeminado y teatral, no frases simétricas y colocadas con afectación pueril, no metáforas, no alegorías, no figuras hacinadas con estudio insolente para embelesar necios y negociar su aplauso con la horrenda profanación de la enseñanza del Altísimo. En ellos habló la elocuencia con divina expresión por la conformidad grande que supieron acomodar entre la alteza de sus asuntos y la manera de persuadirlos.[111]

Lanuza, Jerónimo Bautista de (1553-1625)
In the procession with the sacred orators.[112]
Larraga, Francisco (18th century)
When commenting on the orators of the eighteenth century, he refers to the "moral en el prontuario de *Larraga.*"[113]
Larramendi, Manuel (?-c.1750)
This Biscayan, defender of the Basque as the primitive language of Spain, is shown in the allegory delaying the funeral rites of the Spanish Language.[114]
Las Casas, Fray Bartolomé de (1474-1566)
Forner alludes to the *Brevísima relación de la destrucción de las Indias* of this author. Since the well-known "black legend" condemned by Sepúlveda in the time of Las Casas was revived by Raynal in the eighteenth century, Forner rather ingeniously shows his unfavorable attitude toward Raynal by presenting a heated dispute in Parnassus between those upholding and those opposing the Spanish conquests in the New World. According to Forner, the peoples in the New World had suffered the greatest opposition from Las Casas, whom he describes in the following manner:

> ...cuyo genio ardiente, activo, inflexible, no contento con haber alborotado las Cortes de Carlos V y Felipe II, sobre la que él

---

[111] *Ibid.*, pp. 249-50.

[112] *Ibid.*, p. 249; see Juan de Ávila, Appendix II, p. 149.

[113] *Exequias,* p. 169; see also Losada, Appendix II, p. 153. There is no reference to Larraga in the *Enciclopedia universal ilustrada.* There is a reference to him and his book, the *Promptuario de la Theologia Moral* in the *Manual del librero hispano-americano,* IV, 186. According to this work, the *Promptuario* was published in 1766.

[114] *Ibid.*, p. 171. In all probability, Forner alludes especially to two works by this author, *De la antigüedad y universalidad del vascuenze en España* (1728) and *El imposible vencido, arte de la lengua vascongada* (1729).

Appendix II

llamaba injusticia de las conquistas del Nuevo Mundo, quiso también perturbar el Parnaso, clamando que tal acompañamiento antes sería ignominioso que honroso a España, cuya gloria padecía un borrón feísimo e indeleble por las crueldades inauditas que en la conquista se habían usado con aquellas simples y miserables naciones. Hízole frente allí también, como en España, la gran doctrina y elocuencia de *Juan Ginés de Sepúlveda;* y renovándose la disputa con ardor, se dividió en bandos toda la flor de los filósofos del Parnaso, impugnando y defendiendo la conquista cada uno por los principios del sistema que había jurado. A *Sepúlveda* se arrimaron *Platón, Aristóteles, Cenón, Grocio, Locke, Barbeyrac;* a *Casas, Melchor Cano, Francisco de Victoria, José de Acosta, Robertson, Raynal* y otra turba de modernos, especialmente franceses, que exagerando las cosas para salirse con su porfía, inventaron patrañas y calumnias portentosas en odio de los españoles, a cuyas fatigas (sin iguales en la historia de la ambición humana, que es la historia de todos los imperios) debe ahora esta mitad del globo el conocimiento y participación de la otra mitad.[115]

Latro, Marius Porcius (50 B.C.-4 A.D.?)

Forner calls him by the Spanish name, Ladrón. He speaks of him as "el mayor y mejor Declamador de su siglo" and a man who by the excellence of his genius aroused emulation and awakened a love for study.[116]

León, Fray Luis Ponce de (1528-1591)

Forner's esteem for the works of Fray Luis de León was shown first by having the theologian's doctoral cap rest upon his mystic writings, along with those of Luis de Granada and Saint Teresa;[117] by having the author walk in the procession with the eloquent prose writers and sacred orators;[118] and finally, by having him appear with Bartolomé de Argensola, leading the long line of "varones sabios de España, que con su talento y doctrina habían cultivado, hermoseado y perfeccionado la lengua de su patria."[119] He speaks of him as "magnífico, noble, sublime, igualmente grande en los números, en las galas y en los argumentos."[120] He credits him with adding majesty to the Spanish language,[121] and of contributing to the glory of Spain.[122]

---

[115] *Ibid.*, pp. 230-231.

[116] *Oración apologética*, pp. 120-21.

[117] *Exequias*, p. 214.

[118] *Ibid.*, p. 249; for further comments see Juan de Ávila, Appendix II, p. 149.

[119] *Exequias*, p. 239.

[120] *Ibid.*, p. 240.

[121] *Ibid.*, p. 129.

[122] *Ibid.*, p. 240.

152 *Appendix II*

Herrera, León y Rioja añadieron a la majestad, que ya lograba en sus versos, la grandilocuencia y sublimidad, que no se había dejado aún ver en la estructura de sus períodos.[123]

Leonardo de los Argensolas, Lupercio (1559-1613) and Bartolomé (1562-1631)

Forner admires these writers very much, as is seen from the following passage:

> Ante los dos *Leonardos*
> Pronunciaré encogido
> Palabras con que entiendan
> Cuánto a los dos admiro.[124]

In praise of their work, he writes, "Los dos *Argensolas* juntaron con talento admirable las galas de una poesía varonil a la gravedad de la moral."[125] He speaks of Bartolomé Leonardo de Argensola as "grave, severo, maduro, admirable en la fantasía y en la doctrina."[126] He praises his satires especially.[127] Forner's particular esteem for him and his work is likewise shown when he places him, with Fray Luis de León, at the head of the procession of Spain's "sabios."[128]

López Pinciano, Alonso (late 16th cent.)[129]

"Escritor del arte"; better in his poetics than in his poems.[130]

López de Ayala, Ignacio; pseud. *Gil Porras* (18th cent.)

When Cervantes asks Arcadio if he has read the *Carta crítica del Bachiller Gil Porras de Pachuca a los RR. PP. Mohedanos sobre la Historia literaria que publican* and the latter replies that he has read the *Carta* as well as the Mohedanos' *Historia,* Cervantes remarks: "Dígoos que si habéis tenido tanta paciencia, os pueden llamar, mejor que a *Marco Catón,* devorador de libros."[131]

---

[123] *Ibid.,* p. 129.

[124] *Ibid.,* p. 69.

[125] *Ibid.,* p. 129.

[126] *Ibid.,* p. 240.

[127] *Ibid.,* pp. 76, 143.

[128] *Ibid.,* p. 239; see Luis de León, Appendix II, p. 151.

[129] Although Forner speaks of Fernando López Pinciano, this name is not found in the *Enciclopedia universal ilustrada.* There was a Portuguese chronicler in the fourteenth century named Fernán López, but since Forner speaks of the author as an "escritor del arte," it seems more plausible that he meant Alonso López Pinciano who gained considerable renown as the author of the *Filosofía antigua poética,* which is a commentary on Aristotle's *Poética,* Horace's *Ars Poética,* and Plato's aesthetic ideas.

[130] *Exequias,* p. 247; see also Francisco Cascales, Appendix II, p. 139.

[131] *Exequias,* p. 148.

Appendix II   153

López de Gomara, Francisco (1510-1560)

Forner alludes to this author's work entitled *Hispania victrix, Historia general de las Indias* (1552). He presents him in the allegory as an opponent of Raynal.[132]

López de Mendoza, Iñigo, Marqués de Santillana (1398-1458)

In the procession with the poets.[133]

López de Zárate, Francisco (1580-1658)

Walked in the procession with Cristóbal de Mesa, at the head of a group of epic poets.[134]

Losada, Luis de (1681-1748)

Forner probably refers to this author and his treatise on dialectics which was popular at the time, the *Institutiones Dialecticae, vulgo Summulae* (1721). In condemning the eloquence and oratory of his day, Forner says that when the orators were asked concerning the rudiments of their art they responded that "cuando eran muchachos, decoraron algo de las *Súmulas,* de *Goudini,* y la moral en el prontuario de *Larraga."*[135]

Lucan (39-65)

Forner's regret that Lucan is not given the honor which he thinks he deserves is contained in the following comment: "¡Infeliz joven! No te bastó que Nerón te sacrificase por excelente Poeta: te esperaba todavía la persecución de los modernos Nerones de la literatura."[136]

Comparing Lucan with Lucretius, he writes:

> Canta Lucano la verdadera suerte de la guerra civil: expone los horrores de la discordia, los estragos de la división entre los ciudadanos: retrata con estilo valiente, y espíritu arrebatado los males que produjo la iniqua ambición de la república más poderosa, para que con el lamentable ejemplo escarmiente la posteridad; y materia tan superior a los Átomos de Epicuro, y propósito tan aventajado a los elogios de la irreligión y del fatalismo, no bastaron para igualarle siquiera en el título con el ponderado Tito Lucrecio.[137]

Although Lucan may not be an epic poet, he is a poet of truth and inspires more virtue than Lucretius.[138]

> ...tengo para mí que el que disuade una guerra civil a un pueblo inclinadísimo a ella, no es muy inferior al que majestuosamente

---

[132] *Ibid.,* p. 232; see Raynal, Appendix II, p. 179.

[133] *Exequias,* p. 241; see Pérez de Guzmán, Appendix II, p. 160.

[134] *Exequias,* p. 246.

[135] *Ibid.,* pp. 168-169. It is possible too that Forner may refer to the *Suma de las Súmulas de Pedro Hispano* of Gaspar Cardillo de Villapando (1527-1581), which was also a well-known work at the time.

[136] *Oración apologética,* p. 118.

[137] *Ibid.,* pp. 114-15.

[138] *Ibid.,* p. ix.

154   *Appendix II*

ensalza por hazañas heroicas la usurpación y la perfidia...sean sus libros la lección de los Reyes, el escarmiento de la ambición, el código de la política, y España se satisface con este mérito de su patricio.[139]

According to Forner, Lucan's *Farsalia* is a wonderful piece of work. The vivacity of his style is inimitable; and his expression is remarkable for its images. His ability was such that he might be considered superior even to Virgil.[140]

Luzán, Ignacio de (1702-1754)

"Escritor del arte"; better in his poetics than in his poems.[141]

Manero, Pedro (1599-1659)

In all probability, it was this author's translation of Tertullian's *Apologia* that was included by Forner in the display of translations.[142]

Marcial, Marcus Valerius (b. bet. 38 and 43-?)

"...el festivo y popular Marcial, cuyos libros fueron las delicias y entretenimiento de la ociosidad urbana, no sin fruto en el agudo de sus reprehensiones."[143]

Mariana, Juan de (1536-1623)

Led the historians in the procession. "El arte, la elocuencia robusta y la generalidad del argumento, dieron el primer lugar a *Juan de Mariana*."[144] He possessed a "severidad lacónica,"[145] a "gravedad severa y concisa."[146] His history is characterized by "elocuencia y maravilloso artificio."[147] Great historian though Mariana was, Forner expresses through Arcadio his doubt that Mariana's history would be received with anything but indifference in the eighteenth century.[148] His esteem of Mariana is such that in his allegory he has Ferreras consult him and profit by his definition of history.[149]

Márquez, Juan (1564-1621)

Forner includes the author's *El gobernador cristiano* in the display of works on legislation and politics.[150]

---

[139] *Ibid.*, p. 116.

[140] *Ibid.*, pp. 115-18.

[141] *Exequias*, p. 247; see Francisco Cascales, Appendix II, p. 139.

[142] *Exequias*, pp. 224-25; for further comment see Gracián de Alderete, Appendix II, p. 145.

[143] *Oración apologética*, p. 121.

[144] *Exequias*, p. 252.

[145] *Ibid.*, p. 135.

[146] *Ibid.*, p. 255.

[147] *Ibid.*, p. 153.

[148] *Ibid.*, p. 153.

[149] *Ibid.*, p. 177; see Ferreras, Appendix II, p. 143; see also Forner's comments on history, this study, p. 113 ff.

[150] *Exequias*, p. 218.

Appendix II 155

Martínez Salafranca, Juan (1677-1772)

One of the editors of the *Diario de los literatos de España* commented on by Cervantes in the allegory and disapproved of for his attitude towards Mayans y Siscar. Of him Forner writes, "...dejó por testimonio de su grande ingenio dos tomejos de *Memorias literarias,* esto es, dos cuerpecillos de noticias copiadas tumultuariamente."[151]

Mayans y Siscar, Gregorio (1699-1781)

Not only does Forner deem Mayans worthy of appearing in the procession with the critical historians,[152] but in the allegory he has Cervantes praise him as the last and only defender of the Spanish language.[153] He also makes him the mouth piece, as it were, of many of his own views regarding the eighteenth century. He has Mayans explain how he tried to maintain the propriety and purity of the Spanish language at a time when "no se hablaba sino algarabía."[154] He attributes the unpopularity of his works to the fact that he did not have the ability to "afrancesarlos."[155] Had he written them in the French manner, the number of reprints of his works would have rivalled those of the *Teatro crítico.* Although his *Retórica castellana* would have won favor had he followed the trends of the time, he had his own reasons for the method which he followed, as he explains:

> ...en lugar de proponer ejemplos de autores franceses, para mostrar la elegancia de nuestro idioma, incurrí en la necedad de valerme de ejemplos de autores españoles, puros, castizos y elegantes... Parecíame a mí que en los escritos de una lengua distinta no se debe observar más que el método y modo de pintar, cuando sean dignos de observación; no el estilo, las locuciones, el color y lo demás que penda del carácter y genio de la lengua, y por esto clamaba y gritaba sin cesar que se leyesen nuestros buenos autores, para que, logrado en su lectura el uso de hablar bien, pudiésemos sin miedo de corromper el habla, copiar de los extranjeros lo pertene- ciente al modo de disponer y pensar.... Demás de esto, yo no me precié nunca de epigramático en prosa, a imitación de los ultramon- tanos; porque sabía bien que las agudezas sin tiempo son frialdades ineptísimas, y que llevar los asuntos históricos, filosóficos, políticos y sagrados sobre los filos de epigrama, y no sobre los estribos de la prudencia, es lo mismo que si Virgilio hubiera escrito su *Eneida* en el estilo de Marcial. Enfadábame sobremanera que se hiciese

---

[151] *Ibid.,* pp. 111-112; see Huerta y Vega, Appendix II, p. 146.

[152] *Ibid.,* p. 254.

[153] *Ibid.,* p. 115.

[154] *Ibid.,* p. 107.

[155] *Ibid.,* p. 107; Forner alludes here and in the succeeding comments to the polemic carried on between Mayans and the *Diario de los literatos;* see also Huerta y Vega, Appendix II, p. 146.

156 *Appendix II*

ostentación del ingenio sin juicio alguno, porque preveía lo que ha sucedido después, esto es, que se plagaría el mundo de bufones, que tratarían la historia con agudezas, la poesía con agudezas, con agudezas la filosofia, con ellas la política, y todo, en fin, lo convertirían en agudo y picante, con pérdida inevitable del carácter y genio de cada obra.[156]

Showing further his approval of Mayans' works, Forner has Arcadio and himself designated by Mayans to explain to their countrymen on their return to Spain his motives for writing as he did:

...refieran...que detesto altamente el buen gusto que creen introducir los literatos actuales, trasladándole, no de los consejos de la razón sana y sagaz, sino de la imitación de los escritos de una lengua distinta, y que en los buenos libros, franceses, italianos, alemanes, rusos, romanos, griegos, árabes y chinos, se puede aprender a pensar bien; pero a hablar con elegancia y propiedad, en ningunos, sino en los nuestros de los dos siglos anteriores.[157]

Mejía, Pedro (1500-1552)
Forner refers to him when speaking of philosophical books.[158]
Mendoza, Bernardino de (b.1540 or 1541-1604)
Mentioned in the allegory by Cervantes with other soldier authors; "'...
ladeo hoy en el Parnaso con los Garcilasos, Mendozas y Rebolledos, los cuales me aventajaron en la fortuna, no en el valor...'"[159]
Mercado, Luis (1520-1606)
Made studies of fevers.[160]
Mesa, Cristóbal de (1564-c.1628)
A Spanish epic poet in the procession.[161]
Mira de Amescua, Antonio (bet.1574 and 1577-1644)
In the procession. A dramatist who enriched the Spanish language.[162]

---

[156] *Exequias*, pp. 108-10.

[157] *Ibid.*, p. 111.

[158] *Ibid.*, p. 220. In this passage, Forner refers to "dos Mejías." Sainz y Rodríguez comments in a note that besides Pedro Mejía, Forner probably has in mind a Luis Mejía, "traductor elegantísimo de *Los Coloquios de Erasmo*, Sevilla, 1529." There was no reference to this Mejía in the *Enciclopedia universal ilustrada.* Sainz y Rodríguez also adds in his note that Forner may refer to the Erasmist, Cristóbal Mejía, or to a Pedro Mejía of Toledo, the author of *Tratado de los grados de la vida espiritual*, Toledo, 1550 (*Exequias*, p. 220, n. 13).

[159] *Ibid.*, p. 83.

[160] *Oración apologética*, p. 147.

[161] *Exequias*, p. 246.

[162] *Ibid.*, pp. 242-43; see Guillén de Castro, Appendix II, p. 139.

Appendix II 157

Monardes, Nicolás (1512-1588)
A famous Spanish doctor who wrote "la primera *Historia Medicinal de Indias*, tesoro más exquisito que el del inagotable Potosí."[163]
Montemayor, Jorge de (1520?-1561?)
Made known the riches of the Spanish language by his writing.[164]
Morales, Ambrosio de (1513-1591)
Was with the historians in the procession. He helped to enrich the language.[165] He was noted particularly for his "magisterio para los exámenes."[166] Forner describes him in these words:

> ...grave, maduro, noble, pero embarazada frecuentemente su facundia con los exámenes y discusiones críticas y cronológicas a que le obligó la confusión grande que halló en los hechos de España, cuando trató de reducirlos a narración segura y puntual.[167]

Moreto y Cabaña, Agustín (1618-1669)
Appears in the procession with the dramatists.[168] In the reflections upon the Spanish theatre read by Cañizares, Forner refers to Moreto's *El desdén con el desdén*.

> ...Son innumerables las comedians nuestras en que los reyes y príncipes no hacen otro papel que el que pudieran hacer un D. Luis o un D. Diego, y en que las reinas y princesas no son más que unas Leonores y Violantes. Mudando los nombres y quitando las alusiones a la autoridad Real, estas comedias pasarán por verdaderos dramas de los que llaman de capa y espada, porque entre éstos no hay más diferencia que la de los nombres de las personas. Hágase la prueba con la famosísima de *El desdén con el desdén* y con cuantas no van fundadas en algún hecho histórico. Los mismos lances, los mismos fines, los mismos pensamientos, las mismas bufonadas, la misma complicación de sucesos y de personas.[169]

Muñoz, Luis (?-1646)
Forner speaks of "la dulzura, suavidad y ternura" found in the writings of this historian.[170]

---

[163] *Oración apologética*, p. 148, p. 135.

[164] *Exequias*, p. 129; for further comments see Fernando del Castillo, Appendix II, p. 139.

[165] *Exequias*, p. 128.

[166] *Ibid.*, p. 255.

[167] *Ibid.*, pp. 252-53.

[168] *Ibid.*, p. 242; for further comments see Guillén De Castro, Appendix II, p. 139.

[169] *Exequias*, p. 184.

[170] *Ibid.*, p. 255.

158 *Appendix II*

Navia Osorio y Vigil, Álvaro de, Marqués de Santa Cruz (1684-1732)

Included in the display of legislative works was the *Reflexiones militares*, "corregidas en el estilo y en la erudición."[171] Forner esteems the content of this work more than its form.[172]

Nebrija, Elio Antonio de (1444-1532)

According to Forner, he was declared the prime restorer of the law that Hadrian had founded.[173] He joined to law the humanities which he took from the Greeks of Italy, and began to do away with the barbarity with which Italian jurisconsults had defaced Roman Law.[174] His juridical dictionary was of great value.[175]

Nifo, Francisco Mariano (1719-1803)

When condemning the mercantile pursuits of the literary men of his time, Forner refers a number of times to Nifo. In the "Sátira" at the end of the *Exequias* we read:

Allí el liceo está, donde canina
Me enseña el hambre, en el locuaz *Ninfeo*
A hallar en la barbarie fértil mina.[176]

¡Oh! No permita Dios que de su ciencia
Usurpe yo el comercio al gran *Ninfeo*,
Ni le haga en traducciones competencia.[177]

Again, he refers to him as the sad Lupino, who is trying to make himself a writer.

¿Véis al triste *Lupino* con mil penas
Abortando misiones semanales,
Atado a ser autor cual con cadenas?[178]

In the following passage, Forner refers to Nifo's translations of the works of the Frenchman, Caraccioli, which he writes Caracciolo:

¡Ah! ¡qué fuera de mí si de millares
De heridas traspasado *Caracciolo*,
Aullando ¡ay, ay! a fuerza de pesares,
Saliese de su tumba cuando *Apolo*
Nos retira su lumbre, y entre sueños
Me acometiese a mí, que duermo solo![179]

---

[171] *Ibid.*, p. 219.
[172] *Ibid.*, p. 220.
[173] *Oración apologética*, p. 139.
[174] *Ibid.*, p. 142.
[175] *Ibid.*, p. 139.
[176] *Exequias*, p. 267.
[177] *Ibid.*, p. 272.
[178] *Ibid.*, p. 268.
[179] *Ibid.*, p. 272.

Appendix II 159

Ocampo, Florián de (1499-1558?)

A historian who enriched the language[180] and, as Forner says, "mostró el camino por donde debía caminar la historia."[181] Of Ocampo, he writes further as he describes him in the procession:

> *Esteban de Garibay*, diestro compilador, y *Florián de Ocampo*, restaurador elegante de nuestra historia, pisaban las huellas de los anteriores, y a sus espaldas caminaban *Don José Pellicer de Ossau* y *Don Juan de Ferreras;* y extrañando yo tal mezcla y perturbación en el orden de procedencias, pude saber después que *Ocampo* fué...la media tinta de la arte histórica en España, porque sacando la narración del desaliño y simplicidad con que la habían tratado los cronistas anteriores al reinado de *Don Fernando el V* y *Doña Isabel,* tentaron ennoblecerla y subirla de punto con los ornatos oratorios, cuanto podía permitirlo la infancia en que duraban entonces las buenas letras.[182]

Pablo, Hermenegildo de San (17th cent.)

A critical historian in the procession.[183]

Palencia, Alfonso de (1423-1492)

Forner places this author's translation of Plutarch's *Lives* among the most outstanding translations.[184]

Paravicino, y Arteaga, Hortensio Félix (1580-1633)

Apparently, he was made to walk in the procession as a punishment for his corruption of the Spanish language.

> Iba a lo último el famoso *Hortensio Pavavicino,* caídos los ojos, marchito el semblante, tímidos y avergonzados los movimientos; y no sin razón, porque, desviándose de la sublime simplicidad que debió aprender en los textos mismos sobre que predicaba, subió al púlpito las destempladas novedades de *Góngora* con felicidad tan infeliz, que vinculó en su imitación, para más de un siglo, la extravagancia y el desconcierto de la oratoria. Se le trató sin consideración a la grandeza de su ingenio, porque en ningún estilo dejó cosa imitable, y principalmente porque se obstinó en sus abusos. El testimonio de su conciencia, que le gritaba haber sido padre de la corrupción, era torcedor implacable, que no le permitía gozar con aliento desahogado las glorias de su celebridad. En efecto, las metáforas hinchadas, violentas, remotas; la dislocada

---

[180] *Ibid.*, p. 128; for further comments see Esteban de Garibay, Appendix II, p. 144.

[181] *Exequias*, p. 257.

[182] *Ibid.*, p. 253.

[183] *Ibid.*, p. 254.

[184] *Ibid.*, p. 226.

160 *Appendix II*

colocación de las palabras en su frase ó dicción, dura, áspera, escabrosa, y lo que es peor, obscura y muchas veces incomprensible, no ya a la razón, pero a la misma gramática; la prodigalidad en derramar flores, amenidades, lozanías, brillos, oropeles y relumbrones sin discernimiento, sin elección, sin oportunidad, la intolerable afectación de envolverlo todo en rodeos y perífrasis buscados de intento para evitar la expresión natural y sencilla; los conceptos agudos, fundados en alusiones o semejanzas vagas, que, puestas al yunque de la razón, se desvanecían en sofismas ridículos; las interpretaciones forzadas de los textos santos, trayéndolos por fiadores de bachillerías frívolas; todos estos, en fin, fueron defectos en *Hortensio,* que, aumentados con furiosa monstruosidad en los desatinados émulos de su estilo, produjeron la bárbara y desastrada vanilocuencia que leemos con risa, cuando no con abominación, en el *Florilegio* y los demás monumentos del gerundismo.[185]

Paz, Cristobal (fl. 1. 16th and e. 17th cent.)
Referred to by Forner in his comments on legal study in Spain.[186]
Pellicer de Ossau y Salas y Tovar, José (1602-1679)
In the procession with the historians,[187] Forner also considered him a representative translator.[188]
Pérez de Guzmán, Fernán (bet. 1377 and 1379-1460?)
With the poets in the procession. With the *"Marqués de Santillana, Cristóbal de Castillejo* y cuantos metrificaron desde el rey *D. Alfonso el Sabio* hasta *Garcilaso de la Vega,* desaliñados, simples, escasos en la imaginación, pero los más de ellos robustos y nerviosos."[189]
Pérez de Montalván, Juan (1602-1638)
In the procession with the dramatists.[190]
Pérez de Montoro, José (?-1694)
Forner stresses the insignificance of this author's verse by contrasting him with Garcilaso de la Vega.[191]
Pérez de Oliva, Fernán (1494?-1533)
Walks in the procession with the tragedy writers.[192] He is credited with making known the richness of the Spanish language;[193] and of considering it

---

[185] *Ibid.,* pp. 250-51; see Góngora, Appendix II, p. 145; and Isla, Appendix II, p. 149.
[186] *Exequias,* p. 198.
[187] *Ibid.,* p. 253; for further comment, see Ferreras and Ocampo, Appendix II, pp. 143, 159.
[188] *Exequias,* pp. 224-25; see also Gracián de Alderete, Appendix II, p. 145.
[189] *Exequias,* pp. 241-42.
[190] *Ibid.,* p. 242; see also Guillén de Castro, Appendix II, p. 139.
[191] *Exequias,* p. 190.
[192] *Ibid.,* p. 243; see Jerónimo Bermúdez, Appendix II, p. 136.
[193] *Exequias,* p. 128; see Fernando del Castillo, Appendix II, p. 139.

Appendix II 161

equal to the Greek and Latin for the writing of tragedy, for which reason he grieves over the fact that there were only six tragic poets in the procession.[194]

Prudentius, Aurelius Clemens (384-405 or 410)

This Christian Horace,[195] the greatest poet of his century, Forner considers to be an honor to Spain.[196]

Puig, Leopoldo Jerónimo (?-1763)

One of the editors of the *Diario de los literatos de España,* who, Forner remarks, wrote nothing.[197]

Pulgar, Hernando del (15th cent.)

Helped to build up and enrich the Spanish language.[198]

Quevedo y Villegas, Francisco Gómez de (1580-1645)

In the procession. He manifested the characteristics of the language after the time of Philip IV, which Forner describes as "rápida, lozana, viva, sonora, jovial, galante, florida, deliciosa."[199] Again, Forner speaks of Quevedo's style as "rápido, fecundo, pródigo en cosas y en modos de decir, agudo, conceptuoso, y tan versátil, que habiendo escrito en todos estilos, pareció nacido para cada uno."[200] He mentions the "siempre picante jocosidad de Quevedo,"[201] and he remarks, "Aquel a quien domine el juicio, trabajará inutilmente en querer remedar la travesura, siempre fecunda, de Quevedo."[202] He also alludes with pride to Quevedo's *España defendida* as a defense of the Spaniards in their colonization of the Indies.[203]

Quintilian, Marcus Fabius (35?-95?)

It is Forner's opinion that while Quintilian fared better with the modern Neros than Lucan, he deserved the honor bestowed on him, for he was the "restaurador de la elocuencia en Roma; el maestro más excelente de ella; el hombre de mejor gusto, de juicio más recto entre los latinos."[204] In further praise of him, Forner writes:

> . . . excedió ä Aristóteles, se aventajó a Cicerón, perturbó la gloria de Grecia en la enseñanza de la Oratoria; el que dictó a su posteridad, no sólo preceptos para hablar elocuentemente, sino

---

[194] *Exequias,* p. 244.
[195] *Oración apologética,* p. 120.
[196] *Ibid.,* p. 132.
[197] *Exequias,* pp. 111-113; for further comment see Huerta y Vega, Appendix II, p. 146.
[198] *Exequias,* p. 127; see Garibay, Appendix II, p. 144.
[199] *Exequias,* p. 130.
[200] *Ibid.,* p. 240.
[201] *Ibid.,* p. 76.
[202] *Ibid.,* p. 135.
[203] *Ibid.,* p. 232.
[204] *Oración apologética,* p. 118.

162 *Appendix II*

> prudentísimos documentos para la educación pueril, los cuales ¡ojalá fuesen más admirados y recibidos que los extravagantes sueños del maniaco Rousseau, entre algunas gentes que dan título de filosofía a los delirios, y no ven un grande genio, en el que sencillamente enseña los medios de criar buenos ciudadanos! El Español Fabio fué el mayor y el último apoyo del saber latino, sustentado por sus discípulos, no sin esplendor, en los felices imperios de los Españoles Trajano y Adriano.[205]

While Forner praises Quintilian in this manner, he expresses his lack of agreement with him in the matter of attributing the corruption of eloquence to Seneca.[206]

Raimundo de Peñafort (San) (?-1275)

Gave Christian laws to Rome; and tried to promote the study of the Oriental languages. He was aided in this work by Ramón Lull.[207]

Ramón Lull (bet. 1232 and 1235-1315)

> Fué éste, para el siglo en que vivió, un genio singular nada inferior a Roger Bacon, ni menos digno de los elogios que desperdicía en éste la presente inclinación a las cosas físicas y astronómicas. Si hace servicio a las letras el que anima constantemente su corrección; Lulio, no sólo fundó una secta para mejorarlas, sino que combatió el fundamento de los abusos, persiguiendo a los averroístas, ya con libros, ya con exhortaciones, en toda ocasión y en todas partes: atrevimiento que en aquel siglo se tendría por tan temerario, como si en el presente escribiese alguno contra los errores de Newton.[208]

While the principles of Lull's *Alfabeto* do not show essentials, and while his general notions are of little use when given to experimental examination, yet, Forner thinks, he should not be spoken of so skeptically as Feijóo spoke of him. Forner believes he showed genius in his art of combining but that his followers exaggerated its utility.[209] Lull withdrew from the common manner of philosophizing[210] and worked to improve philosophy.[211]

Rebolledo, Conde Bernardino de (1597-1676)

Led the didactic writers in the procession.[212] Forner expresses his opinion of Rebolledo's writing in the words of Arcadio, "... estimo la doctrina y

---

[205] *Ibid.*, pp. 118-19.

[206] *Exequias*, p. 166.

[207] *Oración apologética*, pp. 136-37.

[208] *Ibid.*, pp. 114-15; see Raimundo Peñafort, above.

[209] *Oración apologética*, p. 200.

[210] *Ibid.*, p. 142.

[211] *Ibid.*, p. 208.

[212] *Exequias*, p. 247.

Appendix II 163

el lenguaje; no le llaméis poema, y no repugnaréis su composición."[218]   In enumerating the books and symbols in the display, which were concerned with legislation and politics, Forner mentions this author's *Selva militar y política* as "entre las magníficas baratijas."[214]   He again refers to this warrior poet when he has Cervantes speak of his association with him in Parnassus.[215]

Rejón de Silva, Diego Antonio (1740-1796)·

Referred to by Forner in his *Sátira contra la literatura chapucera de estos tiempos.*

> Te imploro, languidez; ven a mí cuando
> Prolongar un poema se me antoje,
> Que a un tal *Rejón* le deje tiritando.[216]

Rengifo, Juan Díaz (published his *Arte poética* in 1592)

Forner refers undoubtedly to the popularized form of this preceptist's *Arte poética española,* published by Joseph Vincens in the first part of the eighteenth century.[217]

Rey de Artieda, Andrés (1549-1613)

In the procession with the poets was "el festivo y fisgón *Artemidoro,* cuya naturalidad y gracias desenfadadas agradan por el mismo caso que carecen de estudio y de ornamentos buscados con sudor."[218]

Rioja y Rodríguez, Francisco de (bet. 1580 and 1586-1659)

Forner's comment on this author as he passed in the procession was, "*Francisco de Rioja,* ameno, ufano, sonoro, animado, fecundísimo en la expresión poética, imitador de *Herrera,* y a veces superior a su original."[219] He speaks too of Rioja's increasing the sublimity of the Spanish language.[220]

Rodríguez Mohedano, Rafael and Pedro (bet. 1725 and 1730-bet. 1795 and 1800)

Forner's opinion of the ten volume *Historia literaria de España* of these two brothers is well exemplified by the following incident related in the allegory: "Percibió a este tiempo Cervantes un tomo de la *Historia literaria de España,* y díjonos: '¿Habéis leído aquel libro?', señalándole. 'Por mi desgracia,' respondió Arcadio."[221]

---

[218] *Ibid.,* pp. 219-20.
[214] *Ibid.,* p. 219.
[215] *Ibid.,* p. 83; see Mendoza, Appendix II, p. 156.
[216] *Exequias,* p. 271.
[217] *Ibid.,* p. 97.
[218] *Ibid.,* p. 241.
[219] *Ibid.,* p. 240.
[220] *Ibid.,* p. 129; see Luis de León, Appendix II, p. 151.
[221] *Exequias,* p. 148; see López de Ayala, Appendix II, p. 152.

164 *Appendix II*

Rojas Zorrilla, Francisco de (1607-1648)
In the procession with the dramatists.[222]
Rueda, Lope de (e. 16th cent.-1566?)
Walked in the procession with Bartolomé de Torres Naharro and other early dramatic poets.[223]
Rufo Gutiérrez, Juan (1547?-1620?)
Presided with Alonso de Ercilla over the historical poets.
Described by Forner as "grave, natural, aliñado, más elocuente que poeta."[224]
Sa de Miranda, Francisco de (1495-1558)
In the procession with the bucolic poets.

> *Saá de Miranda,* duro y tosco más de lo conveniente, y *Soto de Rojas,* demasiadamente afeitado, y aun afectado (y por lo mismo uno y otro menos bucólicos que *Garcilaso,* porque el primero no perfeccionó el estilo rústico, dejándole casi en su grosería, y el segundo le engalanó con exceso), iban detrás de *Francisco de Figueroa* y del misterioso *Francisco de la Torre* .. [225]

Saavedra Fajardo, Diego de (1584-1648)
Brought out the magnificence of the Spanish language in his writings.[226] There is found in his historical writings "la pompa y magnificencia de sus períodos."[227] Forner pays honor to this author's work entitled *Idea de un Príncipe político-cristiano representada en cien empresas* (1640) by placing it in the display of outstanding Spanish books dealing with legislation and politics.[228]
Sabunde, Ramón (?-1436)
Discovered the priniciples of Natural Religion; and "con exactísima profundidad, no muy familiar fuera de España a los Escritores de su siglo, convence la necesidad de la Revelación."[229] Speaking of Sabunde's *Theologia Naturalis,* Forner writes:

> No es la menos la demostración de la existencia y atributos de Dios por la idea de un *ente perfectísimo* que puede y debe formar el hombre; raciocinio que tanto satisfizo a Descartes. Es tan demo-

---

[222] *Exequias,* p. 242; for further comments, see Guillén de Castro, Appendix II, p. 139.

[223] *Exequias,* p. 243.

[224] *Ibid.,* p. 247.

[225] *Ibid.,* p. 245. Compare Forner's spelling of Saá de Miranda with that of the *Enciclopedia universal ilustrada* used in heading.

[226] *Ibid.,* p. 131.

[227] *Ibid.,* p. 256.

[228] *Ibid.,* p. 218.

[229] *Oración apologética,* p. 138.

Appendix II 165

strativo el modo con que lo prueba Sebunde....la demostración Cartesiana es muy inferior a la de nuestro Doctor. Cartesio fué obscuro: para entenderle con más facilidad es menester leer el resumen de su demostración en la *censura* de Pedro Daniel Huet.[230]

Sandoval, Fray Prudencio de (c.1560-1621)

In the procession. A general historian whose works showed him "puro, blando, templado en el estilo, pero feliz investigador, y relator no del todo desaliñado."[231]

San José, Fray Jerónimo de (1587?-1654)

In the procession with the historians was *"Jerónimo de San José,* autor del *Genio de la Historia."*[232]

Sempere y Guarinos, Juan (1754-1830)

Referring to this author's *Ensayo de una biblioteca española del reinado de Carlos III,* Forner writes:

> ¿De *Guarinos* la infausta Biblioteca,
> Tablado donde España comparece
> A hacer ostentación de lo que peca;
>   Celo tonto, que piensa que ennoblece,
> · Y en la calle nos pone nuestros trapos
> Y a la irrisión del mundo nos ofrece?[233]

Seneca, Lucius Aeneus (c. 4 B.C.-65 A.D.)

Forner praises Seneca for his contributions to philosophy, legislation, oratory, and drama. He considers him the only original Roman philosopher able to compete with the Greeks,[234] and regards his services to Rome as far greater than those of any other philosopher.[235] It is Forner's belief that Seneca gave to the Latin language "las obras más santas que conoció la verbosa filosofía del Paganismo."[236] He further remarks that Seneca "... sacó del fondo de su rectitud los puros documentos con que enseñó a los hombres los oficios de su naturaleza."[237] He admires him for the virtue which he taught and he regrets that critics overlook this and see only the defects of his eloquence. His contribution to legislation in the form of sound interpretation was also worthwhile.[238] Forner speaks of him as an

---

[230] *Ibid.,* pp. 205-07. Compare Forner's spelling of Sebunde with that of the *Enciclopedia universal ilustrada* used in heading.

[231] *Exequias,* pp. 252-53.

[232] *Ibid.,* p. 254.

[233] *Ibid.,* p. 285.

[234] *Oración apologética,* p. 127.

[235] *Ibid.,* pp. 111, 122.

[236] *Ibid.,* pp. 112-13.

[237] *Ibid.,* p. 112.

[238] *Ibid.,* p. 233.

166   *Appendix II*

orator who did not copy the Greeks as Cicero did. He refers to him as "el mejor crítico de los Declamadores de su tiempo."[239] He considers him a worthy competitor of Euripides in "Oedipus" and "Phaedra."[240] Although many critics have regarded Seneca as a corrupter of literature,[241] and although Italy has been ungrateful to him,[242] Spain has admired this son of hers.[243] Forner believes that much of the discredit that has fallen upon Seneca is due to the fact that many have not known how to imitate him. Seneca, Forner says, was and is lovable for his defects.[244] He cannot understand what reason Quintilian had for attributing the corruption of eloquence to "los vicios halagüeños de Seneca" since Seneca's works were badly copied by the Roman youth. Forner believes that inferior talent is capable of copying only the defects of the great.[245]

Sepúlveda, Juan Ginés de (c. 1490-1573)

Forner speaks of the "gran doctrina y elocuencia" of Sepúlveda. In the allegory he has Sepúlveda defend the Spanish conquest in the New World against Las Casas. He pictures Plato, Aristotle, Zeno, Grotius, Locke, Babeyrac on the side of Sepúlveda, each one defending the conquest according to his own system.[246]

Sepúlveda de Espinosa, Pedro de (1578-1650)

He is described as the "gran pintor de la naturaleza;" he walked in the procession with the poets.[247]

Sigüenza, José (1544-1606)

Forner admired in this post and historian his "despejo y gracia nativa."[248]

Silveira, Miguel (1576-1636)

Appeared in the procession with the gongorists.[249]

Solís y Rivadeneira, Antonio de (1610-1686)

Dramatist and historian. In the procession with the dramatists.[250] His works bring out the magnificence of the Spanish language.[251] His writing is characterized by an "elegancia florida."[252] In his history is to be noted especially "su fertilísima amenidad."[253]

---

[239] *Ibid.*, p. 121.

[240] *Ibid.*, p. 121.

[241] *Ibid.*, p. 112.

[242] *Ibid.*, p. 111.

[243] *Ibid.*, pp. 121, 113.

[244] *Exequias*, p. 165.

[245] *Ibid.*, p. 166.

[246] *Ibid.*, p. 230; see Las Casas, Appendix II, p. 150.

[247] *Exequias*, p. 241.

[248] *Ibid.*, p. 255.

[249] *Ibid.*, p. 248; for further comment, see Juan de Tarsis, Appendix II, p. 167.

[250] *Exequias*, p. 242; see Guillén de Castro, Appendix II, p. 139.

[251] *Exequias*, p. 131.

[252] *Ibid.*, p. 135.

[253] *Ibid.*, p. 255.

Appendix II   167

Solórzano Pereira, Juan (1575-1653 or 1654)

This author's *Política indiana* was included in the display of works on jurisprudence.[254]

Soto de Rojas, Pedro (c.1590-1655)

A bucolic poet of note.[255]

Tarsis or Tassis y Peralta, Juan de, Conde de Villamediana (1580-1622)

His appearance in the procession was for chastisement.

> En pelotón confuso dentro de las filas se dejaban ver los cultos *Villamediana, Silveira* y sus conmilitones en la tenebrosidad *gongorina*, pero ufanos del sudor grande que les debió de costar la fatiga de hacerse ridículos entre sus venideros. No iban para honor, sino para escarmiento; no para gloria de la difunta, sino para ignominia propia. Comenzó en ellos la hidropesía de nuestra lengua y la destrucción de su robusto temperamento. Palabras peregrinas, frases huecas, períodos rimbombantes, metáforas desmesuradas, rodeos afectados, traslaciones violentas, balumbo de adornos impertinentes, conceptos falsos, ponderaciones gigantescas, fueron las pócimas con que destruyeron su salud a título de hermosearla.[256]

Tejada Páez, Agustín de (1567-c.1618)

In the procession with the poets was "El Dr. Tejada, lleno, numeroso, diligente en excusar palabras vulgares y usar las más cultas y escogidas."[257]

Teresa de Jesus, Santa (1515-1582)

Her works were praised with those of the other famous Spanish mystics.[258]

Torre, Francisco de la (c.1534-c.1594)

A pastoral poet in the procession.[259]

Torres Naharro, Bartolomé de (?-1531?)

Walked in the procession with *Lope de Rueda,* behind the dramatic poets who wrote from the time of Lope de Vega to Cañizares.[260]

Trigueros, Candido María (1736-1800)

Forner's opinion of Trigueros is clearly manifested when he has one of his works used as a wick for the funeral pyre. He makes the following comments concerning the author and his works:

> Con horrible impiedad arrolló otro en forma de torcida, descuartizándolo antes, un rollizo tomo de versos alejandrinos en frigidísimo

---

[254] *Ibid.,* p. 217; see Castillo de Bobadilla, Appendix II, p. 139.

[255] *Ibid.,* p. 245; see Sa de Miranda, Appendix II, p. 164.

[256] *Exequias,* p. 248; see also Góngora, Appendix II, p. 145 and Paravicino, *ibid.,* p. 159.

[257] *Exequias,* p. 241.

[258] *Ibid.,* p. 214; see Luis de Granada, Appendix II, p. 145.

[259] *Exequias,* pp. 245-46; see Figueroa, Appendix II, p. 144.

[260] *Exequias,* pp. 242-43.

Appendix II

y barbarísimo romance, cuyo autor tuvo la ·moderación de apellidarse *poeta filósofo;* porque claro está que para ser poeta y para ser filósofo no es menester más que bautizarse uno a sí mismo con la friolerilla de los dos títulos. La rancia novedad de la poesía alejandrina mereció solemnísimos silbos de la mosquetería del Parnaso, viendo que los cuatro martillazos que a unas mismas distancias, en cada dos versos, descarga la tal poesía sobre la pobre oreja española, destruían en ella la varia y fecunda armonía de nuestra lengua, que hasta ahora no ha necesitado tomar lecciones de las fraguas ni de los batanes para construir sus versos; y desde luego convinieron en que un poeta filósofo, que desempeñaba su título echando por tierra la gala, soltura y belleza de nuestros números, debía tener una filosofía orejuda y una poesía muy machacona, semejante al ruido que hace un mulo de Arévalo, o sea de la Laponia, cuando camina lentamente, bien cargado de barras de plomo, por una calzada.[261]

Arcadio's inquiry when Forner awakens from his dream also contains a satirical note in regard to Trigueros. Arcadio asks, "Habéis estado meditando alguna oda pindárica en elogio del inmortal Frigerion..."[262]

Ulloa Pereira, Luis de (?-1663)

Manifested the beauty of the Spanish language in his writings.[263]

Valbuena, Bernardo de (1568-1627)

Led the epic poets in the procession, *"Valbuena, Ariosto* de España y semejantísimo a él en la prodigalidad de ingenio y fantasía pudiéndose decir de su Bernardo que es más bien una mina de poesía que un poema."[264]

Valladares y Sotomayor, Antonio (18th cent.)

Referred to by Forner when he rails against the mercantilism among the writers of his day.

> No quiera Dios que el cómico trofeo
> Robe yo al siempre excelso *Valladares,*
> Vendiendo un *Tabernero* al coliseo.[265]

Vanegas del Busto, Alejo (1493?-1572?)

Although he helped to enrich the Spanish language by his writings,[266] he was not noted for his eloquence.[267] Some of his books are displayed with the philosophical works.[268]

---

[261] *Ibid.,* pp. 262-63.

[262] *Ibid.,* p. 290.

[263] *Ibid.,* p. 130.

[264] *Ibid.,* p. 246.

[265] *Ibid.,* p. 272.

[266] *Ibid.,* p. 128; see also Fernando del Castillo, Appendix II, p. 139.

[267] *Exequias,* p. 220.

[268] *Ibid.,* p. 220.

Appendix II 169

Vega, Garcilaso de la (1503-1536)

Forner speaks of Garcilaso's helping to form the Spanish poetic style.[269] Proof of the author's admiration of Garcilaso is shown when, in imagination, he pictures himself at the peak of Pindus where he will meet and reverence this poet:

> Doblada la rodilla,
> Veneraré a *Salicio*
> Honor del grave Tajo
> De las Musas hechizo.[270]

In the procession, Garcilaso leads the bucolic poets.

> Anduvo a este punto el entierro, y aparecieron los poetas bucólicos, presididos del dulcísimo *Garcilaso,* cuyo candor, cuya ternura, cuya simplicidad, cuya rustiquez elegante, dudo yo que tenga igual, en ninguna lengua de las que hoy se hablan, porque no sé de cierto si en alguna de ellas hay tanta disposición como en la nuestra para tratar con elegancia el estilo pastoril y campestre, sin que por la cultura pierda el sabor de la rustiquez.[271]

Again, the author emphasizes Garcilaso's poetic genius by contrasting him with Montoro, remarking that inclination inspires the writing of verses equally in a Garcilaso and a Montoro.[272]

Vega Carpio, Lope Felix de (1562-1635)

With Calderón, Lope led the dramatists in the procession.[273] Forner regards Lope and Calderón as masters worthy of the study and imitation of those of his generation; but it was his conviction that those who had tried to imitate them caught their defects but failed to bring out the beauties which their dramas contained.[274] In praise of Lope, Forner writes:

> Lope, redundante en todo, llenó sus versos y prosas de descripciones amenas, de metáforas ricas, trasladando desde su imaginación al papel cuantas imágenes le ofrecía la portentosa variedad de ideas que depositaba en ella. En este tiempo fué cuando la lengua empezó a tomar diverso semblante del que había tenido en el tiempo anterior.[275]

---

[269] *Ibid.,* p. 127; see Boscán, Appendix II, p. 136.

[270] *Exequias,* p. 69.

[271] *Ibid.,* pp. 244-45; see also Sa de Miranda, Appendix II, p. 164.

[272] *Ibid.,* p. 190.

[273] *Exequias,* p. 242. See Calderón Appendix II, p. 136.

[274] *Exequias,* pp. 185-86.

[275] *Ibid.,* p. 130.

170   *Appendix II*

Of Lope as an epic poet, Forner makes this passing comment, "Como *Lope, Virués* y *Cueva* iban entre los dramáticos, no pudimos notar el grado que gozan en el Parnaso en calidad de poetas épicos."[276]

Velez de Guevara, Luis (1578?-1645)

In the procession with the dramatists.[277]

Viana, Carlos, Infante de Aragon y Príncipe de (1421-1461)

Designated in the allegory to carry the bier, along with Alfonso X, Alfonso XI, and Juan Manuel.[278]

Villegas, Esteban Manuel de (1589-1669)

Forner's esteem for Villegas is first manifested in his clever description of what he would do if he spied Villegas in Parnassus, and of what happened when he met him, also in the comments which he has Villegas make about himself. Of his imaginary meeting with Villegas, Forner writes:

> Y si a dicha en la tropa
> A *Villegas* percibo,
> Negado a ostentaciones
> De civiles oficios,
> Por más que retozando
> Se ocupe sin peligros
> Con el viejo *Anacréon*,
> Trocando al viejo en niño,
> Romperé por la turba,
> Y de su cuello asido,
> Daréle un dulce beso
> Sin que él pueda impedirlo.[279]

Repeating his expressions of surprise on seeing the poet, he describes the meeting as follows:

> «Pobre, desvalido, émulo del dulce Anacreonte, del fácil y blando Ovidio del sublime y juicioso...—¡Que! ¿Vos sois?» Y arrojándome precipitadamente a sus brazos, estampé tres veces mis labios en las venerables arrugas de su rostro.[280]

Forner has this poet compare the honor which he receives in Parnassus with that which he received from his countrymen:

> A buena cuenta, algunos de los poderosos que me desatendieron son hoy nombres execrables o despreciables entre los que viven;

---

[276] *Ibid.*, p. 246.

[277] *Ibid.*, p. 242; see Guillén de Castro, Appendix II, p. 139.

[278] *Exequias*, p. 258.

[279] *Ibid.*, pp. 69-70.

[280] *Ibid.*, p. 121.

Appendix II

171

yo, sentado a la sombra de estos laureles, gozando de la apacibilidad
de esta mansión amena, coronado de rosas, cual me veis, alegre
por haber carecido de los peligros de la riqueza, digo las alabanzas
de mi ingenio, mezcladas con una tierna compasión por mi
infelicidad, converso con un Dios, sin que las cenizas de los
poderosos de mi tiempo sean de mejor calidad que las mías, y
sin que sus días hayan sido más durables, más tranquilos ni más
justos que los que pasaron por mí.[281]

Villegas speaks of his own writing in these terms:

...yo (permitid esta libertad a mis canas), salido apenas de la
edad pueril traduciendo e imitando al dulce y alegre *Anacreonte,*
di, si no me engaña mi amor propio, el primer ejemplo de aquella
lozanía que no conocía aún nuestra lengua, y que con excesiva
prodigalidad se dejó después ver en los escritos de los reinados
posteriores.[282]

Honoring Villegas' translations, Forner places them in a prominent
place in the display with a few other translations which he considered
representative.[283]

The esteem in which the author holds Villegas is further manifested by
letting him pass judgment on the important Spanish writers and their
contribution to the development of the Spanish language and literature.[284]

Virués, Cristóbal de (1550?-c.1614)

In the procession with the tragic poets;[285] but also pointed out as an
epic poet.[286]

Vitoria, Francisco de (1486-1546)

Forner alludes to his *De Indis.*[287]

Vives, Juan Luis (1492-1540)

To Forner, Vives was the bright star that lighted the way for man.[288]

¿Carecería del conocimiento de toda la Encyclopedia o ciencia
universal, el grande, el inmortal Vives; aquel expugnador inflexible
de los abusos; sagacísimo escudriñador de cuanto superfluo, vano,
desordenado, pernicioso han metido en las ciencias el descuido o

---

[281] *Ibid.,* pp. 122-23.

[282] *Ibid.,* p. 130.

[283] *Ibid.,* pp. 224-25; for further comment see Gracián de Alderete, Appendix II, p. 145.

[284] *Exequias,* pp. 126-170

[285] *Ibid.,* p. 243; see Jerónimo Bermúdez, Appendix II, p. 136.

[286] *Exequias,* p. 246; see Lope de Vega, Appendix II, p. 169.

[287] *Exequias,* p. 231.

[288] *Oración apologética,* p. 146.

172 *Appendix II*

> la sofistería; promovedor indefatigable de la utilidad; verdadero
> y primer padre de la restauración; a cuyos desengaños, no aprendidos
> en la entonces bárbara París o tenebrosa Bolonia, sino sacados del
> inestimable fondo de su prudencia es deudor el entendimiento de
> cuantos progresos sólidos ha hecho después de sus días en el
> estudio de la verdad?[289]

> ... su universal saber en suma, consagrado, si no a la escrutación
> de la Naturaleza, que eternamente se resistirá a las tentativas del
> entendimiento; por lo menos a las mejoras de éste y a la utilidad
> con que le convida la inmensa variedad de objetos le oprimen por
> el abuso; son en verdad méritos, que no sin fundamento obligan
> a reputarle en su patria por el talento mayor que han visto las
> edades.[290]

The philosophical enlightenment of Vives led to every science and art.
He formed theologians and jurists. The international law of Grotius was
built upon matter established by him, as was also the jurisprudence of the
Monarchs.[291] He led the way for Bacon's work. He showed the errors of
knowledge in its very origins; he reduced reason to its limits. He taught
the learned what they were not and what they ought to be.[292] Forner points
out that while Descartes passes as a diffuser of wisdom in Europe, Vives is
disregarded; whereas, he should be given credit for doing more.

> Juan Luis Vives que enseñó los caminos de hacer útil la sabiduría,
> que descubrió los extravíos del entendimiento, que manifestó de
> qué modo se había errado en la formación de las ciencias, que dictó
> las leyes del buen gusto y de la verdad, apenas dará materia a
> un elogio lánguido y pasajero; y el país que le produjo, y el
> clima que inspiró en él aquel talento reformador pasará por rudo
> y bárbaro en la boca de aquellos mismos que venerarán Descartes,
> como al ídolo de la filosofía.[293]

In speaking of Vives' works, Forner asks:

> ¿Quién osará negar que estas tareas son más provechosas al género
> humano que la ordenación de un mundo imaginario que sirvió sólo
> para entretener cosa de medio siglo la habitual discordia de los

---

[289] *Ibid.*, pp. 100-101.

[290] *Ibid.*, p. 145.

[291] *Ibid.*, p. 148.

[292] *Ibid.*, pp. 143-44.

[293] *Ibid.*, pp. xii-xiii. Forner discusses further the value of a number of
his philosophical works in the notes appended to the *Oración apologética*
(pp. 210-15); see also Dupin, Appendix II, p. 177.

Appendix II 173

Filósofos, y cayó después en el olvido en que sucesivamente van cayendo todos los sistemas?[294]

According to Forner, Vives was the first to philosophize without a system.[295] In the seven books of *De la Corrupción de las Artes,* he taught the manner of avoiding "los escollos del error, del engaño, de la opinión del sistema."[296] In comparing this work with Descartes' *Discours de la méthode,* Forner writes:

> Su tratado Del Método es nada en comparación de los libros *De la corrupción de las artes* de Juan Luis Vives, que le antecedió buen número de años. Las obras morales de éste, solas por sí, valen tanto por lo menos como toda la filosofía Cartesiana: y ojalá pueda yo demostrar en algún tiempo a los jactanciosos Filósofos de nuestro siglo, que en el conocimiento del hombre y en la enseñanza de sus deberes no han adelantado una sola verdad a lo que dejó escrito aquel gran varón.[297]

In the three volumes of the *Del alma y de la vida,* Vives surpasses the splendor of this ambitious philosophy, teaching man with proper observation what he is and to what he ought to aspire.[298] Forner believes that the five books of *De la verdad de la fe cristiana* should be read with veneration and admired "con encogimiento, donde triunfa perfeccionada la filosofía del hombre, llevándole irresistiblemente a la verdad del culto."[299]

He praises too, *Del arte de decir,* pointing out that Vives expanded the ancient styles of eloquence "a cuantos razonamientos puede emplear el ejercicio de la racionalidad."[300] .He admires his treatises on education, his satires against the barbarism "apoyada entonces en la Dialéctica,"[301] and his condemnation of the "libros de caballería."[302] In speaking of the censure of the frequent use of octosyllabic verse found in Feijóo's *Teatro crítico,* Forner remarks that Vives regarded this criticism as unjust and ridiculous.

> Bien es verdad que esta represión pareció no sólo injusta, pero ridícula, al perspicacísimo *Juan Luis Vives,* que, poco satisfecho de este dogma retórico de la antigüedad, procuró persuadir que la

---

[294] *Oración apologética,* p. xii.
[295] *Ibid.,* p. 144.
[296] *Ibid.*
[297] *Ibid.,* pp. xi-xii.
[298] *Ibid.,* pp. 144, 214.
[299] *Ibid.,* pp. 144-45.
[300] *Ibid.,* p. 144.
[301] *Ibid.,* p. 145.
[302] *Ibid.,* p. 148.

174   *Appendix II*

introducción de los versos en la oración 'suelta, lejos de afearla, la hermosea y adorna. Pero ¿quién lo creerá? El juicio de los oídos, razón única en que fundó aquella regla la antigüedad, pudo más que los agudos razonamientos del sabio valenciano.[303]

In the following passages, Forner shows his deep regret at the fact that Vives has not been duly appreciated in Europe, although he did so much for the world:

¿Cuánto no comunicó a Europa, al universo, el penetrante, el descubridor, el sagacísimo Juan Luis Vives? ¡O fatal suerte de los talentos: tinieblas vergonzosas con que el descuido y la ingratitud obscurecen la memoria de los que más sirven al género humano![304]

. . . .

Cuando sean más leídas sus obras: cuando más cultivadas las innumerables semillas que esparció en el universal círculo de las ciencias: cuando más observadas las nuevas verdades que en grande número aparecen en sus discursos; los innumerables desengaños con que reprimió los vagos vuelos e intrépida lozanía de la mente, y la facilidad de adoptar por verdad lo que no lo es; entonces confesará Europa que no el amor de la patria, sino el de la razón, me hace ver en Vives una gloriosa superioridad sobre todos los sabios de todos los siglos.[305]

. . . .

Por qué mi España, mi sabia España, no ostenta en la Capital de su Monarquía estátuas, obeliscos eternos que recuerden sin intermisión el nombre de este ilustre reformador de la sabiduría?[306]

Zamora, Antonio de (?-c.1740)
In the procession with the dramatic poets.[307]
Zárate, Agustín de (1. 16th cent.)
Forner alludes to this author's work entitled *Historia del Perú*. In the dispute which takes place in Parnassus, Forner presents him as opposed to Raynal's views on the Spanish conquests.[308]
Zurita y Castro, Jerónimo (1512-1580)
Early Spanish historian who helped to enrich the Spanish language.[309]

---

[303] *Exequias*, p. 192.
[304] *Oración apologética*, p. 143.
[305] *Ibid.*, pp. 145-46.
[306] *Ibid.*, p. 143.
[307] *Exequias*, p. 242; see Guillén de Castro, Appendix II, p. 139.
[308] *Exequias*, p. 232.
[309] *Ibid.*, p. 128; see Esteban de Garibay, Appendix II, p. 144.

Appendix II

He walked in the procession to the right of Mariana, which fact indicates Forner's esteem of him and explains his writing of him as follows:

> *Jerónimo de Zurita,* más sencillo, más natural, de menor artificio en el decir y en el disponer, pero diligente, exacto, ingenuo, y más atento a la sustancia de las cosas que a los accidentes del arte, que descuidó a pesar de las instancias de su íntimo amigo y censor Don Antonio Agustín.[210]

Another reference to Zurita's simplicity of style is contained in the following comment: "...aquél en quien domine el ingenio, aunque lo solicite, no podrá ceñirse jamás...a la naturalidad sencilla de Zurita."[211]

La Celestina

Without specific reference to the author of *Celestina,* Forner remarks that the procession of the dramatists came to an end with the author and continuator of *Celestina.*[212]

---

[210] *Exequias,* p. 252.
[211] *Ibid.,* p. 135.
[212] *Ibid.,* p. 243.

FRENCH AUTHORS

Alembert, Jean le Rond d' (1717-1783)

Forner notes that while d'Alembert regards the censuring of books as an interference with man's reason and freedom, there are other Frenchmen just as learned as d'Alembert who see in this freedom a miserable license of reason.[1]

Alexandre, Noël (1639-1724)

Forner speaks of him as a man of great veracity and of his *Historia ecclesiástica* as a valuable source for information on the University of Paris in the Middle Ages.[2]

Barbeyrac, Jean (1674-1744)

In the allegory, Forner has him defend the Spanish conquest, against Las Casas.[3]

Bayle, Pierre (1647-1706)

Forner places Bayle in the same class with Rousseau, Helvetius, and Voltaire, remarking that the libraries in Spain are not less excellent without the works of "un Baile, patrono y orador de cuanto se ha delirado con título de filosofía."[4]

Boileau Despreaux, Nicolas (1636-1711)

In advising Forner concerning the writing of poetry, Arcadio tells him that it will be useless for him to expect to bring about reforms and that the favor which Horace and Despreaux won will not be his.[5]

Bossuet, Jacques-Bénigne (1627-1704)

His preaching according to Forner was "excelente, alta, maravillosa."[6]

Bouhours, Dominique (1628-1702)

Forner refers to this French grammarian and purist when he has Villegas praise the Spanish language as the best instrument of expression that Europe knows, "diga lo que quiera el francés Bohours."[7]

Bourdaloue, Louis (1632-1704)

Forner groups him with Bossuet and Massillon, applying the same terms to his preaching.[8]

---

[1] *Oración apologética*, p. 154; see Vives, Appendix II, p. 173.

[2] *Oración apologética*, p. 161.

[3] *Exequias*, p. 230.

[4] *Oración apologética*, p. 22.

[5] *Exequias*, p. 77.

[6] *Ibid.*, p. 155.

[7] *Ibid.*, p. 147.

[8] *Ibid.*, p. 155.

Appendix II 177

Caraccioli, Louis-Antoine (1721-1803)

Forner refers to Nifo's translations of some works by this author.[9]

Corneille, Pierre (1606-1684)

When showing the importance of the drama, Forner makes the following reference to the *Cid:*

> No ha habido ni hay pueblo sabio, cuyos primeros pasos hacia la sabiduría no hayan empezado por la poesía dramática... Francia no empezó a ser sabia hasta después que vió representar el *Cid.*[10]

Descartes, René (1596-1650)

Forner says that while there are those who consider Descartes to be the idol of philosophy, he was "indubitablemente menos que Aristóteles, y que valió al poco más o menos tanto como un Zenón o como un Demócrito."[11] As regards his *Discours de la méthode,* Forner thinks it to be nothing in comparison with Vives' *De la corrupción de las artes* which was written many years before Descartes' work.[12] Apparently, Forner recognized the fact that Descartes had a great mind since he remarks that, in reality, he was no more than a Lulio, born in better times.[13] He considers the French philosopher far inferior to Ramón Sabunde.[14] He is happy that Spain did not increase the catalog of celebrated dreamers with a Cartesian.[15]

Dupin, Louis-Ellies (1657-1719)

Referring to the *Bibliothèque universelle des auteurs ecclésiastiques* of Dupin, Forner remarks that this author's judgments of Vives are the most ignorant of all. It is his opinion that Dupin never read Vives' works or did so only in a cursory manner and with a prejudiced mind.[16]

Gassendi, Pierre (1592-1655)

Forner mentions his *Exercitationes paradoxicae adversus Aristoteleos, Lib. I,* as a good literary history of the Middle Ages.[17]

Genlis, Stéphanie-Felicité du Crest de Saint Aubin, Comtesse de (1746-1830)

In his allegory Forner has the works of this French poet and novelist used as wicks for the pyre.[18]

---

[9] *Exequias,* p. 272; see Nifo, Appendix II, p. 158.

[10] *Exequias,* pp. 180-181.

[11] *Oración apologética,* p. xii; for further comment see Vives, Appendix II, p. 172.

[12] *Oración apologética,* p. xi; for further comment see Vives, Appendix II, p. 173.

[13] *Oración apologética,* p. 202.

[14] *Ibid.,* p. 206; see Sabunde, Appendix II, p. 165.

[15] *Oración apologética,* p. 12.

[16] *Ibid.,* pp. 210-211.

[17] *Ibid.,* p. 159.

[18] *Exequias,* p. 262.

178 *Appendix II*

Goudin, Antoine (1639-1695)

Forner alludes to Goudin's book on philosophy, showing that the work had been used a great deal in the early part of the century.[19]

Helvétius, Claude-Adrien (1715-1771)

It is Forner's opinion that the libraries in Spain are not less excellent because they do not possess the works of "un Helvetius, que colocó en la obscena sensualidad los incitamentos del heroísmo, y extrañó la virtud de entre los mortales."[20] He points to him as one of the leaders of the group of writers who possessed little fundamental knowledge and spoke of everything in a superficial way.[21]

Huet, Pierre-Daniel (1630-1721)

Forner recommends the reading of this author's *Censure de la philosophie cartésienne* for a better understanding of Cartesianism.[22]

Launoy, Jean (1603-1678)

Forner speaks of him as a man of great veracity and refers to his *De varia Aristotelis fortuna in Academia Parisina* as a good source of information on the University of Paris in the Middle Ages.[23]

Massillon, Jean-Baptiste (1663-1742)

Forner speaks of his preaching as "excelente, alta, marvillosa."[24]

Masson de Morvilliers, Nicolas (c.1740-1789)

Forner calls him the "inexorable Massón"[25] and condemns him for his malign ignorance in thinking that Europe owes nothing to the Spaniards.[26] Forner describes Masson's ideas of cultured nations as those in which

> ...se haga particular mérito de las ficciones sistemáticas: a aquéllas en que las investigaciones del entendimiento sirvan del la mayor parte para embelesarnos, no mejorarnos o socorrernos: a aquéllas en que la administración pública corra a cuenta del ciudadano imperito, empleándose en tanto los Filósofos en formar estados y legislaciones fútiles, imposibles de reducirse a la ejecución: aquéllas, en fin, en que, puesto que haya mayor número de libros, sistemas, opiniones, bullicio y hervor ardientísimo en el cultivo y fomento de algunas ciencias, no por eso se logre mejor legislación, mejores costumbres, juicio más recto, virtudes más desinteresadas, constitución más feliz para lo general del cuerpo político.[27]

---

[19] *Ibid.*, pp. 168-69.

[20] *Oración apologética*, p. 22.

[21] *Ibid.*, p. 8.

[22] *Ibid.*, pp. 205-207; see Ramón Sabunde, Appendix II, p. 165.

[23] *Ibid.*, p. 161.

[24] *Exequias*, p. 155.

[25] *Oración apologética*, p. xv.

[26] *Ibid.*, p. 72.

[27] *Ibid.*, pp. 72-73.

Appendix II 179

Montesquieu, Charles de Secondat, Baron de (1689-1755)

Forner questions his ideas on government, as is seen in the following apostrophe:

> Grave Platón, sutil Aristóteles, y tú no sé si digno de acompañarte con ellos, fastidiosamente ponderado Montesquieu, ¿a qué estados de los que hoy existen podrán aplicarse vuestras meditaciones, de tal suerte que perpetuamente produzcan el bien a que decís que las encamináis?[28]

Rapin, René (1621-1687)

Forner shows his lack of esteem for this author's *Réflexions sur la Poétique d'Aristote et sur les ouvrages des poètes anciens et modernes* by using the work as a wick to light the pyre.[29]

Raynal, Guillaume-Thomas-François (1713-1796)

Forner expresses his condemnation of this author and his *Histoire des Deux Indes* by having Quevedo, Fernández de Oviedo, López de Gomara, Zárate and Bernal Díaz rail against him in Parnassus, speaking of him as "un soñador francés, que no conocía el mundo sino en el mapa."[30] Through a bitter argument carried on between Raynal with his supporters and Bernal Díaz with his ardent supporters of the Spanish conquistadores, he condemns Raynal's attitude toward the Spanish colonizers.[31]

Rousseau, Jean-Jacques (1712-1778)

Forner has no respect whatever for Rousseau. He mentions him along with Voltaire and Helvétius, as a man who was slightly learned in the fundamentals of science and concealed his ignorance under irony.[32] In Forner's opinion the libraries in Spain have lost nothing in not possessing the works of a "Rousseau que solicitó inutilizar la razón, reduciendo al estado de bestia al que nació para hombre."[33] Comparing the educational documents of Quintilian with the educational theories of Rousseau, Forner expresses the wish that the prudent documents of Quintilian were more admired and better received than the extravagant dreams of the maniac, Rousseau. He regrets that there are people who apply the term "philosophy" to Rousseau's "delirios" and fail to recognize the great genius of one who teaches the manner of making good citizens.[34] Probably with the idea of substantiating his antagonism toward Rousseau, he quotes from a letter which Walpole wrote to Hume, declaring himself the author of a

---

[28] *Ibid.*, p. 31.

[29] *Exequias*, p. 262.

[30] *Ibid.*, p. 232.

[31] *Ibid.*, pp. 230-39.

[32] *Oración apologética*, p. 8.

[33] *Ibid.*, p. 22.

[34] *Ibid.*, p. 119.

180 *Appendix II*

satire against Rousseau: *"Todos los talentos del mundo* (le deciá) *no me impedirán reirme del que los posee, si con todos sus talentos no veo en él más que un charlatán."*[85]

Voltaire (Arouet, Francois Marie) (1694-1778)

Forner classes Voltaire with Helvétius and Rousseau and the sophists who, though lacking in the fundamentals of the sciences, introduced the new and convenient art of speaking entirely by caprice.[86] He refers to him as the "extravagante Voltaire" who set the example and led the way for the group which Forner addresses as "sofistas malignos, ignorantes de los mismos principios de la filosofía que tanto os jactáis profesar."[87] It would seem that Forner makes Voltaire indirectly responsible for the calumnies hurled against Spain and the Catholic religion. He asserts that men who knew nothing of Spain turned not to reliable sources, but to fiction, and manufactured "fábulas" and "novelas" that were as absurd as those of the ancient "escritores de caballerías." Subjecting their knowledge to vain glory, setting up a few sentences that hinted at their philosophy, they considered their few phrases and witticisms sufficient to compensate for their ignorance and their lack of study. Voltaire did this, Forner says. He points out that Voltaire wrote a "fábula" in his *Ensayo sobre la historia universal* and that his learned followers then had to divide the general map and write fables for each province. The French, he notes, invented them about the Italians, and the Italians about the French. Then forgetting their disesteem for one another, they wrote about Spain.

> ...se unen entre sí, y se abalanzan a ella, no de otro modo que los jactanciosos jefes de la moderna incredulidad, combatiéndose motejándose, y viviendo en continua guerra unos con otros por la discordia en las opiniones y por la ambición de la primacía, se unen sólo cuando se trata de impugnar la verdad en la más santa y más magnífica de todas las religiones.[88]

It is Forner's belief that the libraries in Spain are not less excellent in not possessing the works of a "Voltaire, gran maestro de sofistería y malignidad, que vivió sin patria, murió sin religión, y se ignora en todo que creyó o dejó de creer."[89] He regrets that Voltaire is held in such esteem by his contemporaries. On this point, he writes, "...según la recta y consecuente lógica de nuestros tiempos habrá gentes que consagrarán el nombre de Voltaire, pertinacísimo escarnecedor del Cristianismo, en bien

---

[85] *Ibid.,* p. x.

[86] *Ibid.,* pp. 7-8.

[87] *Ibid.,* p. 18.

[88] *Ibid.,* pp. 11-12.

[89] *Ibid.,* p. 22.

Appendix II   181

ridículas apoteosis."[40] He recognizes Voltaire's abilities, but condemns the use to which he put them.

> ¿Qué utilidad ha traído a los hombres toda la agudeza y buen gusto de un Voltaire, si toda aquella agudeza y buen gusto se empleó en sobreponer apariencias artificiosas a los sofismas, y en escarnecer, no mejorar a sus semejantes?[41]

[40] *Ibid.,* p. 130.
[41] *Ibid.,* p. x.

ITALIAN AUTHORS

Ariosto, Ludovico (1474-1533)
Restored to the stage the ancient Greek magnificence.[1]
Caro, Annibale (1507-1566)
Forner speaks of the "pureza de *Annibal Caro.*"[2]
Chiabrera, Gabriel (1552-1638)
Mention is made of the "sublimidad de *Chiabrera.*"[3]
Machiavelli, Nicolò di Bernardo (1469-1527)
Restored to the state the ancient Greek magnificence which had been lost for seven centuries.[4]
Muratori, Ludovico Antonio (1672-1750)
Forner shows his attitude toward Muratori by having Arcadio describe his condemnation which took place in Parnassus when Isocrates, Lycias, Aeschines, Hortensius, Pliny the Younger, and other Greek and Roman authors called him to task for belittling the value and use of Greek and Roman oratory in modern tribunals of justice.[5]
Tasso, Torquato (1544-1595)
Tasso restored to the stage the ancient Greek magnificence which had been lost for seven centuries.[6] Forner considers him an epic poet of the rank of Homer and Virgil.[7] It is of interest to note that the author does not forget the insanity ascribed to Tasso, and places him with Lucretius and other "locos" in Parnassus.[8]
Tiraboschi, Girolamo (1731-1794)
Forner asks why this author goes out from his prudent Italy to look for corrupters of Latin taste.[9]
Trissino, Gian Giorgio (1478-1550)
Trissino, Ariosto, Machiavelli, and ·Tasso brought back to the stage the ancient Greek magnificence which had been lost in darkness and barbarity for seven centuries.[10]

---

[1] *Exequias,* p. 181.

[2] *Exequias,* p. 133.

[3] *Ibid.,* p. 133.

[4] *Ibid.,* p. 181.

[5] *Exequias,* pp. 199-202.

[6] *Ibid.,* p. 181.

[7] *Ibid.,* p. 246.

[8] *Exequias,* p. 136.

[9] *Oración apolgética,* p. 109.

[10] *Exequias,* p. 181.

ENGLISH AUTHORS

Bacon, Francis (1561-1626)

It was Forner's belief that Bacon and Vives were the only men capable of appraising the wisdom of nations,[1] because they were the only ones who recognized the intrinsic merit and the real value of "la sabiduría." The author maintains, however, that Vives led the way for Bacon.[2] He comments at considerable length on the value of the "tópica," invented by Aristotle, and makes the point that the moderns while bitterly detesting the "tópicas" of Aristotle,[3] lavishly praise the *Novum Organum* of Bacon, although it is written after the manner of Aristotle's *Organon*.

> . . . arte tópico particular o un agregado de lugares comunes, que señalan las sendas por donde se debe ir al examen de la naturaleza, así como la *Tópica de Aristóteles* es un conjunto de notas a asientos generales para hallar pruebas en la confirmación de los argumentos, donde no tiene cabida la demostración evidente, y que si aquel buen viejo no se hubiera tomado el trabajo de inventar el artificio y uso de los tópicas, es muy probable que no existiese hoy este *Nuevo Organo,* que tanto ruido ha hecho.[4]

Bacon, Roger (1214-1294)

Forner's reference to him is made in connection with Ramón Lull, who, he remarks, is a singular genius, not inferior to Roger Bacon.[5]

Newton, Isaac (1624-1727)

Forner says he will grant that Spain has not had a Descartes or a Newton; but it is manifest that he considers this no loss.[6] In his opinion it would have been easier for Newton and Descartes to find their worlds without mathematics than it would have been for Magellan to find the famous strait without it.[7] He points out also that Newton contributed no more to humanity than did the Spanish doctor, Luis Mercado.[8]

Robertson, William (1721-1793)

Named in the allegory as a supporter of the views of Las Casas.[9]

---

[1] *Oración apologética,* pp. 6-7.

[2] *Ibid.,* pp. 143-44.

[3] Forner attributes the opposition of the moderns against the "tópica," to their antagonism toward anything belonging to antiquity and to their hatred of the Scholastics who always included the teaching of the "tópica" in their studies *(Oración apologética,* p. 216).

[4] *Ibid.,* pp. 143-44.

[5] *Ibid.,* p. 200; see Ramón Lull, Appendix II, p. 162.

[6] *Oración apologética,* p. 12.

[7] *Ibid.,* p. 99.

[8] *Ibid.,* p. 222.

[9] *Exequias,* p. 231; see Las Casas, Appendix II, p. 151.

LATIN AUTHORS

Albucius, Silius Caius (fl. in reign of Augustus)

Forner mentions this orator when speaking of the philosophizing found in the French eloquence of his time.

> ...es fastidiosa y ridícula la ostentación afectada de la filosofía en los artes de imitación...razón que hace frigidísima para mí, muy cansada y muy árida, la moderna elocuencia de los franceses, al modo que lo eran para los romanos las declamaciones de *Albucio,* por su importuno e impestivo filosofar.[1]

Cicero, Marcus Tullius (106 B.C.-43 B.C.)

Cicero was the only orator, according to Forner, who could worthily imitate a Demosthenes.[2] When speaking of the imitation of authors, Forner notes that Cicero surpassed Crassus because he was not a slavish imitator of the latter's works, but rather, an emulator.[3] Referring to Cicero's *Brutus,* Forner writes,

> Quien lea el libro de *Cicerón,* intitulado *Bruto,* hallará un buen número de oradores desemejantes entre sí, pero laudables los más de ellos en la diversidad misma de los caracteres de su elocuencia, aun cuando Roma se desdeñaba de ser discípula de Grecia.[4]

In setting forth his views on translating as an art, Forner refers to Cicero as an authority in this matter, remarking: "Cicerón dijo de sí que se propuso traducir las dos famosas oraciones de *Esquines* y *Demóstenes,* no como intérprete, sino como orador."[5] In praise also of Cicero's power, he remarks that in the works of Cicero, appear "la magnificencia de un pueblo que acaba de sojuzgar al orbe."[6] To show further Cicero's importance, he pictures him with Quintilian in Parnassus condemning Feijóo for the octosyllabic verse in his work,[7] making fun of his Latin,[8] and showing him the need of artificial aids to make the understanding function properly.[9]

---

[1] *Exequias,* pp. 169-70.

[2] *Ibid.,* p. 156.

[3] *Ibid.,* pp. 108, 163.

[4] *Ibid.,* p. 162.

[5] *Ibid.,* pp. 228, 108.

[6] *Ibid.,* p. 128.

[7] *Ibid.,* p. 192.

[8] *Ibid.,* p. 189.

[9] *Ibid.,* p. 190.

Appendix II

Cornelius Nepos (1st cent. B.C.)

An allusion is made to Nepos when a modern "sabio" in Parnassus displays his ignorance of him by boasting of being a better philosopher than the great Roman.[10]

Crassus (Lucius Licinius Crassus) (140 B.C.-91 B.C.)

Was surpassed by Cicero.[11]

Ennius, Quintus (239 B.C.-169 B.C.)

Was surpassed by Virgil.[12]

Horace (Quintus Horatius Flaccus) (65 B.C.-8 B.C.)

Horace's name is also linked with that of Cicero, Livy and Virgil, who, Forner claims, were responsible for bringing Latin eloquence to a place where it could not be surpassed.[13]

Juvenal (Decimus Junius Juvenalis) (47 B.C.-127 A.D.?)

Forner refers to the "cólera" of Juvenal.[14]

Lactantius (Lucius Caecilius Firmianus) (e. 4th century-340?)

In his effort to explain the proper way to study the masters, Forner asks the question: "¿Cómo hubiera *Lactancio* impugnado tan elocuentemente la filosofía de *Cicerón*, sin haber antes estudiado muy a propósito la elocuencia de los libros filosóficos de Cicerón?"[15]

Livy (Titus Livius) (59 B.C.-17 A.D.)

He is designated by Forner as a model historian.[16] In the works of Livy appear the "magnificencia de un pueblo que acaba de sojuzgar al orbe."[17] His name is linked with that of Cicero, Horace, and Virgil for his part in the development of Roman eloquence.[18]

Lucretius (Titus Lucretius Carus) (94 B.C.?-53 B.C.)

Forner points out that whereas the fastidious grammarians prefer Lucretius to Lucan, he would give the preference to Lucan. In his opinion, Lucretius is an historian of nature and Lucan, an historian of a civil war. Lucretius sings of dreams, fables, and fiction which he takes from a mad, impious school; but he sings of all as truth, of which he wishes to persuade men, "y con todo es Poeta, y admirable Poeta."[19] Lucan, on the other hand, sings of the real lot of those engaged in a civil war. He exposes the horrors of it

---

[10] *Ibid.*, p. 98.

[11] *Ibid.*, p. 163.

[12] *Ibid.*

[13] *Ibid.*, p. 261.

[14] *Ibid.*, p. 76.

[15] *Ibid.*, p. 168.

[16] *Ibid.*, p. 152.

[17] *Ibid.*, p. 128.

[18] *Ibid.*, p. 261.

[19] *Oración apologética*, p. 114.

186 · *Appendix II*

and traces in valiant style the evils of ambition so that he may correct posterity by the pitiable example.[20] Again, Forner writes,

> Lucrecio fué más elegante que Lucano pero Lucano inspira más virtud que Lucrecio en aquel su estilo hueco e imeptuoso. He aquí el mérito sólido y real por más que no sea el más fino.[21]

When speaking of the imitation of authors, Forner remarks that Lucretius was excelled by Virgil.[22]

It is interesting to note that he manages to make reference to the supposed insanity of Lucretius by placing him with a group of "locos" in Parnassus.[23]

Mela, Pomponius (1st cent. A.D.)

Forner alludes to Mela's geographical work.[24]

Ovid (Publius Ovidius Naso) (43 B.C.-17 or 18 A.D.)

Forner speaks of him as the "fácil y blando Ovidio."[25] Forner alludes to the *Fasti* of this author by having a modern "sabio" in Parnassus display his ignorance as he boasts of his knowledge of the "poems sobre el *fausto*."[26]

Persius (Aulus Persius Flaccus) (34-62)

Forner refers only to his "severidades."[27]

Plautus, Titus Maccius (c. 254 B.C.-184 B.C.)

Because he believes that dramatic poetry marks the first step towards the wisdom of a nation, Forner says that Plautus and Terence opened the way to Roman culture.[28]

Pliny the Elder (Caius Plinius Secundus) (23-79)

Forner alludes probably to Pliny's *Historia Naturalis* as a source book.[29]

Sallust (Caius Sallustius Crispus) (86 B.C.-34 B.C.)

Referred to as an historian of note. In his works appears the "magnificencia de un pueblo que acaba de sojuzgar al orbe."[30]

Tacitus (Publius Cornelius Tacitus) (bet. 54 and 57 B.C.-?)

Referred to as an historian of note.[31] Forner believes that the *Annales* of Tacitus could have been published only in the reign of Trajan, for his

---

[20] *Ibid.,* pp. 114-15.
[21] *Ibid.,* p. ix.
[22] *Exequias,* p. 163.
[23] *Ibid.,* p. 136.
[24] *Ibid.,* p. 86.
[25] *Ibid.,* p. 121.
[26] *Ibid.,* p. 98.
[27] *Ibid.,* p. 76.
[28] *Ibid.,* p. 180.
[29] *Ibid.,* p. 86.
[30] *Ibid.,* pp. 128, 152.
[31] *Ibid.,* p. 152.

Appendix II 187

ability and knowledge would have brought him to the gibbet under Nero or Caligula.[83]

Terence (Publius Terentius Afer) (185 B.C.-159 B.C.)

Terence and Plautus, Forner says, opened the way to Roman culture.[83]

Virgil (Publius Virgilius Maro) (70 B.C.-19 B.C.)

In speaking of imitation, Forner praises Virgil's skill in copying Homer, although he copies some of his defects, for Virgil, he says, increases the divinity of the great deity, the father of poetry.[84] Again commenting on the matter of imitation, Forner writes: "Para expresar la sublimidad de un Homero es menester no menos que la grandeza de un Virgilio."[85] Forner says Virgil excelled Ennius, Lucretius, and Hesiod because he was an emulator and not a slavish imitator.[86] The modern writers, he remarks, are so attached to their petty rules that they will accuse Virgil of being a "solecista."[87] He remarks too that Virgil together with Cicero, Livy, and Horace brought Latin eloquence to a point where it could not be surpassed.[88]

To support his view that poets can write poetry about real facts, he remarks that in the sixth and eighth books of the Aeneid, Virgil sings of facts, and in the rest, of fiction.[89] He alludes again to the Aeneid by having one of the modern "sabios" show his ignorance of the great work by boasting that he knew the author of the "Eneidas."[40]

---

[83] *Oración apologética*, p. 120.
[83] *Exequias*, p. 180; see Plautus, Appendix II, p. 186.
[84] *Oración apologética*, p. 117.
[85] *Exequias*, p. 156.
[30] *Ibid.*, p. 163.
[87] *Ibid.*, p. 145.
[88] *Ibid.*, p. 261.
[39] *Oración apologética*, p. 113.
[40] *Exequias*, p. 98.

GREEK AUTHORS

Aeschines (399 or 389 B. C.-314 B. C.)

Forner names as a model translation Cicero's version of Aeschines' oration against Ctesiphon.[1]

Anacreon (599 B. C.-c.478 B. C.)

Forner speaks of him as the "dulce Anacreonte";[2] also, as the "dulce y alegre Anacreonte."[3]

Aristotle (384 B. C.-322 B. C.)

The author refers to him as "sutil Aristóteles"[4] and again as the "grande Aristóteles," the inventor of the "artes analítica y tópica."[5] Forner regrets that this work of the Stagirite was not appreciated by so many of the moderns, for without Aristotle's *Tópica* Bacon's *Novum Organum* would never have existed.[6]

In his effort to show that dramatic poetry in every nation has always marked the first step towards wisdom, Forner remarks that Aristotle did not reduce poetry to art until many years after the immortal works of Sophocles, Euripides, and Menander had been seen in the theatres of Athens.[7]

Satirizing the "reglitas modernas," he speaks of "todas las ridiculas menudencias del pobrete Aristóteles."[8]

Cratylus (younger than Socrates)

Was surpassed by Plato.[9]

Democritus (bet. 480 B. C. and 460 B. C.-?)

According to Forner, he was nothing more than a "gran sistemático."[10]

Demosthenes (384 B. C.-322 B. C.)

Demosthenes was such a great orator that only a Cicero could worthily imitate him.[11] With Demosthenes, Homer, and Plato, Greek eloquence was brought to such a climax that it could not be surpassed.[12]

---

[1] *Exequias,* p. 108; see Cicero, Appendix II, p. 184.

[2] *Exequias,* p. 121.

[3] *Ibid.,* p. 130.

[4] *Oración apologética,* p. 31.

[5] *Exequias,* p. 191.

[6] *Ibid.,* pp. 191-192.

[7] *Ibid.,* p. 180.

[8] *Ibid.,* p. 75.

[9] *Ibid.,* p. 163.

[10] *Oración apologética,* p. 67.

[11] *Exequias,* p. 156; see Cicero, Appendix II, p. 184.

[12] *Exequias,* p. 261.

Appendix II 189

Epicurus (341 or 342 B. C.-370 B. C.)

Forner asks of what use to mankind are the Atoms of Epicurus.[18]

Euripides (480 B. C.-406 or 405 B. C.)

Forner speaks of the immortal works of Euripides,[14] as also of his "grandeza de la locución."[15]

Herodotus (c.484 B. C.-c.425)

Forner remarks that the history written in the eighteenth century in Spain would never have passed for history in the days when Herodotus, Xenophon, Thucydides, Livy, Sallust, and Tacitus were read.[16]

Hesiod (fl. in 9th cent. B. C.)

Was surpassed by Vergil, because the latter knew how to imitate.[17]

Homer (9th or 10th cent. B.C.)

Forner speaks of him as the "father of poetry."[18] In praise of him, he writes: "Para expresar la sublimidad de un *Homero*, es menester no menos que la grandeza de un Virgilio,"[19] and again, "La elocuencia griega no pudo pasar más allá de los términos adonde la llevaron *Homero, Platón* y *Demóstenes.*"[20]

Menander (340 B.C.-c.292 B.C.)

Mention is made of his "inmortales obras."[21]

Moschus (fl. c. 200 B.C.)

Referred to as a model bucolic poet.[22]

Pindar (522 B.C.-443 or 441 B.C.)

The author speaks of the "lira" of Pindar.[23]

Plato (428 B.C.?-317 B.C.?)

Forner speaks of him as the "grave Platón."[24] He questions the utility of some of his ideas,[25] especially, the practicality of his theories on government.[26] He would excuse Plato's failure to form men because he considers his intentions good. According to Forner, Plato thought that by developing the intellect of man he would accomplish his aim; but by giving too much attention to the training of the intellect, he failed.[27]

---

[18] *Oración apologética,* p. 2.

[14] *Exequias,* p. 180.

[15] *Ibid.,* p. 119.

[16] *Exequias,* p. 152.

[17] *Ibid.,* p. 163.

[18] *Oración apologética,* p. 117.

[19] *Exequias,* p. 156; see Virgil, Appendix II, p. 187.

[20] *Exequias,* p. 261.

[21] *Ibid.,* p. 180.

[22] *Ibid.,* p. 246.

[23] *Ibid.,* p. 78.

[24] *Oración apologética,* p. 31.

[25] *Ibid.,* p. 2.

[26] *Ibid.,* p. 31.

[27] *Ibid.,* p. 82.

190   *Appendix II*

Forner pays special honor to Plato when he writes: "La elocuencia griega no pudo pasar más allá de los términòs adonde la llevaron Homero, Platón y Demóstenes.[28] In speaking of the matter of imitation, Forner remarks that Plato excelled Cratylus because he was an emulator and not a slavish imitator.[29]

Sophocles (497 or 495 B.C.-406 or 405 B.C.)

Forner speaks of the immortal works of Sophocles,[30] and refers to the grandeur of his diction.[31]

Strabo (middle 1st century B.C.?-20 A.D.?)

Forner alludes to him as an authority on geography.[32]

Theocritus (end of 4th century B.C.-?)

When speaking on pastoral poetry Arcadio names Theocritus as the master.[33]

Thucydides (c. 460 B.C.-398 B.C.)

Through the remarks of Arcadio, Forner praises Thucydides as an historian.[34]

Xenophon (c. 430 B.C.-after 355 B.C.)

Forner likewise shows his esteem for Xenophon as a great historian.[35]

Zeno of Citium (336 or 335-264 or 263)

In the allegory, Forner has him defend the Spanish conquest of the New World, according to the principles of his philosophy.[36]

---

[28] *Exequias*, p. 261.

[29] *Ibid.*, p. 163.

[30] *Ibid.*, p. 180.

[31] *Ibid.*, p. 119.

[32] *Ibid.*, p. 86.

[33] *Ibid.*, pp. 77, 260.

[34] *Ibid.*, p. 152; see Herodotus, Appendix II, p. 189.

[35] *Exequias*, p. 152; see also Herodotus, Appendix II, p. 189.

[36] *Exequias*, p. 230; see Ginés de Sepúlveda, Appendix II, p. 166.

BIBLIOGRAPHY

Adler, Mortimer J. *Art and Prudence.* New York: Longmans, 1937.

Alonso Cortés, Narciso. "El siglo XVIII." *Historia de la literatura española.* 2. ed. Valladolid: Imprenta castellana, 1935.

Babbitt, Irving. *Rousseau and Romanticism.* Boston: Houghton Mifflin, 1919.

Bertrand, Louis, and Petrie, Sir Charles. *The History of Spain.* New York: Appleton-Century, 1937. Pp. 405-35.

Boak, Arthur, Hyma, Albert, and Slosson, Preston. *The Growth of European Civilization.* New York: Crofts, 1938.

Bonilla y San Martín, Adolfo. *Luis Vives y la filosofía del renacimiento.* Madrid. Rubio, 1929.

Brou, A. *Le dix-huitième siècle littéraire.* Vol. II. 2. ed. Paris: Téqui, 1925.

Brunetière, Ferdinand. *Histoire de la littérature française classique.* Vol. III. Paris: Delagrave, 1913.

Bruun, Geoffrey. *The Enlightened Despots.* New York: Holt, 1929.

Butler, Kathleen T. *A History of French Literature.* Vol. I. London: Methuen, 1923.

Castro, Américo. "Algunos aspectos del siglo XVIII." *Lengua, eseñanza y literaria.* Madrid: Suárez, 1924.

Cejador y Frauca, Julio. *Historia de la lengua y literatura castellana.* Vol. VI. Madrid: Tip. de la "Rev. de arch., bibl., y museos," 1915-22.

Chapman, Percy A. and Others. *An Anthology of Eighteenth Century French Literature.* Princeton: Princeton University Press, 1930.

Colford, William E. *Juan Meléndez Valdés.* New York: Hispanic Institute, 1942.

Cotarelo y Mori, Emilio. *Iriarte y su época.* Madrid. Rivadeneyra, 1897.

Cueto, Leopoldo Augusto de, Marqués de Valmar. "Bosquejo histórico-crítico de la poesía castellana en el siglo XVIII," *Poetas líricos del siglo XVIII,* I. Madrid: Sucesores de Hernando, 1921. (Biblioteca de autores españoles. Vol. LXI.)

————. *Poetas líricos del siglo XVIII.* Vol. I. Madrid: Sucesores de Hernando, 1921. Vols. II-III. Rivadeneyra, 1871-1875. (Biblioteca de autores españoles. Vols. LXI, LXIII, LXVII.)

Delpy, Gaspard. *L'Espagne et l'esprit européen. L'oeuvre de Feijóo (1725-1760).* Paris: Hachette, 1936.

Denina, Carlo. "Réponse a la question, Que doit-on à l'Espagne? Discours lu a l'Académie de Berlin dans l'assemblée publique du 26 janvier l'an 1786 pour le jour anniversaire du roi." Appendix in Forner's *Oración apologética.* Madrid: Imprenta Real, 1786.

192 *Bibliography*

Desdevises du Dezert, V. G. "La société espagnole au XVIIIᵉ siècle." *Revue Hispanique*, LXIV (1925), 255-654.

———. "La richesse et la civilisation espagnoles au XVIIIᵉ siècle." *Revue Hispanique*, LXXIII (1928), 1-488.

Dubray, Charles Albert. *Introductory Philosophy*. New York: Longmans, 1920.

Enciclopedia universal ilustrada europeo-americana. Barcelona: Espasa-Calpe, 1907?-30. 70 vols. in 72.

Eyre, Edward. *European Civilization, Its Origin and Development*. Vol. VI. New York: Oxford University Press, 1937.

Faguet, Émile. *Études littéraires*. Vol. III. Paris: Société française d'imprimerie et de librairie (Ancienne maison, Lecène, Oudin, 1890.

Fernández y González, Francisco.. *Historia de la crítica literaria en España desde Luzán hasta nuestros días con exclusión de los autores que aun viven.* Madrid. Gómez Fuentenebro, 1867.

Folkierski, Wladyslaw. *Entre le classicisme et le romantisme.* Paris: Champion, 1925.

Forner, Juan Pablo. "Carta de Don Juan Pablo Forner a Don Ignacio López de Ayala." Cueto, *Poetas líricos del siglo XVIII*. Vol. II. Madrid: Rivadeneyra, 1871.

———. "Contestación al Discurso CXIII del Censor." Appendix in Forner's *Oración apologética*. Madrid: Imprenta Real, 1786.

———. "Discursos filosóficos." Cueto, *Poetas líricos del siglo XVIII*. Vol. II. Madrid: Rivadeneyra, 1871.

———. *Exequias de la lengua castellana.* Edición y notas de Pedro Sainz y Rodríguez. Madrid: La Lectura, 1925.

———. "Exequias de la lengua castellana." Cueto, *Poetas líricos del siglo XVIII*. Vol. II. Madrid: Rivadeneyra, 1871.

———. "Noticia del licenciado Pablo Ignocausto y razón de la obra, todo en un pieza." *Exequias de la lengua castellana.* Madrid: La Lectura, 1925.

———. *Oración apologética por la España y su mérito literario: para que sirva de exornación al discurso leído por el abate Denina en la Academia de Ciencias de Berlin, respondiendo a la questión ¿Que se debe a España?* Madrid: Imprenta Real, 1786.

———. "Sátira contra los vicios introducidos en la poesía castellana." Cueto, *Poetas líricos del siglo XVIII*. Vol. II. Madrid: Rivadeneyra, 1871.

Gaudeau, Le P. Bernard. *Les prêcheurs burlesques en Espagne au XVIIIᵉ siècle:* Étude sur le P. Isla. Paris: Retaux-Bray, 1891.

González-Blanco, Andrés. "Ensayo sobre un crítico español del siglo XVIII." *Nuestro Tiempo*, XVII (1917), 157-170.

González Palencia, Angel. *The Flame of Hispanicism.* (An Address given at Stanford University, 1938.) New York: Peninsular News Service, n.d.

Havens, George R. *Selections from Voltaire*. New York: Century, 1925.

Bibliography 193

Hayes, Carlton J. H. "The Intellectual Revolution." *A Political and Cultural History of Modern Europe.* Vol. I. New York: Macmillan, 1932.

Honegger, Johann Jakob. *Kritische Geschichte der fransösischen Cultureinflusse in den letzten Jahrhunderten.* Berlin: Oppenheim, 1875.

Hurtado y Jiménez de la Serna, Juan, y González Palencia, Angel. *Historia de la literatura española.* 3. ed. Madrid: Tip. de la "Revista de arch., bibl., y museos," 1932.

Isla, El P. José Francisco. *Historia del famoso predicador Fray Gerundio de Campazas, alias Zotes.* Leipzig: Brockhaus, 1885. (Colección de autores españoles, Vols. XLII-XLIII.)

Jourdain, Eleanor Frances. *Dramatic Theory and Practice in France 1690-1808.* London: Longmans, 1921.

Madariaga, Salvador de. *Englishmen, Frenchmen, Spaniards.* London: Oxford University Press, 1937.

Maritain, Jacques. *Freedom in the Modern World.* Tr. by Richard O'Sullivan. London: Sheed and Ward, 1935.

——. *An Introduction to Philosophy.* Tr. by E. I. Walkin. London: Sheed and Ward, 1930.

——. *Science and Wisdom.* New York: Scribner's, 1940.

Masson de Morvilliers, Nicolas. "Espagne." *Encyclopédie Méthodique.* Vol. I. Paris: 1782.

McClelland, Ivy Lilian. *The Origins of the Romantic Movement in Spain.* Liverpool: Institute of Hispanic Studies, 1937.

——. "Tirso de Molina and the Eighteenth Century," *Bulletin of Hispanic Studies,* XVIII, 182-192.

Menéndez y Pelayo, Marcelino. *Historia de los heterodoxos españoles.* Vol. III. Madrid: Librería Católica de San José, 1881.

——. *Historia de las ideas estéticas en España.* 4. ed. Vols. IV, V. Madrid: Hernando, 1932-33.

——. Same. 3. ed. Vol. VI. Madrid: Artes Gráficas Plus-Ultra, 1923.

Mercier, Désiré Felicien, Cardinal. *A Manual of Modern Scholastic Philosophy.* Tr. from 8. ed. by T. L. Parker and S. A. Parker. London. K. Paul Trench, 1916-17.

Mérimée, Paul. *L'Influence française en Espagne au dis-huitième siècle.* Paris: Les Belles Lettres, 1936.

Miller, Leo Francis. *A History of Philosophy.* New York: Wagner, 1927.

Monner Sans, Ricardo. "El siglo XVIII." *Introducción el estudio de la vida y obras de Torres de Villaroel.* Buenos Aires: Herrando, 1915.

Montolíu y de Togores, Manuel de. "El siglo XVIII." *Literatura castellana.* Barcelona: Editorial Cervantes, 1930.

Morel-Fatio, Alfred Paul. *Études sur l'Espagne.* Paris: Vieweg, 1888.

Morley, John. *Diderot and the Encyclopedists.* London: Chapman and Hall, 1886.

Mornet, Daniel. *La pensée française au XVIIIᵉ siècle.* Paris: Colin, 1926.

Noyes, Alfred. *Voltaire.* New York: Sheed and Ward, 1936.

194   *Bibliography*

Palmer, R. R. *Catholics and Unbelievers in Eighteenth Century France.*
Princeton: Princeton University Press, 1939.

Palau y Dulcet, Antonio. *Manual del librero hispano-americano.* Vol. IV.
Barcelona: Antiquaria, 1926.

Pellissier, Georges. *Voltaire philosophe.* Paris: Colin, 1908.

Pellissier, Robert E. *The Neo-Classic Movement in Spain during the
XVIII Century.* Stanford: Stanford University Press, 1918. (Leland
Stanford Junior University Publications. University Series.)

Poulet, Charles. "International Rationalism." *A History of the Catholic
Church.* Vol. II. Tr. by Sidney A. Raemers. St. Louis: Herder,
1937.

Rio,' A. del. "Algunas notas sobre Rousseau en España." *Hispania,* XIX
(1936), 105-116.

Rubio, Antonio. *La crítica del galicismo en España (1726-1832).* Mexico:
Universidad Nacional de México, 1937.

———. *Comments on 18th Century Purismo.* Philadelphia: 1935.

Sainz y Rodríguez, Pedro. "Estudios sobre la historia de la crítica literaria
en España: Don Bartolomé José Gallardo y la crítica literaria de su
tiempo." *Revue hispanique,* LI (1921), 211-595.

———. "Introducción." *Exequias de la lengua castellana.* Madrid: La
Lectura, 1925.

———. *Las polémicas sobre la cultura española.* Madrid: Fortanet, 1919.

Salvio, A. de. "Voltaire and Spain." *Hispania,* VII (1924), 69-110; 157-
164.

Sempere y Guarinos, Juan. *Ensayo de una biblioteca española de los
mejores escritores del reynado de Carlos III.* Madrid: Imprenta
Real, 1785-89.

Shaw, Charles Gray. *Trends of Civilization and Culture.* New York:
American Book, 1932.

Sorrento, Luigi. *Francia e Spagna nel settecento: Battaglie e sorgenti di
idee.* Milano: Vita e Pensiero, 1928. (Pubblicazioni della Università
Cattolica del Sacro Cuore.)

———. *Italiani e Spagnuoli contro l'egemonia intellettuale francese nel
settecento.* Milano: Vita e Pensiero, n.d. (Pubblicazioni della Università Cattolica del Sacro Cuore.)

Sotelo, Joaquin María. "Elogio del señor Don Juan Pablo Forner." (Leído
en la junta general extraordinaria de la Real Academia de Derecho
Español el día 23 de mayo de 1797.) Cueto, *Poetas líricos del siglo
XVIII.* Vol. II. Madrid: Rivadeneyra, 1871.

Spell, Jefferson Rea. *Rousseau in the Spanish World before 1883.* A
Study in Franco-Spanish Literary Relations. Austin, Texas: University of Texas Press, 1938.

Staubach, Charles N. *The Influence of French Thought on Feijóo.* Ann
Arbor, Michigan: University of Michigan, 1937. (Doctoral dissertation.)

Bibliography 195

Ueberweg, Friedrich. *History of Philosophy from Thales to the Present Time*. Tr. from the 4. ed. by George S. Morris. New York: Scribner's, 1909.

Vial, Francisque, and Denise, Louis. *Idées et doctrines littéraires du XVIIIe siècle*. Paris: Delagrave, n.d.

Villanueva, Luis. "Don Juan Pablo Forner. Noticia biográfica." Cueto, *Poetas líricos del siglo XVIII*. Vol. II. Madrid: Rivadeneyra, 1871.

INDEX

Academicians, 54, 55, 82.
Aesthetics, 31, 70, 79, 91, 93, 100, 123, 173.
Afrancesados, 31, 90, 122, 126.
Alarcón, 105 n.
Albert the Great, 40 n.
d' Alembert, 76, 176.
Alexandrine, 88, 91, 120, 167-8.
Alfonso VIII, 41.
Alfonso X, 39 n., 60, 61 n., 134, 160, 174.
Anacreon, 170, 171.
Antiquity, 71, 90, 93, 106, 109, 122, 124, 125, 129.
Apologies, 80, 118-19.
El Apologista universal, 12 n., 25.
Arabs, language, 17; learning, 42, 59, 60-2; philosophy, 39, 40, 42.
Archimedes, 60.
Argensola, 10, 18, 99 n., 151.
Ariosto, 102, 182.
Aristotle, 26, 42 n., 69, 70 n., 93, 100, 102, 151, 161, 178, 179, 183, 188.
Arnoldus de Villanueva, 41 n.
Art, 72, 73, 75, 76, 79, 107, 113.
Arte tópica, 42 n., 137.
Artists, 72, 73-74.
Authority, 31.
Authors commented on by Forner; English, 183; French, 176-81; Greek, 188-90; Italian, 182; Latin, 184-87; Spanish, 134-73.
Avicenna, 62.

Bacon, Frances, 1, 24, 42 n., ,57 n., 65, 80, 137, 172, 183.
Bacon, Roger, 40 n., 135, 162, 183.
Báñez, 41 n.
Bayle, 53 n., 69, 176.
Beauty, 74; 78.
Bermúdez, Jerónimo, 105 n., 108 n., 136.
Bettinelli, 7, 59.
Bible, 50, 51.
Boileau, 10, 176.
Bonilla y San Martín, 65 n.
Borja, Francisco de, 84, 99, 136.
Borrego, Antonio, 25 n.
Borrego, Tomás, 6, 22 n., 26 n.

Bourgoing, 22 n.
Bruun, Geoffrey, 33 n.

Cabrera, 113, 136, 149.
Cadalso, José, 1 n., 90 n.
Calderón de la Barca, 7, 78, 84, 95 n., 101, 105, 107, 124, 129, 136-7, 139.
Campomanes, 22 n.
Cano, 24, 41 n., 42 n., 137-8, 151.
Cañizares, 81, 105 n., 120, 138-9.
Capmany, 90 n.
Carassa, María del Carmen, 3 n.
Caro, Annibal, 71, 182.
Cartas de un español residente en París, 25.
Cartesianism, 40 n., 165, 173, 177.
Casticistas, 31.
Castillo de Bobadilla, 58 n., 139.
Castro, Guillén de, 105 n., 139.
Catholicism, 49, 179; *see also* Church and Revealed religion.
Cavanilles, Antonio, 132.
Celestina, 105 n., 108 n., 175.
El Censor, 12 n., 25.
Cervantes, 18, 26, 78, 86, 87, 88, 95, 116, 120, 125, 140, 146.
Charles II, 78, 99.
Charles V, 84.
Chemistry, 62.
Chiabrera, 71, 182.
Christ, 48.
Christian philosophy, 23, 35, 63, 93.
Christianity, 48, 130.
Church, 34, 41, 47 n., 50; *see also* Catholicism.
Cicero, 96, 111 n., 142 n., 161, 184, 185.
Cienfuegos, 90 n.
Classicism, 70 n., 72; *see* Neo-classicism and Precepts.
Classics, 124.
Clere, Daniel de, 62.
Conscience, 48, 51.
Copernicus, 60.
Cordero, 132.
El Correo, 108 n.
El Corresponsal, 12 n.

196

Index

197

Cotarelo y Mori, 5 n., 6, 23 n., 24 n., 27, 30, 31, 132.
Criticism, 116-18, 123, 125, 129.
La Crusca, 71.
Cruz, Juana Inés de, 96, 141.
Cueto, 3 n., 14, 31, 139 n.
Cueva, Juan de la, 105 n., 108 n., 141.
Culteranistas, 111.
Culture, 77, 80, 90, 100, 123, 126.

Decorum, 83.
Deism, 32 n.; *see* Natural religion.
Denina, Carlos, 22 n., 132.
Descartes, 26, 39, 164, 172, 173, 177.
Dialectics, 42-3, 50, 173.
Diario de los literatos, 121, 146, 161.
Dictionaries, 56, 79, 86, 119-20.
Dictys the Cretan, 54.
Drama, 10-11, 14, 97-8, 100-9, 120, 123, 124, 186.
Duns Scotus, 40 n.
Durand, William, 40 n.

Education, 173, 179.
Eighteenth century, 14, 20, 23, 27, 31, 32, 36, 41 n., 42 n., 53-6, 64-8; Europe, 70-2; Forner's condemnation of, 83, 86; literature, 75, 78, 79, 82, 83-4, 86, 88, 94, 97, 98, 115, 116-17, 118, 120, 123, 124, 129, 138; *see* Philosophy and Religion.
Eloquence, *see* Oratory.
Encyclopedia universal ilustrada, 129-30, 134.
Encyclopédie Méthodique, 132, 133.
Encyclopédistes, 21, 22, 29, 31, 32 n., 35, 36, 38, 55, 56, 64, 65 n., 76, 92, 126, 127, 128; *see also Philosophes*.
England 71; authors, 183.
Epicurus, 40 n., 112, 153, 189.
Escartín, 26, 121, 141.
Estala, 1, 122 n.
Euclid, 60.
Euripides, 89, 102, 189.

Farinelli, Arturo, 131.
Fatality, 39.
Feijóo, 29, 86, 90 n., 121, 141-3, 155, 162, 173, 184.
Ferdinand the Catholic, 39 n., 84, 88, 159.
Fernández de Moratín, Leandro, 5 n., 19, 90 n., 107 n., 122 n.

Ferreras, 114, 120, 143-4, 154, 159.
Fiction, 115, 123, 125, 180.
Florian, 5 n.
Floridablanca, 4, 22, 24, 31, 133.
Forner, early life and education, 1-3; law career, 3-4; literary career and works, 2, 3-12; marriage, 3 n.; personality and character, 3-5; summary of his critical views, 31, 64-9, 91-2, 122-30; *Exequias*: purpose and plan, 12-15, 30; allegory, 15-19; critical comments on, 19-21; *Oración apologética*: purpose and plan, 21-24, 31; critical comments on, 24-30.
Fornés, Bartolomé, 143.
France, 31, 32, 70, 71, 102; authors, 176-181; hegemony, 32, 71, 90, 125, 131; language, 86, 87, 88, 89, 90, 91, 109, 125, 128.
Free-thinkers, 34.
Free will, 45, 67, 127.
Freind, 62.

Gallardo, 90 n.
Gallicisms, 71, 77, 84, 85, 86, 87, 88, 90 n., 97, 98, 109, 111, 112, 115, 122, 123, 124, 125, 128, 143, 148.
Gallophiles—*see Afrancesados*.
Gallophobes, 24 n., 35, 90, 93, 128, 133.
García de la Huerta, 5 n., 6, 11 n., 12, 25, 90 n.
Genius, 105, 107, 125; *see* Inspiration.
Genlis, Comtesse de, 130, 177.
Germany, 71.
God, 34 n., 43, 44, 45, 46, 47, 48, 49, 51, 52, 67, 81, 127, 164.
Gongora, 145, 159, 167.
Gongorism, 86, 100 n.; *see Culteranistas*.
González-Blanco, 29, 31.
Goodness, 78, 81, 104.
Good taste, 30, 74, 76-9, 86, 99, 107, 122, 123, 172, 181.
Gothic language, 18.
Government, 67, 179.
Granada, Luis de, 47 n., 113, 145-6, 149.
Greece, 71, 86, 88, 102, 109, 113; authors, 88, 188-90; language, 17, 109.
Grotius, 151, 172.

198   *Index*

Hadrian, 158, 162.
Havens, G. R., 35 n.
Helvetius, 37 n., 53 n., 69, 75, 177, 178, 179.
Heredia, 61, 146.
Herennius, 142.
Herrera, Fernando de, 10, 99 n., 146, 152, 163.
Hispanicism, 130.
Hispano, Pedro, 40 n., 41 n., 43 n., 146.
History, 113-15, 120, 123, 125, 143.
Horace, 54, 176, 185.
Hortensius, 160.
Hosius, 47 n.
Huerta, Manuel de, 121, 146-7.
Humanism, 33, 52, 64, 128.
Humanitarianism, 67 n.
Hume, 179.

Iglesias, 1, 5, 78, 120, 147.
Imagination, 75, 80, 99, 100, 103, 107.
Imitation, 72-3, 109, 112, 124, 125; *see* Nature.
Inspiration, 73, 74, 75, 78, 95, 96, 99, 100, 105, 107, 124, 125, 135.
Iriarte, Bernardo, 24.
Iriarte, Domingo, 25 n.
Iriarte, Tomás de, 5 n., 6, 11, 90 n., 120, 148-9.
Isabella, 39 n., 159.
Isla, 90 n., 121, 149.
Italy, 71; authors, 182.

Jovellanos, 90 n.
Juan de Ávila, 113, 149-50.
Justice, 40, 41 n., 56 n.

Lacedemonians, 82.
Laguna, 24.
Lanuza, 113, 149, 150.
Latin, authors, 88, 184-87; language, 17, 88, 160, 165.
Laviano, Fermín, 11 n.
Las Casas, 129, 130, 150-1.
Law, natural and supernatural, 126; *see* Revelation.
Laws, 57, 58, 145, 164, 167.
Learned nation, 54-7, 178.
Lema, Francisco P. de, 5.
León, Luis de, 18, 47 n., 99 n., 113, 145, 149, 151-2.
Lessing, 29.
Liberty, 45, 48, 79, 82, 127, 129, 176; liberty of thought, 75, 76; *see* License and Reason.

License, 76, 82, 176.
Listo, 29.
Literary merit of a nation, 71-2.
Literary principles, 123; *see* Aesthetics.
Logic, 42 n.
López de Ayala, Ignacio, 10, 14 n., 121, 152.
Lucan, 80, 95, 153-4, 185.
Luzán, 74 n., 80, 93 n., 121, 154.

Machiavelli, 102, 182.
Maldonado, 41 n.
Man, 43-6, 48, 51, 52, 66-7, 75, 76, 82, 126, 127, 173.
Marchena, 90 n.
Mariana, 73, 113 n., 114, 125, 154.
Martínez Salafranca, 121, 155-6.
Masson, 22, 24, 59, 130, 131-3, 178.
Materialism, 66.
Mathematics, 41 n., 57 n., 59, 60.
Mayans, 77-8, 86, 90 n., 93, 121, 146, 155-6.
Medicine, 62.
Meléndez Valdés, 1, 120, 122 n.
Menander, 102, 189.
Menéndez y Pelayo, 5, 11 n., 14 n., 19, 26, 29, 31, 35, 36.
Mercado, 24, 61, 156.
Mercantilism in literature, 87, 98, 123.
Metaphysics, 42 n.
Military art, 57 n.
Monardes, 61, 157.
Montalván, 105 n.
Montesquieu, 24, 26, 46, 50, 131, 179.
Morales, Ambrosio de, 113 n., 157.
Morals, 48, 51, 66, 82.
Moreto, 105 n., 157.
Montoliu y Togores, 20, 29, 31, 35 n.
Muratori, 76 n., 110, 182.
Murillo, 75 n.
Mystics, 44, 47, 84, 145.

Nationalists, 121.
Natural law, 34, 67, 126.
Naturalists, 39.
Nature, imitation of, 72, 74, 75 n., 79.
Nava, 4.
Neo-classicism, 70, 90, 91, 93, 107 n., 121, 125; *see* Classicism.
Nepos, 54, 185.
Newton, 39, 162, 182.
Nipho, 11 n., 121, 158.
Nominalists, 39, 40.

Index 199

Novelas de caballerías, 173, 180.
Novelists, 115; *see also* Fiction.
Novelty, 72, 79, 87.

Ocampo, 115, 159.
Optimism, 39.
*Oración apologética por el África
  y su mérito literario,* 25.
Oratory, 82, 109-13, 124, 150, 161,
  166, 173, 182, 184, 187.
Original sin, 127.
Ovid, 96, 170, 186.

Palmer, 33 n., 34 n.
Pellissier, Robert E., 5 n., 28, 30, 31.
Pérez de Oliva, 105 n., 108, 160, 161.
Perfectibility, 126, 127.
Peripatetics, 40 n., 82.
Philip II, 84.
Philip IV, 39, 78, 84, 99.
Philosophes, 28, 31, 32 n., 33-5, 37-
  8, 46, 47, 49, 51, 65, 66, 67,. 68,
  69, 70, 83, 127, 173, 178; *see*
  Encyclopédistes.
Philosophic fables, 80, 125, 178, 180.
Philosophy, 23, 32-45, 49, 64-7, 68-9,
  75, 116, 126, 127, 162, 165; *see*
  Philosophes.
Physics, 62, 63.
Piquer, Andrés, 1, 65 n.
Piquer, Juan Crisóstomo, 3 n.
Piquer y Zaragoza, Manuela, 1.
Plato, 40 n., 44, 151, 179, 189-90.
Plautus, 102, 186.
Pliny, 110, 186.
Poetry, 80, 94 *ff,* 123, 186; *see also*
  Drama.
Pope, 8.
Precepts, 73-4, 97, 98, 106, 122, 123,
  125, 129, 138, 173-4.
Prevost, Abbé, 131.
Progress, 49.
Propriety, 77.
Prosaicism, 100 n., 123.
Prose, 97, 99.
Providence, 49, 51, 67.
Ptolemy, 60.
Puig, Leopoldo, 121, 161.

Quadrio, 7.
Quevedo, 73, 84, 99 n., 161-2.
Quintana, 90 n.

Ramón Lull, 41 n., 143, 162-3, 173.
Rapin, 130, 179.
Rationalism, 33 n., 70.

Rationality, 45, 127; *see* Reason.
Raynal, 69, 130, 141, 150, 151, 153,
  179.
Realists, 39.
Reason, 33, 34, 37, 40, 42 n., 48, 53,
  66, 75, 76, 79, 80, 104, 126, 127,
  173, 176.
Rejón de Silva, 120, 163.
Religion, 34, 40, 44-52, 58, 60, 67-8,
  126, 127; natural, 46, 49, 50, 67,
  164; revealed, 46, 47, 49, 50, 51,
  67, 68, 126, 127; *see* Catholicism
  and Revelation.
Renaissance; 33.
Rengifo, 96, 163.
Revelation, 33, 46, 50, 81, 127, 164.
Rhasis, 62.
Rhyme, 97.
Rioja, Francisco de, 99 n., 152, 163.
Rivera, Mariano, 132.
Robertson, 151.
Rodríguez Mohedanos, 121, 152, 163.
Rome, 37 n., 71, 102, 113, 165.
Roscelin, 40 n.
Rousseau, 46 n., 53 n., 56 n., 69, 75,
  162, 179-80.
Rubio, Antonio, 27, 30, 31, 90.
Rules, *see* Precepts.

Saavedra Fajardo, 19, 84, 113 n., 164.
Sabunde, Raymundo, 50, 164-5, 173.
Saint Simon, 131.
Sainz y Rodríguez, 5, 21, 25, 27, 31,
  132, 139 n., 156 n.
Sánchez Tomás Antonio, 6, 12, 132.
Sátira contra los abusos, 6, 13, 14,
  101.
Satire, 35.
Scepticism, 48.
Scholasticism, 39, 40, 41, 42, 66,
  183 n.
Science, 41, 51, 56, 58, 59, 60, 61,
  62, 63, 64, 125, 126, 127, 172.
Sempere y Guarinos, 121, 165.
Seneca, 129, 165-6.
Society, 48-9, 67, 76.
Socrates, 82.
Solís, 73, 84, 105 n., 113 n., 166.
Sophocles, 89, 102, 190.
Sorrento, 30, 31.
Sotelo, 2 n., 4 n., 6, 20, 31.
Soto, 41 n.
Spain, antagonism toward, 7, 38, 58,
  70, 76, 83, 85, 90, 119, 131-3,
  178, 180; authors, 134-75; cul-
  tural contribution, 24, 31, 39, 42,

200 *Index*

54, 56, 57-64, 70, 80-1, 90; language, 14, 15, 16, 18, 50, 71, 77, 84, 85, 86, 87, 88-90, 98, 100, 109, 113, 115, 120, 124, 125, 128, 134, 136, 138, 144, 160, 161, 164, 166, 168; legislation, 24, 39 n. 58; literature, 14, 71, 72, 80, 81, 84, 94-109, 120, 123-5, 129; literary merit, 26, 70, 80; philosophy, 35, 39, 44, 47, 83; religion, 44, 50, 58, 60; "vulgo," 78, 98, 103.

Spanish Academy, 6, 93.
Sparta, 37 n.
Spell, Jefferson R., 29 n., 35 n.
Spinoza, 48.
State, 34, 45.
Stoics, 40 n., 82.
Style, 83, 84, 97-8, 99, 100, 109, 111, 113, 123, 125, 159-60.
Suárez, 41 n.
Supernatural, 34, 66, 67, 126; *see* Revelation.
Superstition, 49 n.

Tasso, 71, 102, 182.
Teresa, Saint, 47 n., 145, 167.
Theatre, 81, 100-3; *see* Drama.
Theology, 41.
Thomas Aquinas, 40 n.
Thought in literature, 75, 76, 94-5, 124, 125; *see* License and Reason.
Tiraboschi, 7, 59, 182.
Tirso, 105 n.
Tradition, 32, 33, 34, 50, 70.
Traditionalism, 35, 65, 66, 70 n., 130.
Tragedy, 97, 108, 109, 124.
Translations, 15, 72, 86, 88, 125, 148.
Trevisano, 76 n.
Trigueros, 6, 11 n., 12, 120, 132, 167-8.

Trissino, 102, 182.
Truth, 40, 66, 78, 79, 80, 81, 83, 113, 115, 123, 127, 172, 174.

Unities, 109.
Universities, Alcalá, 50, 58, 61; Bologna, 41, 172; Ferrara, 41; Oxford, 41; Naples, 41; Padua, 41; Paris, 41, 172, 175, 178; Salamanca, 1, 3 n., 4, 41, 57, 60, 61.
Utility, 39, 40 n., 63-4, 66, 83, 104, 126, 127, 172, 181.
Utopia, 67-8.

Valencia, 41 n.
Valladares, 11 n., 120, 168.
Valmar, 139 n.; *see* Cueto.
Vega, Garcilaso de la, 54, 96, 156, 160, 169.
Vega, Lope de, 7, 95 n., 101, 105, 124, 129, 139, 169-71.
Verisimilitude, 78, 100, 102, 115-6, 124, 125.
Vitoria, 41 n., 151.
Villegas, 54, 84, 85, 86, 145, 171.
Vincens, Joseph, 163.
Virgil, 95, 96, 187.
Virtue, 44, 48, 51, 67, 70, 81, 82, 104, 113, 123, 126, 165.
Vives, 1, 24, 26, 27, 21 n., 57 n., 65, 75 n., 77 n., 80, 137-8, 142, 171-4, 177.
Voltaire, 32 n., 35 n., 37, 38 n., 46 n., 47 n., 49 n., 50 n., 53 n., 56 n., 69, 75, 83, 131, 179, 180-81.

Walpole, 179.
Wit, 84.

Zamora, 105 n., 120, 174.
Zurita, 73, 113 n., 174.

DATE DUE

868
F76Z
L3

Laughrin, Sr. M. F., I.H.M.
   Juan Pablo Forner as
a critic

DATE	ISSUED TO

868
F76Z
L3

CPSIA information can be obtained
at www.ICGtesting.com
Printed in the USA
BVHW031222280722
643247BV00015B/858